LITERATURE AND LIFE: AMERICAN WRITERS
Select list of titles in the series:

Complete list of titles in the series available from the publisher on request.

WALT WHITMAN

Bettina L. Knapp

A Frederick Ungar Book
CONTINUUM • NEW YORK

1993

The Continuum Publishing Company
370 Lexington Avenue
New York, NY 10017

Printed in the United States of America

Library of Congress Cataloging-in-Publication Data

Knapp, Bettina Liebowitz, 1926–
    Walt Whitman / Bettina L. Knapp
        p.   cm. — (Literature and life. American writers)
    "A Frederick Ungar Book"
    Includes bibliographical references and index.
    ISBN 0-8264-0566-5 (hardcover : acid-free)
    1. Whitman, Walt, 1819–1892. 2. Poets, American—19th century–
—biography. I. Title. II. Series.
PS3231.K58 1993
811'.3—dc20
    [B]   93-248
                                                                               CIP

Contents

Introduction

How is it that Walt Whitman's poetry and prose grip and excite certain contemporary readers while embarrassing and repelling others? Why are Whitman's writings recited, sung, and danced by one group and cast aside or kept under cover by another? What is that basic element or that energetic charge in his works that reaches directly into the heart and viscera of some, that fascinates and hypnotizes them, yet is considered facile, flamboyant, and trite by others?

Since Whitmanians and anti-Whitmanians are alive and well today, I should like to take to the "Open Road" to journey *into* Whitman's writings, and on the *way*, to question their intent and meanings from a variety of vantage points. Perhaps then we may better understand the reasons for the dichotomy of opinion his works have always elicited. After which — let the reader decide!

Do Whitman's writings enthrall the reader as they whisper the sounds of sea and land, of nature in all its garbs and moods, because one is faced with the natural environment's possible destruction? Do the variety of rhythms inhabiting Whitman's pieces act as escape mechanisms, carrying the reader away from the workaday world into the infiniteness of cosmic consciousness? Or could it be that this great primitive, infusing his tropes with magic and epic lyricism, has brought a new poetics into being, taking poetry back to its source, its original function: a divine language? Or are readers captivated because he sings of the *oneness* of body and soul? "And I say that the soul is not greater than the body, / And I say that the body is not greater than the soul" — an attitude that addresses the conflict between flesh and spirit that has been imposed upon the Western world for two thousand years.

Does Whitman's message again bear hearing? A fighter for freedom of expression in the arts, both with regard to form and thematics, he suffered greatly for a courageous stand that may be meaningful to us today, now that we are in grave danger of having this liberty shorn from us. While favoring an authentic and personal feeling of love and awe for Divinity and things natural, Whitman rejected the strictly enforced Christian propriety of churches. Their restrictive doctrines, hierarchies, pomp, and corruptive practices, which sought to govern by intruding in political, economic, and social domains, were anathema to him. Whitman brought out into the open the very real danger of losing what is basic to American society: free thought and the equally crucial separation of church and state. No church, no government, no political group, no society, he reiterated, is to be given the power of muzzling the poet or any other individual.

Is Whitman still praised and/or damned because he preached balance between individualism and the increasingly collective and automated society he saw as a future reality? Although he favored the machine, he warned that its overuse would lead to pollution and robotism. He believed in the work ethic rather than in the welfare state. High on his list of priorities was the pride each being should take in labor, whether the job performed was highly esteemed or not by society. An individualist and enemy of conformism, he fostered the idea of self-help and self-growth.

Perhaps the poet is still so controversial because he advocated women's rights and the beauty of motherhood, expressing all the while his faith in the female's ability to compete in the marketplace, as well as her right to decide on issues governing her life, rather than allowing one sex or one powerful group to subvert the dignity of another. In this respect, as in all his other convictions, he was deeply committed to the democratic spirit and to America — to brotherhood, to humanitarian causes, to a world in which harmony of spirit and love of neighbor prevailed.

Whitman's frequently apocalyptic verse conveyed a fear of the extremes to which a pluralistic society could lead — even to the atomization of America, to the breakup of the union. He foresaw the economic and social problems America would experience with mass immigration. He spoke forth against corruption in government; against public officials who used whatever arguments possible to win the approval of the collective. A man with few personal possessions, Whitman had renounced comforts and the soft life of the effete. He believed in an egalitarian society, respectful of the individual's needs as well as those of the collective. More important to him than gold, and all it could buy, were the riches of spirit, of heart, of mind, and of physicality. He *lived* his world of uninhibited exhilaration, of awe, of sacred terror — of rhapsody.

Whitman was unique in his day and in ours. His *Leaves of Grass, Specimen Days, Democratic Vistas,* journalism, correspondence — and such tropes as "I wear my hat as I please indoors or out," from "Song of Myself" — disclose a lifelong quest for spiritual and intellectual independence, authenticity of purpose, forthrightness of expression in a continuous battle against censorship, be it social, religious, esthetic, or sexual. Reviled by many, he was also admired by many for favoring sexual liberation for women and for men, be their preferences hetero- or homosexual. His sexually explicit poems in the *Children of Adam* and *Calamus* clusters poignantly convey his erotic and turbulent impulses and longings. Free expression was Whitman's law. Always open to new ideas, be they ancient or modern, he approached life and art by wading intrepidly into their currents, countercurrents, and crosscurrents, thus deepening and expanding his writings during the course of his life.

Opting for Dionysian, uninhibited leaps into the private and the sacred world of phenomena and being, Whitman experienced nature as the supreme healer. Alive and dynamic, charged with mysterious powers, it spoke to him and renewed him, and he responded to its moods, which so frequently paralleled his own. Nature invited him to experience its sacrality, its unending givingness. And Whitman, the mystic, journeyed forth into nature, human and nonhuman, as well as into space and time — to dialogue with hosts of secret voices.

"I launch all men and women forward with me into the Unknown," he wrote in "Song of Myself" — into a world where imagination, fantasy, and musicality roamed free and inspired him to create. Like the writings of the ancient bards, Whitman's were connected to oral traditions, to the epic poems of Homer and Virgil, and the anonymous *Song of Roland.* To experience their flavor and succulence, they should be read aloud: especially, for example, the harmonious and/or cacophonous sonorities of "Song of the Open Road," "Song of the Broad-Axe," "I Sing the Body Electric," or "A Song for Occupations."

"But for opera [and Italian opera in particular] I could never have written *Leaves of Grass,*" Whitman stated. Because music was his guide, along with nature, such poems as "As I Ebb'd with the Ocean of Life," "Out of the Cradle Endlessly Rocking," or "There Was a Child Went Forth" are replete with immense ranges of tones floating, like so many breaking waves, in and out of the written text in long or short, or peaking and descending, folds. His parallelisms, catalogings, repetitions, imagings, and inner rhymes and rhythms bear biblical magnitude, accounting for the intensity and emotional value of the dramas enacted.

Whitman, who rejected the tyranny of tradition and its metrics, struck down what he considered to be artificial forms and constraints imposed on his animalistic hunger for free expression. Nevertheless, although liberal in form and thematics, Whitman's poems were chiseled with the precision and deftness of the sculptor, and the sensitivity and mathematical accuracy of the musician. Meticulously worked and reworked, each trope, patterned frequently upon inner erupting energies, obeyed a law of its own. Discarding verse or line when arbitrarily rigidified by predetermined metrical patterns and regulations, Whitman composed in units, clauses, and sentences, stressing not one vowel necessarily, but using "hovering accents" that distributed emphasis on a word or grouping of words. For example, the plenitude and depth of the panoramic images stamped in "Crossing Brooklyn Ferry," while replicating thought and feelings by fusing rhythm and tone, also introduced a time/space dimension. Although impressionistic mobile images and tremulous luminosities atomized the scene in the poem, a dual displacement followed suit: the forward moving light of the sun splattered its diminishing rays on the ferry as the oncoming subdued glimmerings of the moon were descending.

The creative individual, Whitman contended, is a kind of forerunner of what is to be: a prototype of many people, a person who sees into the future. Like the founding prophets of all the great movements, whether artistic, religious, or philosophical, who have been able to make far-reaching predictions and perform miracles, artists are endowed with special gifts. They respond more powerfully to the deepest layers within themselves — to transpersonal realms, they sense the unknown and transmute the impalpable into the palpable, the evanescent into the eternal. As the artist shapes his or her words, forms, colors, rhythms, and moods (which the public later experiences in poems, paintings, novels, musical compositions), he or she is conditioned by inner psychic realities. These are not merely personal revelations, not simply individual offerings extracted from the depths, but an indication of what lies hidden behind the scenes — that which will impact on future generations. Readers and audiences must, therefore, pay attention to the offerings of artists in every medium. They must be *conscious* at all times of what is being produced and *act* accordingly, so as to avert disaster.

Whitman's message was manifold: as visionary, living in the world of the imagination; as realist, coping with everyday life; as humanitarian, giving unstintingly of himself to the needy, the ill, the wounded, and the dying. From 1862 to 1872, the "wound-dresser," as he was called, visited casualties of the Civil War in Washington, D.C., caring lovingly for them in makeshift and permanent hospitals while also learning how to deal with the horrors of death.

Whitman believed in the existence of two principles that cohabited in each individual: Good and Evil. "I am not the poet of goodness only, I do not decline to be the poet of wickedness also," he wrote in "Song of Myself," shocking a great many of his contemporaries, as well as some of his readers today. Only through the direct experience of all aspects of life — "Look for me under your boot-soles," he wrote in "Song of Myself" — could the beauty or the chilling reality of an incident and its emotional aftermath be transcended in the crystalization of the work of art.

D. H. Lawrence considered Whitman a "pioneer...the first heroic seer to seize the soul by the scruff of her neck and plant her down among the potsherds...the first white aboriginal." Ezra Pound, the antithesis of Whitman in almost every way, wrote that "mentally I am a Walt Whitman who has learned to wear a collar and a dress shirt (although at times inimical to both)....And to be frank, Whitman is to my fatherland...what Dante is to Italy...the first great man to write in the language of his people" (Pearce, *A Collection,* 9).

Even T. S. Eliot, who would have found Whitman repugnant had he known him, had fewer acerbic tidbits to direct his way than was his habit, he called him "a great master of versification." Edith Sitwell compared Whitman to Blake, whose mission was "to lead poetry back to the 'divine original, concrete.' " Hart Crane declared that Whitman "better than any other, was able to coordinate those forces in America which seem most intractable, fusing them into a universal vision which takes on additional significance as time goes on." William Carlos Williams considered Whitman to be at the vanguard of modern "American" poetry, the creator of "a new language, an unnamed language which Whitman could not identify or control." Anthony Burgess spoke of Whitman's "rhetorical sweep" as "symphonic," and of the America he created as a "visionary country, built in an epic fantasia...an America, roamed by the linker, the joiner-of-hands, the Answerer." Wallace Stevens imagined him "walking along a ruddy shore.... Nothing is final, he chants. No man shall see the end. / His beard is of fire and his staff is a leaping flame" (Norton, *Anthology,* 901, 902, 905, 972, 992).

A lyrical and epic voice for poets and novelists, Whitman opened a door onto the creative process for such poets as John Berryman, Robinson Jeffers, Carl Sandburg, Robert Lowell, Allen Ginsberg, Charles Olsen, A. R. Ammons, Karl Shapiro, Robert Creeley, and John Ashbery, and prose writers such as Ernest Hemingway, John Dos Passos, Henry Miller, William S. Burroughs, Jack Kerouac, and Paul Bowles.

Karl Shapiro wrote: Whitman "sprouted... out of nowhere into the role of prophet and seer.... He is the one mystical writer of any consequence America has produced; the most original religious thinker we have; the poet of the greatest achievement; the first profound innovator; the most accomplished artist as well — but nobody says this nowadays" (Norton, 941).

And now Whitman's Song:

> Smile O voluptuous cool-breath'd earth!
> Earth of slumbering and liquid trees...
> Earth of the vitreous pour of the full moon just tinged
>   with blue... ("Song of Myself").

Chronology

1819 Born on May 31, West Hills, near Huntington, Long Island.

1823 Family moves to Brooklyn.

1830–34 Learns printing trade. 1835: employed as printer.

1836–38 Teaches in various schools on Long Island.

1838–39 Edits *Long Islander.*

1840–46 Works as printer, editor, and writer.

1846–48 Works on the Brooklyn *Daily Eagle;* from February to May 1848 works on the *Crescent.* Pursues work as editor, printer, and free-lance journalist.

1855 Publication of *Leaves of Grass.* Emerson's letter to Whitman on July 21.

1856 Second edition of *Leaves of Grass.*

1860 Third edition of *Leaves of Grass.*

1861 Civil War begins on April 12. Whitman's brother George enlists.

1862 Whitman goes to Fredericksburg, Virginia.

1865 Meets Peter Doyle. *Drum-Taps* printed.

1868 Fourth edition of *Leaves of Grass.*

1870 Fifth edition of *Leaves of Grass.* Publication of *Democratic Vistas.*

1873 Suffers paralytic stroke on January 23. Mother dies on May 23. Moves into George's house in Camden, New Jersey.

1876   Meets Harry Stafford. Arrival of Mrs. Gilchrist.

1879   Travels to the West.

1880   Visits Dr. R. M. Bucke in London, Ontario.

1882   Publication of *Specimen Days and Collect.*

1884   Buys house on Mickle Street, Camden, New Jersey.

1891   "Death-bed edition" of *Leaves of Grass* printed.

1892   Dies on March 26, buried in Harleigh Cemetery, Camden, New Jersey.

Part 1

The Life

Camerado, this is no book,
Who touches this touches a man....
Dear friend whoever you are take this kiss....
I give it especially to you, do not forget me....

— "So Long!"

1

"Dear Friend Whoever You Are Take This Kiss"

Walt Whitman, poet of nature, of the city, and especially of the people, was born in West Hills, Long Island, on May 31, 1819. In an environment peppered with farms, vast expanses of fields, and seemingly endless forests, he enjoyed the drama of the ocean's angry cries and hoarse murmurs, and the feel of its bracing breeze against his skin. His eyes, frequently focusing on distant vessels illuminated by the glistening sun, or hidden by haze or the darkness of night, experienced these as mysterious presences. As a lad, he loved to fish, to dig for clams, or just to sit and watch the sea gulls fly above.

Although Whitman pleasured in aloneness, the future poet also empathized with people, particularly his jolly, ruddy-complexioned, and fun-loving maternal grandfather, Major Cornelius Van Velsor. Of Dutch-Welsh origin, this Quaker farmer and breeder of horses was a fine storyteller, who knew just how to regale his grandson on each of his visits. Whitman also felt close to his grandmother, "Amy" (Naomi), to whose gentle and harmonious personality he responded with ease. She, like her husband, had a gift for amusing and fascinating the young child, recounting tales about her adventurous father, Captain John Williams. Not only had he served under John Paul Jones, but he had also been involved in the West Indies trade. Amy's premature death in 1829, and Cornelius Van Velsor's remarriage, which Whitman described years later as "not a very good investment," cut the child off from this wonderful source of warmth and comfort (Allen, *The Solitary Singer,* 14).

After swimming, fishing, or just tramping through the fields and beaches of Long Island, he would visit his paternal grandmother, Hannah Brush Whitman, a former schoolteacher. When reminiscing in *Faint Clews and Indirections,* the poet tells how she kept him entertained for hours on end with stories about her ancestors. Some had played heroic roles in the Revolution, and a great-grandfather,

Nehemiah Whitman, had owned five hundred acres of farmland with slaves enough to work it.

The closeness Whitman felt with his grandmothers he experienced to an even greater extent with his mother, Louisa. A stocky, blue-eyed woman, with a pleasant personality, she, too, "excelled in narrative — had great mimetic power; she could tell stories, impersonate; she was very eloquent in the utterance of noble moral axioms — was very original in her manner, her style" (*WWC*, II, 113). She must have been born with great patience as well as enormous fortitude because she was able to put up with her husband, Walter, a stern, obstinate, quarrelsome, and moody man. Worse, she could rarely count on him to furnish a steady income. Of strong stock, his Puritan ancestors having moved from England to Huntington, Long Island, in the seventeenth century, he was not afraid of hard work and was a highly trained and fine carpenter. Unfortunately, he had bad luck and lacked business acumen. By 1823 the construction market had become so depressed that he had been forced to earn his living as a farmer during the summer months, and as a cutter of firewood in the winter. More frightening to both parents was their continuously growing family: five-year-old Jesse; nearly four-year-old Walter, two-and-a-half-year-old Mary, and another expected in November.

Hoping to improve their material circumstances, the Whitmans moved to Brooklyn in 1823. Although it was still a village comprising only six or seven thousand people, Brooklyn, for an enterprising man, offered enormous possibilities. Its harbor and the ferry linking it with New York City not only attracted commerce, manufacturing, and shipping, but its large and luxurious estates and its working farms on Brooklyn Heights also enticed entrepreneurs to its shores. The Whitmans, intending to take advantage of these, moved to a house on Front Street, not far from the United States Navy Yard.

Walter senior took employment as a carpenter, then began speculating in houses. He started modestly, buying one lot for around $250, on which he built a house and into which the family moved. Selling it after a few months, he now had the money to buy a second lot, and he repeated this process so often that the Whitmans moved on an average of once a year. The constant moving, in addition to the unpaid mortgages leading to the subsequent loss of houses, was in no way conducive to the well-being of the family members. That Mrs. Whitman kept giving birth to more and more children — Hannah Louisa in 1823, an infant who died shortly after birth in 1825, Andrew Jackson in 1827, and George Washington two years later — helped neither the family's financial status nor its sense of security.

The onus of continuous financial failure was due, Whitman wrote, to his "straightforward father [who] was nearly swindled out of his boots" by a Methodist "elder," and later by a "minister" (*WWC*, I, 256). Such a statement may help explain Whitman senior's freethinking stand in matters of religion. Although father and son did not get along, there is no doubt that as a youngster, the future poet was influenced by the eider Whitman's liberal attitudes toward Divinity as well as by his deep-seated admiration for America and the principles upon which it had been founded.

He must have been impressed by the fact that his father, a radical democrat, identified with laborers, farmers, and tradespeople. More important, perhaps, was his father's respect for the English pamphleteer Tom Paine. From Paine's harrowing existence, Whitman learned that the lot of the innovator — no matter what the field — was fraught with obstacles. Upon arriving in America in 1774, Paine had preached revolt rather than reform (*Common Sense; The American Crisis*); later he had militated against western lands becoming the property of one colony rather than of the nation (*Public Good*) and had vituperated as well against monetary inflation (*Dissertations on First-Principles of Government*). Following the publication of *The Age of Reason,* Paine was attacked as an atheist. Although he had participated in both the French and American revolutions, had been made an honorary citizen of France by the Republican government, and had held several official positions in the colonies, his enemies were many. He died in poverty, vilified as a radical, drunkard, and atheist, and was refused burial in consecrated ground. Only years later, after opinions had changed, was Paine considered an American patriot.

That Whitman senior had also been a longtime friend of one of Paine's defenders, the Quaker radical and remarkable orator Elias Hicks, also spoke well of him. This deeply religious but non-doctrinaire man, who had become the head of the liberal branch of the Quaker Church (the Hicksites) had courageously instigated the schism in the Society of Friends by stating, "The blood of Christ — the blood of Christ, why, my friends, the actual blood of Christ in itself was no more effectual than the blood of bulls and goats" (*PW*, II, 645). Whitman's father also introduced his son to *The Ruins,* a work attacking superstition and Christianity, by the French Deist philosopher Count C. Volney.

A socialist, Whitman senior subscribed to the socialist paper *Free*

Inquirer published by Robert D. Owen and Frances Wright. Owen, a philanthropist and inaugurator of programs for adult education, sought to reorganize society on the basis of small, cooperative communities. It was he who inspired the founding of New Harmony Community (1825) in Indiana. Wright, a much-maligned Scottish-born feminist, was a preacher of equal rights, organizer of workers, and promulgator of a more rational approach to education. Her motto, as enunciated in her pamphlet *A Few Days in Athens,* was "think for *yourself.*" Years later Whitman called her, "a woman of the noblest make-up . . . one of the best in history though also one of the least understood" (*WWC,* II, 30, 204). Given such early influences, it seems natural for Whitman to have expressed his antagonism to restrictions of any kind: "I was never made to live inside a fence" (*WWC,* II,19).

Not surprisingly, this open and winsóme lad reacted negatively to the rote learning techniques and harsh disciplinary measures to which he was subjected during the six years he attended school. Teachers called for corporal punishment for the slightest infraction, be it talking in class or swearing. Paradoxically, despite his father's dislike for organized religion, Whitman was sent to a variety of Sunday schools, including Saint Ann, run by the Episcopal Church.

So precarious had Whitman's father's economic situation become that the future poet's formal education ceased when he was eleven. He took a job in the law offices of James B. Clark and his son, Edward, who were kind and well disposed toward the young lad. They helped him improve his handwriting and composition, and gave him a subscription to a circulating library so that he could continue his readings, which were to become one of Whitman's lifelong pleasures.

After leaving the Clarks, Whitman held many jobs. One of the most important of these was in 1831, when he was employed by Samuel E. Clements, editor of the *Long Island Patriot,* a newspaper to which his father subscribed. At the age of twelve, Whitman was invited to contribute "sentimental bits" to the *Patriot,* although exactly which articles were his is not known (*WWC,* V, 33). The paper's foreman printer, William Hartshorne, not only taught Whitman a great deal about his trade, namely typesetting, but also about American history, particularly when reminiscing about Washington, Jefferson, and other American heroes.

A year later Whitman started working on Alden Spooner's successful weekly, the Whig-oriented *Long Island Star,* identified with big business and manufacturing. That he also wrote short anonymous articles for such prestigious papers as New York City's *Mirror* must have filled him with a sense of self-worth, since he decided to remain alone in Brooklyn, after his family, for financial as well as for health reasons (a cholera epidemic), had returned in May 1833 to West Hills, Long Island.

The young reporter was most fortunate to receive free passes to attend performances at the Bowery Theater and elsewhere, including such popular melodramas as *Jonathan Bradford; or, The Murder at the Roadside Inn, Napoleon's Old Guard,* and many of Shakespeare's works, including *Richard III,* starring the all-time favorite, Junius Brutus Booth, about whom he wrote:

Though fifty years have pass'd since then, I can hear the clank, and feel the perfect following hush of perhaps three thousand people waiting. (I never saw an actor who could make more of the said hush or wait, and hold the audience in an indescribable, half-delicious, half-irritating suspense.) And so throughout the entire play, all parts, voice, atmosphere, magnetism, from "Now is the winter of our discontent," to the closing death fight with Richmond, were of the finest and grandest. (*PW,* II, 596)

To experience theater as frequently and as momentously as Whitman did was crucial to his formation as poet. Voice, tone, rhythm, and gesture were, to be sure, important to his emotional enjoyment of the particular play, but these factors were also developing in him a whole, aesthetic dimension.

By 1835 Whitman, "the journeyman printer," now grown stocky and strong, found work as a compositor in Manhattan. Passionately attached to the big city, he was oblivious to its dangers. Gangs were forever fighting each other; riots were breaking out every now and then; and fires, which had become a scourge, the worst occurring in 1835, were destroying whole sections of Manhattan near Wall Street, including the Customs House and the Merchants' Exchange. Moreover, New York City was going through a periodical depressed financial condition, bankruptcies being par for the course. Not only did many people lose their jobs, including Whitman, but the extreme cold of the winter of 1935 added to the suffering of the poor and the homeless.

By May 1836 Whitman had moved back into the family home, now located in Hempstead. To add to the already stressful condition of dealing with a one-year-old retarded brother, Edward, was the dissension existing between the future poet's father and himself. The former, having taken on the lucrative business of farming, wanted his son to follow suit. When he refused, tempers grew hot.

Mrs. Whitman, coming between the two warring parties, hoped to instill peace.

Always close to his mother, Whitman grew increasingly attached to her, helping her to care for the younger children, Edward in particular. Lovingly, and with great understanding, he unconsciously took on the role of surrogate father, the one he now realized that his own stern, morose, irritable — and perhaps even alcoholic — father was incapable of fulfilling. Years later, when Whitman had become the family's provider, some of his friends began referring to him as "the mother-man." His paternally tender feelings toward his siblings is evident in his depiction of them in "My Boys and Girls," a narrative piece written in 1835–36. Such a close relationship, however, is double-edged. To be sure, Whitman was all-giving to his family, both materially and emotionally. In so being, he also disclosed the void within him: a desperate need for relatedness. To add to his psychological dependency upon his mother was his increasingly implicit and explicit desire for masculine camaraderie.

For one whose formal education had ceased at the age of eleven, it is an irony that Whitman began teaching in a district school, near Cornelius Van Velsor's farm. But his work as a journalist and his inveterate reading had broadened his mind and enriched his English style; he stood head and shoulders above the country schoolteachers of the time — especially for his ultramodern ideas.

Despite their long hours, from eight in the morning until four or five at night, teachers in country schools were neither well paid nor treated with consideration. Whitman's lot was no exception. Although specific texts, such as Webster's "blue-backed speller," were supposed to be used in class, most students availed themselves of books their parents owned and had themselves used. The lack of unity in learning techniques was appalling: each child memorized a specific lesson from the book he happened to have. Very little uniformity existed in the texts. Equally deleterious was the burden placed upon the teacher, who, while listening to an individual recitation, was also expected to sharpen the students' quills and to write down the sentences and phrases the class was then ordered to copy. During the winter months, teachers were obliged to tend the fire.

Whitman, not one to follow standard rules and regulations, had, by 1838, developed his ideas on teaching: rather than obliging the students to learn by rote, he questioned them orally on what they had read, conversed with them, and tried all the while to practice what he termed *mental arithmetic* — stimulating their minds. If he noticed that a child had lied or misbehaved, he did not resort to corporal punishment, as was customary. Without alluding to the student by name, he would tell a story with a moral to it in which the guilty lad would recognize himself. Whitman's understanding approach to his pupils had evidently made a deep impression upon them, for many had grown deeply attached to the future poet.

Teaching, however, did not fulfill the energetic Whitman's needs. To sharpen his mind and activate his inborn argumentative streak, he joined Smithtown's debating society. The society's get-togethers made it possible for him to meet prominent townspeople. Surprisingly, the eighteen-year-old Whitman succeeded in holding his own against the best-educated adversaries.

A wanderer by nature, Whitman kept on the move, looking toward different vistas to fulfill an inner, still-unsatisfied urge. Journalism must have tempted him more than any other career, since in 1838 he decided to found a weekly in Huntington, the *Long Islander*. Not only had he borrowed money for this venture, he also elicited his brother George's help to run the enterprise. After the initial enthusiasm, Whitman spent less and less time harnessed to his work. The paper failed. His backers, it is surmised, sold the *Long Islander*, after which Whitman returned to New York City.

Was the year 1839 propitious for such a move? Perhaps not, since the city was again economically depressed. When Whitman failed to find work, he reasoned that since James J. Brenton, the editor of the *Long Island Democrat*, had published some of his essays and poems, he could apply to him for a job. He did so and was accepted. During his leisure time, he taught at the Little Bay Side school.

It was in 1840 that the restless, dreamy, impractical, and for some, slovenly Whitman began writing poems and essays for Brenton, namely, the "Sun-Down Papers from the Desk of a School-Master." The modern reader of Whitman's pedestrian prose, with its highly sentimental and didactic edge, and his poetry, based thematically and stylistically on à la mode verses, finds it hard to imagine him capable of eventually authoring *Leaves of Grass*.

Although his writing had not yet showed it, he was learning and broadening himself in every way possible. By May 1841 he was not only writing for the *New World*, a literary weekly, but also became involved in the Democratic electoral campaign. Part of the speech he delivered on July 30, at a Democratic rally near City Hall, was quoted in the *Post*, edited by the renowned William Cullen Bryant, a fighter for liberal causes and author of *Thanatopsis*; and in the *New Era*, a Tammany newspaper. Adding to his feelings of accomplishment was the fact that the prestigious literary magazine, the

Democratic Review, in which such celebrities as Poe, Bryant, Hawthorne, Whittier, and Lowell published, had bought some of his poems and stories, namely, "Death in the School-Room," "Wild Frank's Return," and "Bervance."

The themes of Whitman's morose, romantic, and moralistic tales were drawn, to a great extent, from experience. In the ultramelodramatic "Death in the School-Room" he pointed up the evils of corporal punishment. "Wild Frank's Return," based perhaps in part on a tale his mother had told him, discloses some of Whitman's own psychological torments: a deep-seated rivalry with his siblings. "Bervance," even more acute in its psychological revelations, narrates events revolving around a father's guilt-ridden hatred for his son.

Meanwhile, Whitman was siphoning off some of his pent-up but justified anger against the lack of integrity of some newspaper publishers in parodies printed in the democratic, *Aurora,* of which he became editor on March 28, 1842. Not arrogance, but the pride he took in his new and prestigious position, encouraged Whitman to alter his dress. His formerly sloppy but comfortable clothes, were now exchanged for the stylish garb of a dandy: he wore a high hat and a frock coat ornamented on the lapel with a boutonniere, and sported a small cane.

Although Whitman labored hard, he still made time to wander about the city, chatting with friends and strangers and delighting in the excitement offered him by the frenzied activities of political parties. Openly and brashly, perhaps even foolhardily, he declared himself against any government appropriations for parochial schools, advocated so militantly by the new Irish immigrants. To meddle in religious education, he believed, was an infraction of the fundamental democratic doctrine of separation of church and state. When Tammany yielded to the demands of the Irish, Whitman castigated the Democrats, labeling them weak and deceitful. Predictably, no sooner had Bishop John Hughes succeeded in winning approval for his school bill than riots between Catholics and Protestants became the order of the day.

Not only was Whitman an individualist who believed in the Jeffersonian dictum "The best government is that which governs the least," but he was also a deeply compassionate man. That he took pity on the poor and the oppressed would have been commendable in and of itself. But feelings alone do not remedy unjust realities. Actions must follow. In editorials in the *Aurora,* Whitman expressed his outrage at the arrest of fifty prostitutes on Broadway. So strong a statement did he make and so strong was the clamor against his point of view that he was obliged to print an apology. Although losing the first round, Whitman was not one to be stopped. He continued to interest himself in the cause of the pariah, whatever the reason. Whether Whitman was fired from the *Aurora* on May 3, 1842, for indolence or for his unwillingness to tone down his leaders is moot. He had little time for self-pity, having been hired almost immediately by the daily *Evening Tattler.*

Since money was scarce in the Whitman household, and the future author of *Leaves of Grass* was always trying to sniff out good sources of revenue, he found the perfect opportunity in the mushrooming temperance movement. Hadn't Whitman himself signed the pledge of total abstinence when an apprentice journalist in Brooklyn? And again, when teaching on Long Island? It comes as no surprise, then, that when he was asked to write a temperance novel in 1842 he agreed to do so. Much to his delight, his *Franklin Evans; or, The Inebriate* sold twenty thousand copies. As the years passed however, Whitman was ashamed of the sloppiness of his writing and claimed that "it was damned rot — rot of the worst sort — not insincere, perhaps, but rot, nevertheless" (*WWC,* I, 93).

Whitman changed employment rather frequently in 1843: working for the Democratic *Statesman,* he also free-lanced such romantic, Poe-like fantastic short stories as "Eris: A Spirit Record," "Dumb Kate," and "The Little Sleighers," which appeared in the *Columbian* magazine. By 1844 Whitman was editor of the New York *Democrat* and author of short stories appearing in the *New Mirror.* A year later he published in the *Aristidian* and the *American Review* (the latter, which had published Poe's "The Raven," featured Whitman's gripping tale "Richard Parker's Widow").

Whitman was not one to spend his days doing nothing but writing and working. He relaxed by keeping company with New York politicians from whom he learned the ins and outs of corruption. The fun-loving Whitman also frequented the "Bowery Boys," rowdies, toughs, and gangs. All of these avenues, pleasant and unpleasant, furnished him with a broader view of the New World's cultural calendar.

Why Whitman began working in 1845 for the Brooklyn-based *Long Island Star,* a Whig-oriented paper, edited by the son of his former employer, Alden Spooner, is not known. Coincidentally, his family also moved back to Brooklyn that same year, and thus all the Whitmans were reunited. The poet's devotion to his family had not altered.

Whitman's outspoken writings touched upon many subjects: literature, theater, opera, moral tales, educational and school texts, temperance, the evils of smoking cigars, chewing tobacco, obscene language, and war between England and America over the disputed Oregon boundary. Like the Swiss-born writer Jean-Jacques Rousseau, Whitman also condemned theater, although to a lesser degree, for its immorality. While the American poet, a devotee of the performing arts, applied his interdict to contemporary plays alone, Rousseau rejected all theater and opera. Whitman's criticisms were not only leveled at a play's lack of morality, but to its antirepublicanism.

Nevertheless, and antipodal to Rousseau and to his own antagonism toward immorality onstage, Whitman thrilled to many of the performances he attended, especially, Shakespeare's *Macbeth* and *Coriolanus* at the Chatham. Although negatively disposed toward British actors in general, he considered Charles Kean's performance in *King John,* at the Park Theatre, remarkable; and his wife's performance as the queen, in this same play, unforgettable. Indeed, along with *Richard III,* it became Whitman's favorite Shakespearean tragedy.

Why had Whitman been so deeply moved by Mrs. Kean's performance? Had he identified with her portrayal of the queen's agony after the murder of her children? Had her excoriating tragedy, which he experienced through projection, opened him up to his own mother's grieving heart, and hence, to his own motherly and feminine instincts? Whitman's close ties with his mother had made him privy to the pain she had endured during her mature years: living with an irascible husband and difficult children. For example, Jesse, her oldest son, suffered from such violent tempers and severe personality disorders that he was finally sent to a mental hospital; the retarded Eddy needed constant supervision. In addition to the family's financial difficulties, mention must again be made of the incredible burden placed on Mrs. Whitman of moving almost yearly.

Whitman's antidote to low spirits was to attend operas by Verdi, Bellini, Rossini, or Donizetti at the Park Theater, Niblo's Garden, or Palmer's Opera House. The voices of some of Europe's finest artists — Alessandro, Marietta Alboni, Bettini, Henriette Sontag — touched him deeply. His insightful critique "Art-Music and Heart-Music," published in the *Broadway Journal,* edited at the time by Poe, not only gave Whitman the opportunity of expressing his ideas on the vocal art, but also afforded him the pleasure of meeting the celebrated author of "The Raven."

Despite the many plays and operas Whitman attended, his ideas on aesthetics remained incredibly moralistic and limited. He was convinced that ethnic music — for Americans this meant country style — best expressed the essence and soul of a nation. Americans, he reasoned, should listen to what is intrinsically theirs, rather than to European imports. Significant as well was his strangely pragmatic approach to music: he insisted that vocal music should be taught in school, not for its beauty or spiritual content, but to enhance the manners, conduct, and finesse of students. Whitman's change of heart toward music's message occurred after hearing *The Oratorio of St. Paul* sung by the New York Tabernacle Choir. So moved had he been by the performance and his ensuing mystical experience that he believed his soul and his feeling world had been marked forever by this tonal feast.

As editor of the Brooklyn *Daily Eagle*, which he became in 1846, Whitman engaged in communal activities, and was even elected secretary of the General Committee of Queens County. His editorials and articles touched on a variety of subjects: the growth of unemployment caused by the increasing use of machines, the evils of child labor, poor working conditions, low wages for women in general and "sewing-women" in particular. The subjects of women's rights, women's education, and women's health care were important to Whitman. That Whitman had always been drawn to the plight of women is understandable because of his own mother's financially strapped existence. Drawn only to motherly types or career women, as far as is known, Whitman had never had a girlfriend. Although he enjoyed looking at a "well-developed, healthy *naturally* beautiful woman," his attraction, divested of any sexuality, preluded his growing ideological belief in physical exercise and good diet for women.

Some of Whitman's other favorite themes dealt with the hypocrisy related to the building of garish churches with overly comfortable pews, which, rather than spiritualizing parishioners, served to make them complacent and materialistic. Interviews with such great names as Barnum, the circus man, and reviews of works by Goethe, Carlyle, Emerson, Margaret Fuller, the phrenologist O. S. Fowler, and others were also important.

A tendency toward hero worship was also implicit in Whitman's personality. For the moment, he placed his faith in Zachary Taylor who had won a victory against the unstable Mexican government at Buena Vista. Whitman's present belligerent attitude was antithetical to his usual stance as a pacifist. Like Emerson, Thoreau, and

the Boston clergyman Theodore Parker, he had always sided with
antiwar factions. Now, however, he argued that because of Mexico's unwillingness to negotiate for peace, he favored a declaration
of war. Always intent upon finding an outstanding candidate to run
for the presidency, the Whigs adopted the "Old Rough and Ready,"
as Taylor was called, and Whitman seconded their choice.

Not only was Whitman prowar at this time, but he was in no way
averse to America's expansionist policies. To add California, Santa
Fe (New Mexico), Texas, and other lands to the union would, he
believed, not only alleviate the oppressive conditions under which
these territories were administered, but would also spread democratic ideals. Whitman then, and understandably jumped on the
bandwagon of "Manifest Destiny," a phrase that came into use
in 1845 during the dispute over the Oregon territory. Espousing
William Cullen Bryant's view as conveyed in his poem "Oh Mother
of a Mighty Race," Whitman wrote: "The old and moth-eaten
systems of Europe have had their day, and that evening of their existence which is nigh at hand, will be the token of a glorious dawn
for the down-trodden people."

The introduction of the Wilmot Proviso (1846), forbidding slavery in the new territories, which Whitman had advocated, triggered
renewed political activity on his part. As a Free-Soiler, he believed
that to open the new western territories to free labor would be
a paradigm of democracy in action. The emergence of two warring factions in the Democratic party (the conservative "Hunkers,"
backing the South, and the "Barnburners," supporting the proviso), tore it apart. Whitman's attacks on the "Hunkers," including
Isaac Van Anden, the publisher of the *Eagle*, for having abandoned
the Jacksonian ideals, led to his dismissal from the newspaper.
Nevertheless, Whitman was a divided man. While supportive of the
Wilmot Proviso, he also execrated fanaticism in any form, even that
of the abolitionists. Like Lincoln, he felt the union was sacred and
must not be sacrificed even to abolish slavery.

Chance factors frequently intervened in Whitman's life at crucial times, to change his orientation. Such an event occurred on
February 9, 1848. While attending a Broadway theatrical performance, he happened to meet J. E. McClure, who, together with A. H.
Hayes, was in the process of founding a newspaper, the *Crescent*,
in New Orleans. So impressed was McClure with Whitman, and
the poet with him, that a contract was signed. Whitman received
two hundred dollars both to seal the bargain and to pay his fare to
Louisiana. He was thrilled at the thought of escaping the contro-

versies raging in the East, of indulging his passion for travel, and of being able to employ his brother Jeff as office boy for the *Crescent*.

The trip to Louisiana, with detours chosen by Whitman, gave him the opportunity of seeing parts of a country he deeply loved. He took notes, sometimes hastily and at other moments in a more leisurely manner, of his frequently idealized and romanticized impressions of Pennsylvania, West Virginia, Maryland, Ohio, Kentucky, Mississippi, and Louisiana: people, mores, foods, landscapes, clothes, river traffic, commerce, and language. Not only was the poet awakening to the greatness and immense size of his nation and to its incredible potential, but to his own likes and dislikes, thereby firming up a credo of his own.

Although Whitman and his brother remained at the *Crescent* from only February until May 1848, the future poet seemed to have enjoyed his work, particularly during the first few months of his stay. He not only edited news articles, but wrote feature stories: "Crossing the Alleghenies," "Western Steamboats — the Ohio," the "Model Artists," pieces on the bustling markets he visited in the French Quarter of New Orleans, and on the new faces he saw and studied. Nor were satires and parodies omitted from his deft depictions.

Whitman's reasons for returning to New York may have been multiple. His mother's letters were replete with concern over her husband's illness, her troubled finances, and her fear that Jeff might come down with yellow fever, which had reached epidemic proportions in Louisiana. These worries, coupled with Whitman's own desire to go back (his relationship with McClure having soured), may explain his haste in leaving Louisiana. Whitman planned a fascinating sight-seeing return trip, taking his brother to Missouri, Illinois, Wisconsin, Michigan, and New York State, arriving home on June 15.

In October 1848 Whitman ventured boldly into the business world by buying a lot on Myrtle Avenue and having a three-story frame house erected on it. The lower floors would be used for a printing office and bookstore, while the family would occupy the rest of the space. Enterprising in his journalistic endeavors, he decided to work for several papers, including the Brooklyn *Advertiser* and the Brooklyn *Freeman*, a Free-Soiler paper.

So important did Whitman consider the political issues of his day that by 1850 he struck out at the Democratic party, which was dominated, he felt, by a deceitful old guard who would do virtually anything to maintain its majority. That Whitman conveyed his openly hostile ideas in editorials and articles served to increase the number of his enemies and their vitriolic attacks on him.

While revolutions were raging in Europe (France, Austria, Hungary, Ireland, Lombardy, Venice, Denmark, Schleswig-Holstein) and peoples were fighting against the forces of tyranny, Whitman offered his own passionate response to them in "Resurgemus," which appeared in the New York *Tribune* (June 21, 1850).

> Liberty, let others despair of thee,
> But I will never despair of thee:
> Is the house shut? Is the master away?
> Nevertheless, be ready, be not weary of watching,
> He will surely return; his messengers come anon.

Whitman's involvement in political matters made it essential for him to husband some inner resources for an even greater and far more disturbing personal battle: the setting down of his poetry on paper. To introspect at this point of his life, to return to nature, would help him see into his creative instinct. To this end, he programmed his activities, taking long walks on Coney Island.

Alone, and when weather permitted, he strolled about amid the exciting and dramatic landscapes, savoring the experience of rushing into the cool, clear waters, and running or strolling along the beaches or in newly made paths in the neighboring woods. While observing nature in all of its variegated personalities, he also pleasured in listening to himself declaim Homer or Shakespeare, receptive to the rhythms, tonalities, and nuances of his voice and its overtones. When in the mood, he spoke or sang his own poems, overjoyed at the prospect of sharing with nature what was eventually to become *Leaves of Grass*.

Whitman's interest in the body and the necessity of maintaining its health with exercise and clean living was in keeping with his increasing fascination with science in general. For several years now, he had become interested in the relatively new field of phrenology, already lauded by Poe, Horace Mann, Emerson, Daniel Webster, and Oliver Wendell Holmes. Founded by Franz Joseph Gall, a German physician, phrenology posited that a relationship existed between the formation of a person's skull — its bumps and hollows — and the individual's character. Johann Kaspar Lavater, a Swiss divine, with whom Goethe had collaborated, added another dimension to this insightful "science," that of physiognomy, linking facial characteristics to personality traits.

Whitman not only visited the Phrenological Cabinet of Fowler & Wells in New York City, on 131 Nassau Street, but he consulted their complex charts. He even allowed Lorenzo Fowler to thoroughly examine and chart his bumps, which were evaluated as follows.

This man has a grand physical construction, and power to live to a good old age. He is undoubtedly descended from the soundest and hardiest stock. Size of head large. Leading traits of character appear to be Friendship, Sympathy, Sublimity and Self-Esteem, and markedly among his combinations the dangerous faults of Indolence, a tendency to the pleasure of Voluptuousness and Alimentiveness, and a certain reckless swing of animal will, too unmindful, probably, of the conviction of others. (Allen, 103)

Although duly impressed with their assessment of his personality, what must have fixed itself most powerfully in Whitman's mind was the vocabulary used by phrenologists to depict specific emotional tendencies. Words such as *amativeness,* defined as heterosexual love; *philoprogenitiveness,* meaning love of mankind; and *adhesiveness,* identified with "manly love," "the love of comrades," by extension homosexual love, were so provocative that Whitman was to incorporate them in his later prose and poetical works.

Not only was Whitman drawn to phrenology, as he had also been to theater and opera, but as a visualist, the pictorial arts also intrigued him. Particularly alluring were the works of the successful artist William Sidney Mount, whose dictum Whitman might have taken seriously: "Paint pictures that will take with the public — never paint for the few, but the many." The poet responded to the feelings of serenity and homeliness in Mount's scenes of rural life on Long Island — "Farmers Nooning" (1836) and "The Power of Music" (1847). Perhaps their resemblance to Dutch genre painting triggered reminiscences of Whitman's own heritage. He also became friendly with such artists as Walter Libby, known for his "Boy Playing Flute," and Henry Kirke Brown, noted for his bronze statue of Washington in New York's Union Square.

Perhaps because of Whitman's involvement in creativity in general and its impact on verbal images in poetry, he found the company of artists congenial. He enjoyed whiling away hours on end listening to their experiences and also imparting his own to them. Particularly intriguing to Whitman, perhaps because the artist had studied in Europe, were Brown's painterly notions. It is believed that Brown's student John Quincy Adams Ward, whose idealized statues of Indians had been well received, taught Whitman the fundamentals of sketching.

Whitman might have been drawn to the seminude statue of Washington as an Olympian god, by Horatio Greenough, because he, like the sculptor, believed that a human body was never to be looked upon as either evil or dirty, but rather, as the supreme example of God's creation. Greenough's statue, when placed under the Capitol dome, had been scoffed at by the public, the consensus being, at least outwardly, that it smacked of sentimentalism and overly classical influences. Additional, and covert, criticisms were leveled against the sculptor's exposure of the body. To these, Greenough responded in his *Aesthetics in Washington* (1851) that Americans should reject the overwhelming moralism pervading their land; they should be encouraged to create their own art forms in a free and healthful atmosphere. He, like Whitman, felt strongly that the human body was the most beautifully organized network on earth, and therefore, nudes should be depicted if the artist desires it. Significant as well were Greenough's statements concerning functional art, which certainly must have given Whitman pause when he was to write his poems celebrating the locomotive, ferries, steamships, and other machines.

Opera, which Whitman continued to attend, was making increasingly deeper inroads on him as a poet. Tones, rhythms, and diapasons emanating from the stage seemed to translate themselves for the poet into sheer emotion. So "overwhelmed" was he, for example, by the purity of Alessandro Bettini's perfect tenor voice, most particularly when portraying Fernando in Donizetti's *La Favorita,* that it elicited tears.

Although Whitman had attended the performances of many visiting European operatic celebrities, including Jenny Lind, it was Italian opera and bel canto that affected him most deeply. After hearing Marietta Alboni, his favorite operatic star, in Donizetti's *Lucia di Lammermoor,* he wrote, "She used to sweep me away as with whirlwinds.... Her voice is a contralto of large compass, high and low — and probably sweeter tones never issued from human lips" (R. Faner, *Walt Whitman and Opera,* 59).

So important a place had the operatic voice acquired in Whitman's life, that he came to believe that *Leaves of Grass* could not have been written without the influence of opera. Bellini introduced into music a special note, he wrote: "It is a kind of hushed, neurotic ecstasy, a kind of gentle languorous orgasm in moonlit, bloom-pervaded gardens. Long before Verlaine, it was always crying in

Bellini's heart. Chopin heard it, and it is the stuff of his sulphurous, elegant nocturnes" (Faner, 31).

Was vocal music that special element that had eluded Whitman until now? Was bel canto that intensely powerful factor that enabled him to make his genius manifest? In "Shut Not Your Doors" (1865), hadn't he suggested that *everything* must feed poetic fantasy?

> Shut not your doors to me proud libraries,
> For that which was lacking on all your well-fill'd shelves, yet needed
>   most I bring,
> Forth from the war emerging, a book I have made,
> The words of my book nothing, the drift of it every thing,
> A book separate, not link'd with the rest nor felt by the intellect,
> But you ye untold latencies will thrill to every page.

That music was crucial in triggering Whitman's creative act is attested to in his many readings and positive statements referring to George Sand's "masterpiece," *Consuelo,* and its sequel, *The Countess of Rudolstadt* (1842). In his *Notebooks* he writes that the soul, and not the senses alone were of import to Sand's heroine and that it was humanity's soul that spoke through hers. Sand's protagonist, let us recall, a gypsy girl brought up in the streets of Venice and discovered by the maestro Porporo, became one of the greatest of all European opera stars. The manner in which Sand depicts her heroine's magisterial voice in all of its nuances remained with Whitman always. Indeed, it inspired him to transmute into words, in "Song of Myself," the emotions elicited in Consuelo's listeners during one of her extraordinary performances:

> I hear the trained soprano....
> The orchestra whirls me wider than Uranus flies,
> It wrenches such ardors from me I did not know I possess'd them,
> It sails me, I dab with, bare feet, they are lick'd by the indolent
>   waves. (26:603)

Open to everything life and art had to offer, Whitman also became fascinated with Egyptology. Although he had read some books on the subject, it became a living experience for him mainly because of his lengthy discussions with Dr. Henry Abbott, owner and curator of the Egyptian Museum, at 659 Broadway, which opened in 1855. When Dr. Abbott, unable to provide for the collection himself, tried to sell his museum to the city, Whitman offered his help by writing an article on it for *Life Illustrated*. The poet's considerable understanding of Abbott's collection, as well as his knowledge of the Egyptian pantheon and his familiarity with the latest books published abroad on the subject, was impressive. "The theology of Egypt," Whitman wrote admiringly, "was vast and profound. It respected the principle of life in all things — even in animals. It sought truth and justice above all other attributes of man. It recognized immortality" (Allen, 122). Later, Whitman would decant into his *Leaves of Grass* a panoply of sexual symbols and lush green images identified with the God Osiris's procreative power.

Whitman's insatiable appetite for knowledge included ethnology, astronomy, geology, and the evolution of the human race. He attended lectures and read broadly on these subjects, incorporating much of the information gleaned into his poems. Such notions, as the enormity of space, celestial movement, the patterns made by constellations, the trajectory of comets, the rings of Saturn and estimates of its diameter, the concepts of time, both historical and cyclical — these themes were forever infiltrating his poems. Engrossing to him also were the works of such ancient and modern writers as Froissart, Dante, Shakespeare, Spinoza, Milton, Johnson, Burns, Scott, Dickens, Bulwer-Lytton, Kant, Carlyle, Coleridge, Shelley, Keats, Spenser, and Guizot, as well as texts by Hindus, Buddhists, and Taoists.

Direct experience, in conjunction with the impact made upon him by the arts in general, was instrumental in Whitman's creation of his own passionately authentic poetics. Although techniques and stylistics were of import to him, he had refrained early in his writing career from an overuse of both figures of speech and traditional imagery. A good poet, he thought, should suggest and not state didactically. In the *Edinburgh Review* (April 1849), Whitman wrote: "The perfect poem is simple, healthy, natural — no griffins, angels, centaurs — no hysterics or blue fire — no dyspepsia, no suicidal intentions." In the margin of an article he read that same year, Whitman noted that poets should be regarded, as in ancient times, as *vates:* "divine mediums — through them come spirits and materials to all the people, men and women" (Allen, 133). Awakened in this fashion to the poet's inner world, readers would not merely *take in* passively, but would also make an effort to deepen their understanding of the feelings and thoughts involved.

Exactly when and where Whitman began writing his *Leaves of Grass* is not known. Seemingly, he had thought of bringing out such a volume as far back as the 1840s. Evidently, he had to wait for that propitious moment when he felt, both intellectually and emotionally, prepared to act. As previously noted, Whitman was not a *thinking* type. Body and feeling emerged virtually simultaneously with the spiritual orientation, the orientation of the soul. It was a paradox for some, but not for Whitman, to believe that the soul was not only as important as the body, but synonymous with it. Crucial for him as well was his distaste for constrictions, ensnarements, and imprisonments of any kind, be they those of ideology or of human relationships. Outside of his everpresent sense of commitment to his immediate family, Whitman could not be harnessed to anyone or anything for any length of time. Still — and this is the paradox — despite his need of wandering, he forever yearned to experience a long-term love relationship. He now understood something intensely disturbing and unresolvable about himself: "I cannot understand the mystery, but I am always conscious of myself as two — as my soul and I: and I reckon it is the same with all men and women" (*UPP*, II, 66).

After all these years of searching and wandering, Whitman was not only discovering his vocation as poet, but, seemingly, also accepting his sexual inclinations. Still, a paradox remains. Although he certainly did not shun sexual imagery in his poetry (on the contrary, he refused to cast aside autoerotic passages that burst into his mind's eye), facts surrounding his own sexual identification are seemingly nonexistent. Judging from the poet's life-style and his writings, including his correspondence, one may conclude — although not with certainty — that he was homosexual. Perhaps some powerful feelings of guilt prevented him from revealing his thoughts on the subject outright, though these remain implicit in his poems and prose. Time and time again, he castigated others — puritan elements in society in particular — for hiding their real thoughts concerning sexual matters. The gist of his statements focused on speaking openly and brazenly about how one feels concerning one's *secret* inclinations. So far as is known, however, Whitman never did.

What is known is that this many-sided individual, always concealing personal matters, was attracted to strong, handsome, uneducated, and "coarse" young men. Perhaps these outwardly naive and simple types afforded him the visceral pleasures that enabled him to find an outlet for his highly emotional and conflictual nature. Of the many whom he would frequent, Peter Doyle, a bus driver who did not get along with his father, but, like Whitman, loved his mother, was most important to the poet. More about him later.

Sex, along with Whitman's poetic needs, energized him both on terrestrial and on mystical planes. So sensitive was he that everything not only impacted upon him, but also had its syncretistic and symbolic ramifications. Nothing, therefore, was either simple or clear-cut for Whitman. Thoroughly imbued with Emerson's philosophy, as well as that of other transcendentalists, he understood the soul in poetic terms — as an amalgam. For him, it was neither stagnant nor stationary, but existed in a state of eternal becoming in an ascending hierarchical sphere. Such an approach to something so intangible not only helped Whitman struggle through his crushing feelings of sexual guilt, particularly acute in nineteenth-century puritanical America, but it also allowed him to meditate on certain happenings, then to free-associate, as was the habit of many symbolist poets. The *reality* of the ecstatic sensations experienced during Whitman's periods of creative reverie was crucial in ushering him into transcendental realms where pain and ennui did not exist.

Because no commercial house wanted to take the financial risk of publishing Whitman's *Leaves of Grass* (1855), he published it in Brooklyn, on July 4 of that year, at his own expense. The volume's physical aspect was arresting: the engraving opposite the title page featured a bearded workingman wearing a broad hat and shirt open at the neck. The printers, James and Thomas Rome, friends of the poet, allowed him not only to supervise the process, but to set ten pages himself. The phrenologists Fowler and Wells paid for the advertising and sold the volume in their offices. Although around one thousand copies were printed, many were given away, including one to Ralph Waldo Emerson.

Whitman's untitled essay prefacing *Leaves of Grass,* written in the author's innovative but also sibylline style, explained his very personal approach to punctuation, including his frequent use of ellipses. It also summarized his thoughts and feelings concerning an expanding America, and the poet's role in this vast land. He assured his readers that he had not rejected past achievements in poetics, but would, to the contrary, integrate these into a new, fresh, and transcendent vision of this art. Such a composite would, in keeping with Whitman's new vision, reflect American geography, multiplicity of ethnic groups, variety of occupations and diversity of personality types: "Here is not a nation but a teeming nation of nations." Poetry, not an art for escapists, would deal with earthly truths and values: "Whatever satisfies the soul is truth." Reality would be the focus of poetics: "Love the earth and sun and the animals." Sciences and histories of the world would be called upon to enrich the writer's medium, thus transforming language into an all-encompassing art — "transcendent and new." He noted that "Nothing is better than simplicity." Nor would rhyme be the supreme arbiter. In fact, the poet might, if he so chose, not use any at all. Nor would stanzas be uniform in length. Philosophically, the great American poet intended to be an "equalizer," "equable," above pettiness; one who spoke with "candor" and "openness" for he was a "seer" and "complete in himself."

Poetics, the great educator, the inspiration for generations to come, would instill spiritual and physical cleanliness and vigor in the children of tomorrow, as well as friendliness and a sense of equality between female and male. Using the phrenologists' term, Whitman wrote of "the large amativeness — the fluid movement of the population — the factories and mercantile life and labor saving machinery." Poetic themes would replicate neither the melancholia and dissatisfactions of the Graveyard poets (Thomas Parnell and Thomas Gray, among others) nor the didacticism of a Longfellow. Pomposity would be banned; "genuineness" alone would be acceptable. The English language — "brawny enough and limber and full enough" — would be enriched until it could "express the inexpressible."

Not surprisingly, then, mystical themes, and unlimited spaces and time schemes, would also be fleshed out in Whitman's poetics: "The known universe has one complete lover and that is the greatest poet." The poet is not a moralizer. He is a poet of the "kosmos" and is a "kosmos" unto himself: a being in whom "the essences of the real things" cohabit. Within him all events are linked: the *oneness* of body and soul advances "through all interpositions and coverings and turmoils and stratagems to first principles." When the poet "breathes into any thing that was before thought small it dilates with the grandeur and life of the universe." Since no good act is lost, failure itself is to be transformed into success. A prophet, ahead of his times, the poet, knowing what to exalt and how to serve the people, replaces the priest. Like Victor Hugo, Whitman considered the poet as having a messianic function:

A superior breed shall take their place.... The gangs of kosmos and prophets en masse shall take their place. A new order shall arise and they shall be the priests of man, and every man shall be his own priest.... Through the divinity of themselves shall the kosmos and the new breed of poets be interpreters of men and women and of all events and things. They shall find their inspiration in real objects today, symptoms of the past and future.

By immersing himself in infinity — in mythical domains — the poet exists in past, present, and future simultaneously, thus living in "vast stretches of time or the slow formation of density," thereby participating in the flow and pulsation of what mystics term an eternal present.

That Whitman had interwoven in his introduction some of the significant statements made by Emerson in his essay "The Poet" could not but have pleased the older writer. For Emerson, the poet was a person who "stands among partial men for the complete man, and apprises us not of his wealth, but of the commonwealth." Not surprisingly, Emerson continued, the poet

is isolated among his contemporaries, by truth and by his art, but with this consolation in his pursuits, that they will draw all men sooner or later. For all men live by truth, and stand in need of expression. In love, in art, in avarice, in politics, in labor, in games, we study to utter our painful secret. The man is only half himself, the other half is his expression.

Emerson — and here, as we have seen, Whitman would follow his master — did not believe that meters were the sine qua non of poetry; rather, he declared, "a metre-making argument, that makes a poem, — a thought so passionate and alive, that, like the spirit of a plant or an animal, it has an architecture of its own, and adorns nature with a new thing." Each age, he stated, needs a new poet to announce the changing tidings: "I had fancied that the oracles were all silent, and nature had spent her fires, and behold! all night, from every pore, these fine auroras have been streaming." Nature's creatures offer themselves to the poet to be eternalized in symbols because "nature is a symbol, in the whole, and in every part" and is conveyed in "picture-language." The use made by the poet of nature is a measure of his divineness "whereby the world is a temple, whose walls are covered with emblems, pictures, and commandments of the Deity." Emerson's beliefs, also incorporated in Whitman's credo, held that poets "stand before the secret of the world, there where Being passes into Appearance, and Unity into Variety."

Along with the similarities that existed between the Bostonian born sage and Whitman, there were vast differences. Although Emerson's prose was at times sensuous, particularly when depicting nature, his thinking was essentially abstract, his thoughts ordered in logical sequences. Whitman, to the contrary, *felt* into life. Above all, he was instinctual. Nor was Whitman, as was Emerson, puritanical in his demeanor, or his writings. On the contrary, *Leaves of Grass* was to be his springboard: the beginning of what he intended to be his progressive divestiture of constraints; his ejaculation of fears and guilt; his rejection of the puritanical principles that were preventing him from singing out his soul in broad sweeps. These basic personality differences between Whitman and Emerson were, however, still buried in their respective coded and symbolic vocabularies, perhaps not even evident to either of them except subliminally.

When Whitman received a laudatory letter from Emerson, thanking him for sending a copy of *Leaves of Grass,* he was so filled with gratitude that he carried it around for days. Emerson wrote:

I greet you at the beginning of a great career, which yet must have had a long foreground somewhere, for such a start. I rubbed my eyes a little to see if this sunbeam were no illusion; but the solid sense of the book is a sober certainty. . . .
I did not know until I, last night, saw the book advertised in a newspaper, that I could trust the name as real & available for a post office. I wish to see my benefactor, & have felt much like striking my task, & visiting New York to pay you my respects.

What Whitman did not as yet know was that Emerson had recommended *Leaves of Grass* to such friends as Bronson Alcott, the philosopher, teacher, and poet; Henry David Thoreau, the famed transcendentalist, naturalist, and author of *Walden;* Frank Sanborn, an abolitionist and journalist; and Moncure D. Conway, a Unitarian minister who later became a preacher of free thought.

Emerson's endorsement of *Leaves of Grass,* while enhancing Whitman's deficient feelings of self-worth, would also help him stave off — at least emotionally — the crushing negative criticism his twelve nontraditional free-verse poems attracted. Particularly irritating and shocking to the readers of the day, even to Emerson, was Whitman's bold autoerotic and plainly sexual imagery, evident in "Song of Myself," among others. To be sure, Whitman's visualizations were the natural outcome of his mystical doctrine based on his belief in the unity and equality of body and soul. Others considered the equating of body and soul as blasphemous.

Whitman's poems, for many, were paradigms of this newcomer's arrogant, egotistical, immodest, and crude thinking. Emerson, however, and the few other discerning critics of the time who understood the deeper meanings of Whitman's verse, discovered in his stanzas a transcendental philosophy: a belief in, and feeling for, union with God. Whitman's sense of relatedness to everything, be it manifest or not, in a world replete with infinite analogies, endowed the poet with a sense of plenitude and overflowing love. Within Whitman's spiritual visions existed his understanding of the Pythagorean and Swedenborgian framework of *correspondences:* from the smallest to the greatest element implicit in nature's visible and invisible garb, *love* is the supreme catalyst for life's eternally gestating power.

A review by Charles A. Dana, managing editor of the New York *Tribune,* although not unqualified in its praise, and referring to Whitman as an "odd genius" whose language was "too frequently reckless and indecent," did single out the originality of his poetic form when stating that "no impartial reader can fail to be impressed with the vigor and quaint beauty of isolated portions" (James Woodress, *Critical Essays on Walt Whitman,* 18).

Whitman himself felt it necessary to write three praiseworthy articles about his own work, among these, his "Walt Whitman and His Poems." In time, Charles Eliot Norton of Harvard, referring to Whitman's book in *Putnam's Monthly* as "a mixture of Yankee transcendentalism and New York rowdyism," analyzed the pros and cons of *Leaves of Grass* (Woodress, 20). Whitman, fearing adverse criticism, either agreed to Dana's suggestion or suggested himself that Dana print Emerson's letter in the *Tribune* (October 10) without its author's permission. Emerson did not comment on it publicly, but in a note to Longfellow he wrote that Whitman had "done a strange rude thing in printing in the Tribune...my letter of thanks for his book" (Ralph Rusk, *The Life of Ralph Waldo Emerson,* 373). Later, after Whitman again made use of Emerson's letter, and Emerson began receiving notes from friends and strangers decrying his congratulatory missive, he regretted his initial gesture.

Although Longfellow, Holmes, and Lowell preferred not to comment on *Leaves of Grass,* and Whittier, it was reported, threw his copy into the fire, Rufus W. Griswold's review in the *Criterion* stated that it "strongly fortifies the doctrines of Metempsychosis, for it is impossible to imagine how any man's fancy could have conceived such a mass of stupid filth, unless he were possessed of the soul of a sentimental donkey that had died of disappointed love." An anonymous review appearing in the Boston *Intelligencer* declared *Leaves of Grass* to be "a violation of decency" and stated that it "should find no place where humanity urges any claim to respect, and the author should be kicked from all decent society as below the level of the brute" (Woodress 25, 28).

(Had Whitman been aware of a statement made by Henry R. Rankin, a law student working in the offices of Lincoln and Herndon, in Springfield, Illinois, he would have been deeply satisfied. It seems that after *Leaves of Grass* had arrived in some unknown way in the above-mentioned law offices, it became a subject of discussion between Herndon and the students.)

Although Whitman used every journalistic ploy to promote *Leaves of Grass,* it was Emerson's letter and recommendations that brought Whitman many of his influential readers. To the original twelve poems of the first edition, Whitman added another twenty to the second, which appeared in 1856. To ensure its sales, and again without asking Emerson's permission, the author not only printed the sage's laudatory letter, but his own reply addressed to "dear Friend and Master."

Thanks to Emerson's praise, two highly esteemed men came to New York to visit Whitman: Thoreau and Alcott. About Alcott, Emerson wrote: "As pure intellect I have never seen his equal." Thoreau considered him "the sanest man I ever knew." Whitman must have been impressed with the modernity of the New Englander's ideas on education: not only did Alcott favor a conversational method of instruction and the development of the imagination, but the introduction of recreation, gymnastics, organized play, and an honor system into the curriculum. Although a believer in an extremist form of transcendentalism (referred to as personalism), Alcott did not share the group's view of individualism. He believed that all minds are separate, but linked to a central Mind, and "all souls have a Personal identity with God and abide in Him." Alcott and Thoreau had vastly different personalities from Whitman, but both visitors appreciated the poet's qualities. Alcott's restrained and sometimes stiff manner, contrasted sharply with Whitman's, whose usual style was neither decorous nor reticent. When meeting with the self-contained Thoreau, however, Whitman was so reserved that no real contact was made that first time. Nevertheless, after Thoreau's reading of the second edition of *Leaves of Grass,* he wrote to a friend: Whitman "is the most interesting fact to me at present." Some poems, he conceded, were overly sensual — "as if the beast spoke" — and not a celebration of love. Yet he was impressed by their energy and courage, even admitting that what he had judged as arrogance upon the initial New York meeting was not that at all. On the contrary, "He may turn out the least of a braggart of all, having a better right to be confident" (H. D. Thoreau, *Letters of Various Persons,* 142, 146).

Despite the publicity awarded *Leaves of Grass,* it sold poorly. Since Whitman had no other means of support at the time, he found himself obliged to borrow money to see him through the winter of 1857. Although his situation changed by spring — he became editor of George C. Bennett's Brooklyn *Daily Times* — his energies, rather than being devoted to poetry, were siphoned off into his editorials. The articles he wrote dealt with politics, corruption, prostitution, the crash of 1857, bank failures, unemployment, poverty, mob violence, the laying of the Atlantic cable, railroads, waterworks, the ministry, education, and other subjects. Outspoken as usual, he spared neither the clergy nor organized religion in his attacks on their corruption and hypocrisy. The complaints by churchgoers resulted in Whitman's discharge or resignation from the *Daily Times.*

While unemployed, the poet devoted his energies to the preparation of a third edition of *Leaves of Grass* (1860): sixty-eight poems were added to the second edition's thirty-two, of which he revised many. More significant than the additions to his collection of poems was its change in tone: the increasingly spiritual, psychological, and literary cast spelled a deepening understanding of life. It became evident that his still-disparate ideas were in the process of coalescing. More important to him now was his need to sing of America's dramatic physiognomy — its breadth and sweep, the variety of its landscapes and soils — as well as of its culture and art. Nor would its democratic principles be omitted. Expressed also was his approach to love: his use of the phrenologists' terms — *amativeness* and *adhesiveness.*

Whitman's better understanding, and perhaps acceptance, of his own inclinations lead to greater insights into the psychological problems homosexuals faced. Rejected by nineteenth-century society, they were looked upon as deviates, as aberrants, that is, in some way deficient. Siding with majority opinion, as was natural for the time, Whitman unconsciously looked upon his sexual attraction for men as a fault or lack within himself. Until now, he had kept his highly volatile emotions at bay, locked within, masking these in his poetry by referring to "her" or "she when really talking about "him" and "he."

A volcano was seething within the poet's psyche: a struggle between what he *should be* and what *he was,* between the fear of revelation and the backlash that might ensue were he to finally liberate himself of his "secret" by telling all. The question remaining to be formulated was whether or not Whitman would have the emotional stamina to survive the stigma that "others" would brand him with should he confess his sexual proclivities.

Unlike St. Augustine, who equated God with Good and who believed Evil to be nonexistent in a God-created world (what appeared to be Evil was merely a *privatio boni*), Whitman, like the Gnostics, concluded that the dual forces of Good and Evil were continuously present, vying with each other for dominance in the cosmos as well as in the human personality. Humankind, therefore, must be awake at all times, ready and able to fight wrong and injustice.

Whitman's "secret," however, was not Evil. His sexual inclinations were simply his way of expressing his love of life. Although his approach toward "adhesiveness" differed from that of the majority of the heterosexual population, it was authentic, thus pure in intent. Nevertheless, Whitman's rationalizations did not diminish the conflict and feelings of guilt raging within him. Why was he different from others? Did the potential for Evil exist within him? His impulse to reveal his "secret" in the new edition of *Leaves of Grass* was made manifest by the inclusion of *Calamus,* a homoerotic group of poems dealing with male friendship. In veiled and symbolic indications, they yielded glimmerings of the poet's corrosive guilt feelings, but also of opposite extremes, the unbounded joy in his love experiences. The sexual imagery in "Not Heat Flames Up and Consumes" (1860) is more than overt:

> Not these, O none of these more than the flames of me, consuming,
>   burning for his love whom I love,
> O none more than I hurrying in and out;
> Does the tide hurry, seeking something, and never give up? O I the
>   same,
> O nor down-balls nor perfumes, nor the high rain-emitting clouds,
>   are borne through the open air,
> Any more than my soul is borne through the open air,
> Wafted in all directions O love, for friendship, for you.

Nor is there anything veiled in "I Saw in Louisiana a Live-Oak Growing" (1860). Ecstasy in the sensations enjoyed in "manly love" cohabits with chaos, revolving around fears of society's opprobrium and of castration.

> I saw in Louisiana a live-oak growing....
> And its look, rude, unbending, lusty, made me think of myself,

But I wonder'd how it could utter joyous leaves standing alone
    there without its friend near, for I knew I could not,
And I broke off a twig with a certain number of leaves upon it, and
    twined around it a little moss,
And brought it away, and I have placed it in sight in my room,
It is not needed to remind me as of my own dear friends,
(For I believe lately I think of little else than of them,)
Yet it remains to me a curious token, it makes me think of manly
    love;
For all that, and though the live-oak glistens there in Louisiana
    solitary in a wide flat space,
Uttering joyous leaves all its life without a friend a lover near,
    I know very well I could not.

Whitman had very nearly come full swing. He thoroughly rejected any thoughts concerning Christianity's view that sexual love was something unclean, as attested to in such notions as the Immaculate Conception, asceticism, flagellation, and other modes of self-chastisement. Instead, his poetry sings of nature's generative process in all of its manifestations, and most particularly of the love experience. Sexual love for Whitman, as it had been for many ancients, the Hindus, and certain mystical sects, was viewed as the earthly replication of a Divine act.

The love act between male and female and the ensuing miracle- and mystery — of birth would serve to create a new race of human beings whose minds and bodies would, Whitman projected, go forward in unison and evolve in so doing. A eugenicist, he believed in the powers of forward-looking groups, be they politically, scientifically, or culturally oriented. The hope in future progress was for Whitman — as it was for most European thinkers and creative people of the nineteenth century — a reality!

Whitman was no armchair philosopher living in an ivory tower. On the contrary, while preparing his third edition of *Leaves of Grass* he never gave up his extroverted ways. Mingling with the crowd, conversing, and exchanging ideas, serving to refine and sharpen his point of view on many subjects.

Whitman made friends easily and everywhere. Indeed, he had a whole coterie at Pfaff's restaurant. Founded in 1854 by the Swiss-German skeptic and socialist Charles Pfaff, on lower Broadway above Bleecker Street, the restaurant attracted a very special clientele: *Bohemians*. A term borrowed from the French, it referred most overtly to antipuritanical artists and writers. The free and easy tone enjoyed at Pfaff's, together with its intellectually stimulating atmosphere — even its noise — could not but appeal to Whitman's temperament.

Not everyone, however, took to Pfaff's milieu. The Ohio-born novelist William Dean Howells was unimpressed with the restaurant. However, he described Whitman in warm terms, as the poet

leaned back in his chair, and reached out his great hand to me, as if he were going to give it me for good and all. He had a fine head, with a cloud of Jovian hair upon it, and a branching beard and mustache, and gentle eyes that looked most kindly into mine, and seemed to wish the liking which I instantly gave him, though we hardly passed a word, and our acquaintance was summed up in that glance and the grasp of his mighty fist upon my handle. (Allen, 230)

The third edition of *Leaves of Grass* (1860) was published by Thayer and Eldridge, a Boston firm. When in that city to confer with his publishers, Whitman took the opportunity to meet with Emerson as well. Years later, when referring to their March 15 discussion, the poet, speaking with reverence of his "Master," mentioned his advice not to include his cluster of poems, *Children of Adam* (*Enfants d'Adam*), in the new edition. Emerson's reasons must have been motivated by his extreme generosity toward the poet, believing that to include them would damage Whitman's reputation and alienate his readers. Whitman's refusal to be budged in no way altered Emerson's friendly and ever-helpful relationship with him.

Longfellow, Lowell, and Holmes still refused to meet Whitman during his stay in Boston. Thoreau and Alcott, who wanted to invite him to visit their homes, were prevented from doing so by the vociferous protests of their wives and sisters. Whitman did, nevertheless, meet some of his admirers while in Boston: William Douglas O'Connor, journalist, minor official, and author of an abolitionist novel, *Harrington* (1860); Dr. Henry Channing, the Christian Socialist and member of the Transcendental Club; John Townsend Trowbridge, editor and author of such boys' and antislavery novels as *Cudjo's Cave* (1864). It was on a visit to the latter's home that Whitman confessed to the two greatest influences on his poetry: Italian opera and Emerson's writings. The latter had helped him find himself: "I was simmering, simmering, simmering; Emerson brought me to a boil" (Allen, 242).

The publication of the expanded third edition of *Leaves of Grass,* with its superabundance of phallic imagery, its focus on amativeness and adhesiveness, and its haunting leitmotif of death, stunned many a reader by its beauty, colorations, rhythms, and tonal quali-

ties. The poet's depictions of working people, machines, nature, and
the vastness of America were unparalleled for their visceral and hypnotic effects. Whitman's ebullience and adventuresome excitement,
as well as his sense of the aesthetic, caught the readers unaware. The
poet seemed to revel in his need to confess, to liberate himself from
his corrosive feelings of guilt, as he disclosed his yearnings, and his
dislike and distrust of certain people and their ways.

While many heterosexual male critics considered the poems
included in the 1860 edition of *Leaves of Grass* immoral and indecent, certain liberated women came to the author's defense. Mary A.
Chilton of Islip, Long Island, for example, sent a letter to the *Saturday Press* stating that she favored the inclusion of Whitman's
sex poems for their "simple grandeur," as well as for the natural
manner with which he treated the body and its functions.

In childhood there is no blush of shame at sight of a nude form, and the
serene wisdom of maturity covers this innocence with a halo of glory,
by recognizing the divinity of humanity, and perceiving the unity of all
the functions of the human body...and those functions which have been
deemed the most brutal and degrading, will be found to be first in rank
when nature's hierarchy shall be established and observed. (Allen, 263)

Nor should it come as a surprise to learn that many women en-
dorsed Whitman's poetry, because of the author's stand on equality
between the sexes and his help in mounting a campaign for women's
rights. Mention must also be made of women's attraction to the
poet's outgoing, open, and friendly manner. Nevertheless, Whitman
became subject to an increasing number of venomous reviews, parodies, and sarcasms. The destructive onslaught encouraged him to
write more anonymous laudatory critiques of his work. But nothing really seemed to work for him. Sales were poor and his Boston
publisher declared bankruptcy some months after publication.

Still, Whitman was determined to pursue the kind of existence
he felt was right for him and to say the things he felt and thought.
Again, he turned to nature for solace and inspiration, spending long
hours tramping along the Long Island shore. Whitman's gregarious
side also impelled him to take walking tours around the streets of
New York City. Pfaff's restaurant and its "Bohemian" clientele remained a source of amusement and stimulation to him. What he
appreciated most about it were not the conversations or discussions he heard, but the creative people he met there. The satiric
bent of the Irish-born journalist and author Fitz-James O'Brien ex-
cited him, as did the quick and arresting wit of the poet-humorist

George Arnold. Despite his scornful quips, Whitman enjoyed the eloquence of Henry Clapp, the founder of the *Saturday Press* and translator of Fourier. Perhaps it was because Whitman lacked the gift of rapid repartee that he wrote years later: "My own greatest pleasure at Pfaff's — was to look on — to see, talk little, absorb" (*WWC*, I,417).

Throughout these difficult but also pleasurable and eventful years, Whitman had never neglected his family. Whether times were merry or tragic, the poet remained the dutiful son he had always been, extending both money and comfort. However, the fact that he had not been present, through no fault of his own, at his father's death in 1855 had activated his already piercing feelings of guilt. The thought of not having lived up to his father's expectations further haunted him. He rationalized in his own favor, however, arguing that his father had never taken the trouble to appreciate his poetry. Nor, for that matter, had any member of his family begun to understand it. His feelings of responsibility for his sister Hannah's disastrous marriage in 1852, to the French-born Brooklyn landscape painter Charles L. Heyde, may have had some foundation, since he had introduced the couple. Would the newly married Jeff, employed since 1859 as surveyor of the Water Works, fare any better? He looked dimly upon Andrew's future. He had already suffered a severe bout of pleurisy. Jesse, employed at the Brooklyn Navy Yard, was given to violence.

Although deeply involved with his family, Whitman was nevertheless his own man, able and determined to follow his bent. One of his great pleasures was riding the stages, making certain to seat himself in front near the driver. To be a stagecoach driver in nineteenth-century New York City was a difficult and dangerous metier: the hours were long, from four o'clock until midnight; collisions were frequent; and horses getting out of hand on their journey up and down Broadway were common occurrences. Because stage drivers sustained many injuries, Whitman had, whatever the underlying motivations, developed a taste for visiting them when they were patients at New York Hospital (then at Broadway and Pearl Steet). Not only did he enjoy their company, but they too, responded openly to his warmth and fervor. Dr. D. B. St. John Roosa described one of Whitman's visits as follows:

Whitman appeared to be about forty years of age at that time. He was always dressed in a blue flannel coat and vest, with gray and baggy trousers. He wore a woolen shirt, with a Byronic collar, low in the neck, without a cravat, as I remember, and a large felt hat. His hair was iron gray, and he had a full beard and mustache of the same color. His face and neck were bronzed by exposure to the sun and air. He was large, and gave the impression of being a vigorous man. He was scrupulously careful of his simple attire, and his hands were soft and hairy....

His personality was extremely pleasing. It must have been from the gentle and refined caste of his features, which were rather rude, but noble. No one could see him sitting by the bedside of a suffering stage driver without soon learning that he had sincere and profound sympathy for this order of men. Close observation of their lives at that time would convince one that they endured hardships, which naturally invited the sympathy of a great nature. When we found that Walt Whitman was anxious to visit sick stage drivers, the house staff gave him the largest liberty of entrance. (Allen, 268)

The house staff also enjoyed chatting with Whitman. What they most admired about him were his open ways and his compassion for the physically and emotionally needy. Nevertheless, they kept wondering why his interest was limited to this "class" of men. Was it the stage drivers' virile nature, their heroism, and their perseverance that impressed the poet? Whatever the causes behind Whitman's behavior, he felt emotional harmony with the stage drivers as a group.

Nevertheless, Whitman's visits to the hospitalized stage drivers were soon to screech to a halt. With the election of Abraham Lincoln to the presidency in November 1860, the political climate was changing — rapidly and dangerously. The North, fearing violence, had not favored Lincoln's platform. The South had already set matters into motion to secede.

Lincoln was inaugurated on February 18, 1861, and the Confederate batteries fired on Fort Sumter on April 12, marking the beginning of the Civil War. Whitman's brother George enlisted for military service with the Thirteenth New York Regiment. Although generally optimistic, believing, as did so many at the outset of the hostilities, that the "rebellion" would be crushed momentarily, Whitman had a change of heart on July 22, 1861, when Union troops were routed at the first battle of Bull Run. Nor was he alone. Rage, shock, fear, and a sense of helplessness shot through Washington, D.C., as people watched the mud-soaked and exhausted soldiers pour into the city. Lincoln wasted no time reorganizing the troops. As for Whitman, he verbalized his feelings of respect and wonderment at the president's decisive stance with his own call to arms, "Beat! Beat! Drums!" — a poem that was to go down in history.

Beat! beat! drums! — blow! bugles! blow!
Through the windows — through doors — burst like a ruthless force....
Beat! beat! drums! — blow! bugles! blow!
Make no parley — stop for no expostulation;
Mind not the timid — mind not the weeper or prayer;
Mind not the old man beseeching the young man....
So strong you thump, O terrible drums — so loud you bugles blow.

So electrified had Whitman been by the events, that he decided to resume his career as a journalist, focusing his attention on the newly admitted war casualties of Bull Run.

Although he was patriotic in every way, Whitman could not help but be concerned over George's welfare. Proud of the fact that his brother's bravery had earned him a promotion to the rank of lieutenant, he grew ever more anxious when informed of his reenlistment. After, in the New York *Herald* of December 16, he read George's name among the list of wounded at the battle of Fredericksburg, he decided to leave for Washington that very day in search of him.

Whitman's trip, which included several ferry and train rides, was long and arduous. To make matters even more unpleasant, a pickpocket robbed him en route of the fifty dollars his mother had given him for emergencies. Although he was exhausted and penniless by the time he finally arrived in Washington, he immediately began to visit the forty military hospitals in the vicinity. His efforts to locate his brother were unsuccessful. Fortunately, the money he was able to borrow from William D. O'Connor, whom he had met in Boston and who was now working in the Treasury Department, paid his way to Fredericksburg. Perhaps his brother had rejoined his regiment, he reasoned. With the help of another friend, Charles W. Eldridge, the publisher of the 1860 edition of *Leaves of Grass,* now assistant to the army paymaster, he obtained a pass to Fredericksburg.

Although right thinking led him directly to George's regiment, the sight he saw, prior to his meeting with his brother, struck him with horror: "One of the first things that met my eyes in camp was a heap of feet, arms, legs, &c. under a tree in front of a hospital" (*CORR,* I, 59). The thought that one of George's limbs might be among the ghastly heaps was sheer agony. No matter. He was there to find his brother, and find him he would. When finally he located him, he learned joyfully, that his injury had been minor: his cheek had been pierced by a shell fragment and was healing well.

Whitman's eight- or nine-day stay with George was spent mostly visiting soldiers in area hospitals. Just as he had felt immensely drawn to the injured stagecoach drivers with whom he talked in the hospital in New York, he now became emotionally involved, and frequently deeply and quite romantically, with the wounded soldiers.

The inadequacy of the makeshift hospital facilities was appalling. To observe the suffering of the sick men lying about on blankets or directly on the cold ground, while bugles sounded all around, sabers clashed, and horses' hoofs thumped the ground, catalyzed Whitman's need to help them. So competent must Whitman's approach and care have been that on December 28, when leaving for Washington, he was put in charge of a trainload of wounded men. As he made his way amid the countless stretchers, never did he cease trying to comfort the bleeding and pain-racked soldiers: either by touching their heads or holding their hands or arms, or by promising to send messages to their families and loved ones, thereby alleviating, to some degree, their mental anguish.

Back in Washington, Whitman decided to stay on for a week or so in order to visit the hospitals in which Brooklyn soldiers had been confined. Seemingly, he could not tear himself away from what he now began looking upon as a mission. Thanks to the good offices of Eldridge, Whitman received an appointment as copyist in the paymaster's office, which made it financially possible for him to remain in the capital and visit and care for the wounded. To supplement his income, allowing him to continue sending money to his mother, he wrote some war articles. His government job required only two or three hours of work daily, which gave him ample time to visit the military hospitals.

Whitman's magnetic personality, in addition to the cheer and warmth he brought the emotionally deprived soldiers — so important to the recovery process — restored in many the will to live. Generous with his time as well as with his purse, keeping for himself only enough for essentials, Whitman bought the neediest patients fruits, candies, ice cream, stationery, and reading material. Although he was neither a smoker nor a chewer of tobacco, and despite the fact that the authorities at the hospital frowned upon it, Whitman brought them tobacco, believing it might help some patients relax and therefore feel better. His caring nature, and his love for "the beautiful young men in wholesale death & agony," transcended political lines. Never did he distinguish between Confederate and Union soldiers. Not only did he speak to all of them in loving and endearing terms, but at their request, began writing informative letters to their families and friends. Nor was he embarrassed or fearful of expressing to the authorities or to the doctors in charge a soldier's need for additional or more efficacious care.

Because of Whitman's deeply feeling nature and his intuitive faculties, he understood from the very outset how effective genuine affection and companionship was in aiding the healing process. Not only did Whitman derive satisfaction by doing good to others, but their heartfelt response to his ministrations restored a sense of well-being to his seared soul. On March 6, 1863, he wrote of the workings of this dynamic to his brother Jeff.

I never before had my feelings so thoroughly and (so far) permanently absorbed, to the very roots, as by these huge swarms of dear, wounded, sick, dying boys — I get very much attached to some of them, and many of them have come to depend on seeing me, and having me sit by them a few minutes, as if for their lives. (CORR, I, 76)

At this time Whitman was also expending a great deal of effort to find a more remunerative government post that would enable him to be even more generous materially to the soldiers. However, he allowed nothing to interfere with the hours he spent with the ill and dying. Long and harrowing as these hours were, Whitman found his daily visits to the soldiers fascinating, even exhilarating: a reaction that is complex and difficult to explain. Essentially, the visits tapped a whole untouched realm within his psyche. He understood, and rightly so, that *he needed to be needed.*

In my visits to the hospitals I found it was in the simple matter of personal presence, and emanating ordinary cheer and magnetism, that I succeeded and help'd more than by medical nursing, or delicacies, or gifts of money, or anything else. During the war I possess'd the perfection of physical health. My habit, when practicable, was to prepare for starting out on one of those daily or nightly tours of from a couple to four or five hours, by fortifying myself with previous rest, the bath, clean clothes, a good meal, and as cheerful an appearance as possible. (PW, 1, 51)

Is it any wonder, then, that Whitman was sometimes referred to as the "mother-man"?

His hospital visits, despite the feelings of well-being imparted by them, were not easy. Hospitals were poorly supplied and understaffed, the sanitary conditions were primitive. Next to the Judiciary Square Hospital, for example, the dead who were awaiting burial had been piled up naked on a vacant lot. Surgeons did not wear gloves, they sharpened their knives on their boot soles, and they collected the excess blood from a wound with a sponge that had been merely rinsed in water after previous operations. Most wounds became infected, and blood poisoning, tetanus, hemorrhages, and gangrene were frequent. Deaths resulted not so much from battle but as from the lack of sanitation and diseases such as typhoid, dysentery, and malaria. Moreover, some surgeons, physicians, nurses, and attendants were known for their heartlessness and brutality.

Still, despite the agony he witnessed and the mistreatment some soldiers received at the hands of doctors and attendants, Whitman wrote his friends Nathaniel Bloom and John F. S. Gray, on March 19, 1863, about the feelings of redemption he experienced following his visits.

These Hospitals, so different from all others — these thousands, and tens and twenties of thousands of American young men, badly wounded, all sorts of wounds, operated on, pallid with diarrhea, languishing, dying with fever, pneumonia, &c. open a new world somehow to me, giving closer insights, new things, exploring deeper mines than any yet, showing our humanity, (I sometimes put myself in fancy in the cot, with typhoid, or under the knife,) tried by terrible, fearful tests, probed deepest, the living souls, the body's tragedies, bursting the petty bonds of art. To these, what are your dramas and poems, even the oldest and the tearfulest? Not old greek mighty ones, where man contends with fate (and always yields) — not Virgil showing Dante on and on among the agonized & damned, approach what here I see and take a part in. For here I see, not at intervals, but quite always, how certain, man, our American man — how he holds himself cool and unquestioned master above all pains and bloody mutilations. It is immense, the best thing of all, nourishes me of all men. (CORR, I, 81)

Not only was Whitman selfless in his approach to the wounded, but he also remained very much the poet and journalist, keeping careful notes throughout the war that he transformed into newspaper articles, and at a later date, published in *Specimen Days*.

Forever plaguing Whitman, despite his extremely modest life style, was his need for money. He lived in a garret room; owned a cup, bowl, and spoon; cooked on a sheet-iron stove, used a jack-knife to cut his bread, a tin kettle to brew his tea, brown paper for a butter plate, and an oblong pine box as a cupboard. Emerson, responding to Whitman's call for help, wrote two letters on his behalf, as did other well-known men at the time. The O'Connors, husband and wife, offered him daily lunch and supper.

Problems revolving around Whitman's health surfaced: a loss of hearing and a great increase in weight. His two hundred pounds, ruddy complexion, sore throats, and protracted dizzy spells caused alarm. Certainly some of these symptoms were prodromal signs of hypertension due to overwork and to emotional stress. Nor did Washington's damp heat help matters. Whitman's family also gave him cause for concern. His brother Andrew, a longtime alcoholic, was suffering from what was to be diagnosed as tuberculosis of the throat, and died in December 1863. His wife, with whom he had never gotten along, had become a prostitute. Edward, the retarded brother, required more and more care. Jesse, given to bouts of violence, was too ill to work. Although the diagnosis was never proven, critics theorized that he was suffering from advanced syphilis. In 1864, his condition having become dangerous to himself and the family, he was interned in King's County Lunatic Asylum. Jeff, more inconsiderate than ever, suffered increasingly from morosity and mood swings. Nor was Whitman's sister, Hannah, faring well. While Mrs. Whitman became increasingly dependent upon her poet son, his sense of inadequacy with regard to his family mounted progressively.

Still, rain or shine, vertigo or not, sore throats and fevers, Whitman continued both his work for the government and his daily visits to the hospital. His love for the wounded soldiers and their attachment toward him imbued him with a raison d'être. When the surgeons decided to amputate the leg of the twenty-year-old Lewis ("Lewy") Kirke Brown, whose wound refused to heal, Whitman, at the lad's request, was at his side throughout the ordeal, even spending several nights with him at the hospital until the danger of hemorrhage had passed. In his letters to Lewy during Whitman's vacation periods in Brooklyn, he called him "my dear son," "my darling boy," "darling comrade," and wrote, "your letters & your love for me are very precious to me." The poet knew, and was forever reiterating it, that he was always there for those who needed or wanted him.

Whitman was also emotionally involved with a friend of Lewy's, Sergeant Thomas P. Sawyer. Referring first to Lewy in his letter of April 21, 1863, Whitman confessed his feelings for Tom:

Lew is so good and affectionate — when I came away, he reached up his face, I put my arm around him, and we gave each other a long kiss, half a minute long.... Tom I wish you was here. Somehow I don't find the comrade that suits me to a dot — and I won't have any other, not for good.... Dear comrade, you must not forget me, for I never shall you. My love you have in life or death forever. I don't know how you feel about it, but it is the wish of my heart to have your friendship, and also that if you should come safe out of this war, we should come together again in some place where we could make our living, and be true comrades and never be separated while life lasts — and take Lew Brown too, and never separate from him. Or if things are not so to be — if you get these lines, my dear, darling comrade, and any thing should go wrong, so that we do not meet again, here on earth, it seems to me, (the way I feel now,) that my soul could never be entirely happy, even in the world to come, without you, dear comrade....

Good bye, my darling comrade, my dear darling brother, for so I will call you, and wish you to call me the same. (*CORR*, I, 91)

Whitman's need to establish a permanent relationship with Tom and the unguarded and passionate language he used to express his love might have frightened the lad away. Since Whitman's letter remained unanswered, he wrote a second amorous missive on April 26, not only openly erotic, but also tinged with jealousy. He made mention of the fact that Lewy had received two letters from him whereas he had received none.

I was sorry you did not come up to my room to get the shirt & other things you promised to accept from me and take when you went away. I got them all ready, a good strong blue shirt, a pair of drawers & socks, and it would have been a satisfaction to me if you had accepted them. I should have often thought now Tom may be wearing around his body something from *me*, & that it might contribute to your comfort, down there in camp on picket, or sleeping in your tent.

...whatever it is, hoping it may please you, coming from old woolyneck, who loves you.... Not a day passes, nor a night but I think of you. Now, my dearest comrade, I will bid you *so long* & hope God will put it in your heart to bear toward me a little at least of the feelings I have about you. If it is only a quarter as much I shall be satisfied. (*CORR, I, 93*)

When, on May 27, he still had not heard from Tom, he was not loath to express his feelings of hurt, concluding:

My dearest comrade, I cannot, though I attempt it, put in a letter the feelings of my heart — I suppose my letters sound strange & unusual to you as it is, but as I am only expressing the truth in them, I do not trouble myself on that account. As I intimated before, I do not expect you to return for me the same degree of love I have for you (*CORR*, I, 107).

Whitman, in the doldrums, needed a change and tried to accomplish his goal, as he sometimes had previously during times of distress, by creating a new look for himself: that of a dandy. He sported a floppy wide-brimmed hat, a loose-fitting coat, military boots, and carried a knapsack (albeit a threadbare one) filled with gifts for the soldiers. Another change was forced upon him: he had to find other quarters after the sale of the building he occupied. Although he was still obliged to climb stairs (he now lived on the third floor) to get to his more than modest hall-bedroom, his new location at 502 Pennsylvania Avenue, near Third Street, had the advantage of being a pension: he could eat his meals without leaving the premises. Since he was increasingly complaining of fatigue, dizziness, headaches, sore throats, and spells of faintness, the boarding house arrangement seemed more than ideal.

But it was not enough to give him the respite he needed. Added to his tension, overwork, and the emotionally draining visits to the army hospitals, was the news he received, on October 8, 1864, that his brother George had been taken prisoner by the Confederates. Furthermore, his mother's recent illness created a new and far more severe source of worry. All of these trials must have been instrumental in wearing his patience thin with some of the hospital staff and personnel, whose coldness toward the sick shocked him. Before anything else could go wrong, Whitman thought it wise to return to Brooklyn to rest and recuperate from his multiple ailments.

By the time he arrived home in June 1864, he was so ill that he remained housebound until July 8. Upon his return to Washington after his recovery, he realized — none too soon — that to live with his family, no matter the depth of his love for them, was a stifling experience. Their financial and emotional demands were such that he felt utterly devitalized. In the years to come, although he made several trips to Brooklyn, his visits were of short duration.

Whitman's recuperation was seemingly complete. His life was again full, active, and deeply satisfying. He still worked for the government, still visited the soldiers in the hospitals, and still pursued his activities as a journalist with such articles as "Fifty-First New York City Veterans," and "Our Wounded Sick Soldiers — Visits among the Hospitals." His comparative studies of the conditions in the hospitals, blaming management but not the staff for the lamentable state of affairs existing in the wards and operating rooms, were eye-openers to many.

Thanks to the good offices of Whitman's Washington friends, he finally succeeded in obtaining a more remunerative job. On January 12, 1865, he was appointed to a first-class (the lowest grade) clerkship in the Department of the Interior in charge of administrating Indian lands and funds. Although delighted, he did not for one moment forget that his brother was still a prisoner of war. His first priority, now that he had a better job and more time available, was to try to get George released as rapidly as possible from the Confederate Prison in Danville, Virginia. But his maneuverings, in trying to effect an exchange of prisoners, although facilitated by his contacts with army and government officials, failed. Mrs. Whitman was relieved, nonetheless, upon receipt of a letter on February 24 from her son from Annapolis, in which he informed his family of his safety. By April, George had asked for and received permission to return to Brooklyn to spend Easter with his family.

The knowledge that George was safe relaxed Whitman sufficiently to allow him to enjoy fully the second inauguration of his hero, Abraham Lincoln, whom he had admired deeply from the time he first saw him en route to his first inauguration in 1861. Whitman noticed, however, a look of fatigue on Lincoln's face. The war had taken its toll on this leader of state: "The demands of life and death, cut deeper than ever upon his dark brown face; yet [there was] all the old goodness, tenderness, sadness, and canny shrewdness, underneath the furrows." After attending the public reception held at the White House that evening, Whitman wrote that the president was "drest all in black, with white kid gloves and a claw-hammer coat, receiving, as in duty bound, shaking hands, looking very disconsolate, and as if he would give anything to be somewhere else" (*CW*, I, 92, 61).

The news of Lee's surrender to Grant at Appomattox Courthouse on April 12 encouraged a mood of festivity throughout the nation, particularly deeply felt by Whitman whose long years caring for the wounded had been such a heavy, if sought after, burden to him. Moreover, his revered Lincoln would now be able to recover from the ordeal of war. Two days later, however, smiles were replaced by expressions of sorrow, shock, and consternation: President Lincoln had been assassinated. In Washington for the funeral, Whitman commemorated the event the best way he knew how, with a poem, "Hush'd Be the Camps To-day."

The war years, although grim in many ways for Whitman, had matured him as an artist. He had not, to be sure, participated in military campaigns, but he had gone to the battlefront, had treated and consoled many of the wounded, and was still doing so despite the end of the hostilities. The experiences he had undergone had deeply impressed themselves into his poems. A veneer of self-indulgence and narcissism had been discernible prior to the war, but a new power, sense of urgency, and poignant authenticity now dominated. No longer did the poet's universe center around himself. Humankind the world over was his new focus — the American people most particularly.

Whitman, however, did not omit or attempt to nullify the evils perpetrated during the Civil War, either by leaders or by the common man; nor did he minimize the ennobling of those soldiers who deserved the highest praise — for the eminence of their soul. Death, which had been one of Whitman's underlying themes even before the war, took on even greater importance for him in the fifty-three poems included in *Drum-Taps,* published in May 1865. Whitman's close companion for four years, Death was now personified in his poetry, and it haunted him evermore persistently. The excoriating vision of mutilated and bloodied bodies was always there — parading before him night and day. Yet, by facing such painful sights, by dealing with them in his writing, Whitman was beginning to come to terms with the notion of death — accepting it as part of the life process.

Because death's presence had become such an acute part of Whitman's daily existence, love (Eros), had also deepened in intensity. As conveyed in the *Calamus* poems, the poet's understanding of love had been focused on the personal element, and thus, to a certain extent, was egocentric. Whitman's postwar understanding of the Eros principle had taken on amplitude, becoming universalized — mythic in proportion. In "Hymn of Dead Soldiers," for example, he showed that love could never be destroyed, not even in death. Pantheistic in tone, but also deeply mystical in manner, reminiscent at times of Emerson's "Over-Soul," Whitman's hymn implied that the souls of the dead would one day dwell together in harmony. The implication in his "Pensive on Her Dead Gazing, I Heard the Mother of All" is that nothing is lost in death ("let not an atom be lost"), for the earth (nature, or the "Mother of All") absorbs unto herself the beautiful bodies and blood of the men who have left earthly life. In "Pensive on Her Dead Gazing," he wrote:

> Pensive on her dead gazing I heard the Mother of All,
> Desperate on the torn bodies, on the forms covering the battlefields gazing,
> (As the last gun ceased, but the scent of the powder-smoke linger'd),
> As she call'd to her earth with mournful voice while she stalk'd,

Absorb them well O my earth, she cried, I charge you, lose not my
    sons, lose not an atom....
Exhale me them centuries hence, breathe me their breath, let not an
    atom be lost,
O years and graves! O air and soil! O my dead, an aroma sweet!
Exhale them perennial sweet death, years, centuries hence.

In essence, Whitman had taken on the stature of a collective
healer of the lonely and ill, as attested to in the title of another
poem, "The Dresser" (becoming "The Wound-Dresser").

The crush'd head I dress, (poor crazed hand tear not the bandage
    away,)
The neck of the cavalry-man with the bullet through and through I
    examine,
Hard the breathing rattles, quite glazed already the eye, yet life
    struggles hard....
Back on his pillow the soldier bends with curv'd neck and side falling
    head,
His eyes are closed, his face is pale, he dares not look on the bloody
    stump....
I dress a wound in the side, deep, deep,
But a day or two more, for see the frame all wasted and sinking,
And the yellow-blue countenance see....

Thus in silence in dreams' projections,
Returning, resuming, I thread my way through the hospitals,
The hurt and wounded I pacify with soothing hand,
I sit by the restless all the dark night, some are so young,
Some suffer so much, I recall the experience sweet and sad,
(Many a soldier's loving arms about his neck have cross'd and rested,
Many a soldier's kiss dwells on these bearded lips.)

Healer of bodies and souls, Whitman had visions of becoming
America's national poet and of being loved by his people. He was,
therefore, completely unprepared for the rude awakening he received at the hands of Senator Harlan of Illinois. When this former
Methodist minister, who had now become the new head of the Department of the Interior, happened to come upon *Leaves of Grass,*
he was so shocked by its contents that he dismissed Whitman on
June 30, 1865. The poet's financial situation, now more precarious
than ever before, dashed his fondest dream — that of seeing to the
printing at his own expense of a fourth edition of *Leaves of Grass.*
Whatever extra funds he could muster had to go to his mother.

Meanwhile, Eddy, his retarded brother, had become such a problem that the idea of institutionalizing him was seriously considered. The very thought of doing so, however, so disturbed Mrs. Whitman that the family did not act upon it until 1881, long after her death in 1873.

Only through the good offices of Whitman's trusted friend, William O'Connor, who called upon the assistant attorney general, J. Hubley Ashton, did Whitman find a new job. Since Ashton considered Whitman the greatest living American poet and his dismissal an outrage, he saw to his transfer to the attorney general's office. Only now could Whitman's publication plans go forward: a new edition of *Leaves of Grass,* and the publication of the twenty-four-page *Sequel to Drum-Taps.* The latter was to feature what was to become one of Whitman's greatest elegies, "When Lilacs Last in the Dooryard Bloom'd," and one of his most popular poems, "O Captain! My Captain!"

Although Whitman's latest publications were reviewed only desultorily, William Dean Howells's critique and that of the twenty-two-year-old Henry James impacted unfavorably upon the poet's works. Howells found his "artistic method" wanting.

No doubt the pathos of many of the poems gains something from the quaintness of the poet's speech. One is touched in reading them by the same inarticulate feeling as that which dwells in music; and is sensible that the poet conveys to the heart certain emotions which the brain cannot analyze, and only remotely perceives. This is especially true of his inspirations from nature; memories and yearnings come to you folded, mute, and motionless in his verse, as they come in the breath of a familiar perfume. They give a strange, shadowy sort of pleasure, but they do not satisfy, and you rise from the perusal of this man's book as you issue from the presence of one whose personal magnetism is very subtle and strong, but who has not added to this tacit attraction the charm of spoken ideas. We must not mistake this fascination for a higher quality....

So long, then, as Mr. Whitman chooses to stop at mere consciousness, he cannot be called a true poet. (Woodress, *Critical Essays,* 57)

James's review was cruel — even searing: "It has been a melancholy task to read this book; and it is a still more melancholy one to write about it." What hurt Whitman most deeply was the fact that he was accused of having used the entire hospital experience for purposes of self-aggrandizement.

Like hundreds of other good patriots, during the last four years, Mr. Walt Whitman has imagined that a certain amount of violent sympathy with the great deeds and sufferings of our soldiers, and of admiration for our national energy, together with a ready command of picturesque language, are sufficient inspiration for a poet. If this were the case, we had been a nation of poets....

But Mr. Whitman's verse, we are confident, would have failed even of this triumph, for the simple reason that no triumph, however small, is won but through the exercise of art, and that this volume is an offense against art. It is not enough to be grim and rough and careless; common sense is also necessary, for it is by common sense that we are judged. There exists in even the commonest minds, in literary matters, a certain precise instinct of conservatism, which is very shrewd in detecting wanton eccentricities. To this instinct Mr. Whitman's attitude seems monstrous. It is monstrous because it pretends to persuade the soul while it slights the intellect; because it pretends to gratify the feelings while it outrages the taste....

To become adopted as a national poet, it is not enough to discard everything in particular and to accept everything in general, to amass crudity upon crudity, to discharge the undigested contents of your blotting-book into the lap of the public. You must respect the public which you address; for it has taste, if you have not. (Woodress, *Critical Essays,* 62)

O'Connor was quick to come to Whitman's defense with *The Good Gray Poet* (1866), a virtual eulogy of his idol. Not only did he champion Whitman's talent and personal integrity, but spoke out overtly in favor of literary freedom and against expurgation and censorship. Among the laudatory reviews of *Leaves of Grass* was one by Whitman's friend John Burroughs. He was the first, seemingly, to recognize the "dramatic" nature of "When Lilacs Last...."

Meanwhile, Whitman was winning fame in England. The art critic and author William Michael Rossetti not only remarked on the innovative nature of *Leaves of Grass,* but referred to it as "incomparably the largest poetic work of our period." It was he, as well, who brought out *Poems of Walt Whitman* (1868) in England. Unlike James, he praised both their literary and aesthetic worth. Indeed, he ranked the American's poetry with Homer's epics. William Michael Rossetti's brother, Dante Gabriel, was indifferent to Whitman's verses, commenting negatively on their crudity. At opposite poles was Algernon Swinburne's comparison between Whitman's writings and those of William Blake. Whitman considered Swinburne's twenty-two-stanza poem "To Walt Whitman in America" (1871) to be the greatest testimony of his talent he had ever received.

> Send but a song oversea for us,
> Heart of their hearts who are free,

> Heart of their singer, to be for us
> More than our singing can be;
> Ours, in the tempest at error,
> With no light but the twilight of terror;
> Send us a song oversea! (Woodress, *Critical Essays,* 148)

However, it took Swinburne only two years to have a change of heart, labeling Whitman a "formalist" and a "propagandist," and castigating him for his theoretical didacticism.

Meanwhile, Whitman accepted an offer from the Church brothers, the owners of *Galaxy,* to write a reply to "Shooting Niagara: And After," by Thomas Carlyle. Carlyle's article had stated that the growth of democracy and the extension of suffrage in England in 1867 would bring civilization to a halt. Although Whitman had at first rejected Carlyle's vilifications of the United States — he himself having referred to them in *Democratic Vistas,* as "canker'd, crude, superstitious, and rotten" — he was no longer the naive idealist he had once been. He realized only too well that materialism and corruption were rampant throughout the land and "the depravity of the business classes of our country" was equally great. Nevertheless, he considered democracy to be an ongoing process, a form of government undergoing constant purification. As for the people, whom Carlyle alluded to as the "unnamed, unknown rank and file," the Civil War had proven them to be for the most part courageous, ready to sacrifice themselves rather than to yield to "hopelessness, mismanagement, defeat" (*PW,* I, 369).

On a personal level, Whitman had come to experience great happiness when, in December 1865, he met Peter Doyle, an eighteen-year-old Irish lad from Alexandria. A former soldier in the Confederate army, who had been captured by Union forces and released after the war, he was now a horse-car conductor in Washington. He had become one of Whitman's closest friends, in a way neither O'Connor nor Burroughs could ever be. Doyle wrote of their first meeting:

We fell to each other at once. I was a conductor. The night was very stormy.... Walt had his blanket — it was thrown round.... his shoulders — he seemed like an old sea captain. He was the only passenger, it was a lonely night, so I thought I would go in and talk with him. Something in me made me do it and something in him drew me that way. He used to say there was something in me had the same effect on him. Anyway, I went into the car. We were familiar at once — I put my hand on his knee — we understood. He did not get out at the end of the trip — in fact went all the way back with me.... From that time on we were the biggest sort of friends. (*CW,* 8, 5).

Doyle fulfilled Whitman's ideal of a man: almost uneducated and very handsome. The two became inseparable. Doyle accompanied the poet on his long walks around the outskirts of Washington and on boat rides to Alexandria. Nor were Whitman's caring and paternal ways wasted on the lad, who craved for a close and protracted relationship. When writing to Doyle on October 9, 1868, during his vacation, the poet revealed the extent of his affection for him in such phrases as "Yours for life, dear Pete, (& death the same)" *CORR,* II, 57). In another letter (September 29, 1868) Whitman had written:

I think of you very often, dearest comrade, & with more calmness than when I was there — I find it first rate to think of you, Pete, & to know that you are there, all right, & that I shall return, & and we will be together again. I don't know what I should do if I hadn't you to think of & look forward to. (*CORR,* II, 51)

Careerwise, Whitman was finally faring relatively well, despite some negative reviews. "Proud Music of the Sea-Storm" appeared in *The Atlantic Monthly* (1869); there was a fifth edition of *Leaves of Grass* in 1870, and a slim prose work, *Democratic Vistas,* was published in 1870. In the last named, a kind of tour de force, Whitman presents an overview of American democracy, both deprecating the "depravity of the business classes," while praising the courageous and altruistic stand of so many during the Civil War. He also takes this opportunity to extrapolate his notions concerning the functioning of individualism versus the "mass" in democracy; and lyricizes his desire for a "rich, luxuriant, varied personalism" as being the sturdiest and most ethical foundation for democracy. What he yearns for most powerfully is the creation of an "American imaginative literature" with "grand and archetypal models."

A week spent in Providence, at the invitation of Thomas Davis, a former member of Congress, and invitations from William F. Channing and William O'Connor, who lived in the region, did much to make Whitman glow. His meeting of Jack Flood, a streetcar driver, when on vacation in New York, added another note to his pleasure. In a letter to Whitman, his latest love wrote of his possible visit to Washington. The poet answered on November 1868: "I hope you will come truly, for it would be a great comfort to me if we could be together again." At the same time, Whitman seemed to be dissuading him from taking the trip: Washington "is a stupid place compared to New York — but we would have each other's society, and that would be first rate" (*CORR*, II, 70). Whitman's young male friends were increasing in number, including not only streetcar drivers but firemen as well. Although Doyle was his greatest love at this time, Whitman's heart was big enough to embrace them all.

Nevertheless, it became evident that Whitman's physical condition was declining. The dizzy spells, head pains, sore throats, and depressions to which he was subject weakened him. He felt so ill that he returned to Brooklyn to recuperate from what was diagnosed as a severe viral infection. Relaxation, however, was impossible, so concerned was he about Doyle, who had been suffering from a stubborn skin rash that a doctor diagnosed as "barber's itch," and for which he was being treated: the eruptions were cauterized and then lanced with nitrate of silver. Until Doyle's recovery, Whitman's letters, as evident in the one of August 21, 1869 — in which he scolded him for his morosity and perhaps for what he erroneously understood to be his suicidal bent — disclosed a tone of anxiety:

I have thought of you, my darling boy, very much of the...time Dearest Pete must forgive me for being so cold the last day & evening. I was unspeakably shocked and repelled from you by that talk & proposition of yours — you know what...there by the fountain. It seemed to me, (for I will talk out plain to dearest comrade,) that the one I loved and who had always been so manly & sensible, was as gone, & a fool & intentional murderer stood in his place.

My darling, if you are not well when I come back I will get a good room or two in some quiet place, (or out of Washington, perhaps in Baltimore,) and we will live together, & devote ourselves altogether to the job of curing you, & rooting the cursed thing out entirely, & making you stronger & healthier than ever...

Dear comrade, I think of you very often. My love for you is indestructible, & since that night & morning has returned more than before. (*CORR*, II, 84)

In another letter to Doyle, Whitman referred to his worsening dizzy spells and to the fact that for no known reason he had been breaking out into sudden sweats. His doctors diagnosed his condition as "that hospital malaria, hospital poison absorbed in the system years ago." On September 3, 1869, as Whitman's health improved, he began making plans to return to Washington and promised Doyle that "we will soon be together again" (*CORR*, II, 86).

The following year when on vacation in Brooklyn, Whitman's passion for Doyle seemed to have grown even stronger, as indicated in this note of August 2, 1870.

We parted there, you know, at the corner of 7th st, Tuesday night. Pete, there was something in that hour from ten to eleven o'clock (parting though it was) that has left me pleasure & comfort for good — I never dreamed that you made so much of having me with you, nor that you could feel so downcast at losing me. I foolishly thought it was all on the other side. But all I will say further on the subject is, I now see clearly that was all wrong. (CORR, II, 101–2)

In his letter of September 2, 1870, Whitman expressed his feelings of loneliness: "My dear loving boy, how much I want to see you — it seems a long while.... Well, Pete, about half our separation is over." He concluded his missive of September 6, 1870, with "a good smacking kiss, & many of them — & taking in return many, many, many from my dear son — good loving ones too — which will do more credit to his lips than growling and complaining at his father" (CORR, II, 109–10).

Emotionally, Whitman seemed fulfilled. Financially, however, he was strapped. Although he had been promoted in 1866 to the highest rank, that of third-class clerk, he was still only earning sixteen hundred dollars a year, and living in a small room with the barest of material possessions. Any extra funds were siphoned off to his mother, to his brother Eddy, and to Doyle, whenever the latter was either ill or unemployed. Feelings of culpability must have been triggered when the poet learned of his brother Jesse's death on March 21, 1870, and of his burial in potter's field.

More than ever did Whitman's concerns revolve around death and immortality, as attested to in such poems as "Proud Music of the Sea-Storm," "Out of the Cradle Endlessly Rocking," "Thou Vast Rondure," "Swimming in Space" (retitled "Passage to India"), and "The Almighty Leader." Fascinated as always by all the world's religions, Whitman embedded Hebrew, Egyptian, Hindu, and other beliefs into what could be termed his syncretistic approach to art and life. This was as it should be for Whitman, since, as the "true Son of God, the poet," he sought to link religion with ethics while preaching a gospel of love.

There were moments, however, when a return to earthly matters was a necessity. Despite the fact that Whitman was never known to have had any sexual adventures with women, the opposite sex had always been immensely attracted to him. Mrs. Juliette H. Beach, a case in point, considered him a "genius" and wrote in the *Saturday Press* (Spring 1860) that "Walt Whitman on earth is immortal as well as beyond it, God bless him." She predicted that *Leaves of Grass* would surely be "the standard book of poems in the future of America." Mrs. Abbey Price and her daughter Helen also idolized him. He had spent many a memorable evening with them discussing the ideas of the Swedish spiritualist and theologian Emanuel Swedenborg (1688–1772), whose views had also influenced William Blake.

A new lady was now making inroads onto Whitman's horizon. Mrs. Anne Gilchrist, widow of Alexander Gilchrist, Blake's biographer. Not only was she a literary figure in her own right, but she had also earned the friendship of the Rossettis, Carlyle, Swinburne, and Tennyson, among other notables. She sent some flattering statements she had made about *Leaves of Grass* to William Michael Rossetti, who in turn passed them on to O'Connor, who then showed them to Whitman. Needless to say, he was touched by the most favorable impressions of this English lady. Mrs. Gilchrist's laudatory article on Whitman's poetry, which appeared anonymously in the Boston *Radical* (1870), was considered not only a glowing defense of sex in poetry, but one of the finest appreciations of his work. Whitman could not help but be flattered by her remarks. A correspondence between the two ensued. What Whitman failed to realize was the power of Mrs. Gilchrist's passion.

It is for her soul exactly as it is for her body. The strong divine soul of the man embracing hers with passionate love — so alone the precious germs within her soul can be quickened into life. . . . This was what happened to me when I read for a few days, nay, hours, in your books. It was the divine soul embracing mine. I never before dreamed what love meant: not what life meant. Never was alive before — no words but those of "new birth" can hint the meaning of what then happened to me. (Allen, 436)

Although pleased by her compliments concerning his work, Whitman was totally uninterested in Mrs. Gilchrist as a woman. She had, evidently never probed the real meaning of the *Calamus* poems, nor his use of the word *adhesiveness*. She was, however, not one to be stopped.

Great anxiety may be noted in some of Whitman's cryptic entries in his *Notebooks*. On June 17, 1870, he writes of his distress over his "own weakness — REMEMBER WHERE I AM MOST WEAK, & most lacking. Yet always preserve a kind spirit & demeanor to 16. Pursue her no more." By July 15, he seems to be overwhelmed by a sense of humiliation: his "useless undignified pursuit of 164 — — too long, (much too long) persevered in... avoid seeing her, or meeting her, or any talk of explanations — — or ANY MEETING WHATEVER, FROM THIS HOUR FORTH, FOR LIFE" The identities of "her," "16," and "164" still remain a mystery for Whitman scholars. Since he had always shielded his sexual proclivities, the "her" may really be "he," and the numbers, coded references to Doyle or to other young men. What might substantiate such a theory is the following passage in the same notebook: "Depress the adhesive nature / It is in excess — making life a torment / All this diseased, feverish disproportionate *adhesiveness.*"

Whitman's ideas and his poetry, particularly because of his allusions to sexual matters, made him anathema to editors of such reviews as *Macmillan's* and *Contemporary Review.* Yet, despite the plethora of parodies, satires, and insults, Whitman appeared to be weathering the storm. His mood was bolstered every now and then by stunning reviews or invitations to read his poems, such as the one issued by the American Institute in New York to celebrate the fortieth National Industrial Exhibition (September 7, 1871). Other organizations, such as the Smithsonian Institution in Washington and Dartmouth College, also invited him to speak. American, Danish, German, and French magazines began publishing his works.

The joy of growing fame, however, was severely diminished by Whitman's poor health. His dizzy spells became more frequent, and his head pains increased in severity. Nor did his quarrel with his longtime friend and ardent supporter, William Douglas O'Connor, help matters. The misunderstanding revolved around the poet's unwillingness to grant the vote to the newly liberated Negroes.

In January 1873, Whitman suffered a major stroke that left him virtually paralyzed. Some doctors believed that his stroke had been brought on by the accumulation of "poisons" or viruses to which he had been exposed in the military hospitals during the war years. Others blamed his condition on "emotional disturbances." Some scholars suggested that Whitman's suffering over an incident that had occurred in 1870 had drained his energies. It is unknown what that event was.

Unable to work, and so as not to be divested of all funds, he was given permission to hire a young man to replace him at the office. The fifty dollars per month he paid him left the poet sufficient funds to give to his mother and to pay for his brother Edward's board of twenty dollars a month. Bedridden most of the time, each time he tried to get up, he was overcome with dizziness and nausea. Doctors decided to use electric (battery) shock therapy on him. It was to no avail.

The paralyzed Whitman rested at home, surrounded by friends and well-wishers. Many weeks passed before he was able to sit at his desk. The news of his sister Martha's passing on February 19, and, most particularly, of his mother's deteriorating physical condition slowed his recovery. So critical had Mrs. Whitman's condition become that as soon as he was able to stand, Whitman decided to make the difficult trip to Camden, New Jersey. He arrived there on May 20, three days before her death. His heartbreak was devastating. Depression followed, as did extreme weakness.

Lonely, discouraged, and still suffering "some bad feeling in the head," he continued his correspondence with Doyle, and their plans for a future together did much to help the poet through his trauma. On July 10, 1874, his missive to Doyle read:

My darling son, you must not be unhappy about me — I hope & trust things may work so that we can yet be with each other, at least from time to time — & meanwhile we must adapt ourselves to circumstances. You keep on, & try to do right, & live the same square life you always have, & maintain as cheerful a heart as possible — and as for the way things finally turn out, leave that to the Almighty. (*CORR*, II, 308)

When Whitman's health began improving, he started to write some articles focusing mostly on the war and its aftermath, published as *Memoranda during the War.* That he was also inspired to set down some poems — "Song of the Redwood Tree" and "Prayer of Columbus" yielded him the satisfaction of knowing that his creative bent had not aridified. Nevertheless, his outlook on life was far from ebullient. In "Prayer of Columbus," for example, he featured not the young and vibrant explorer, but the desperate and sick old man who wondered why his God had imposed such suffering upon him at the conclusion of his earthly days.

During the days and months spent recuperating, the poet, always an inveterate reader, pursued this same course. That for years he had been drawn to the philosophy of Georg F. Hegel is evident in *Democratic Vistas* and "Song of the Universal." Reality for Hegel, let it be noted was looked upon as a dynamic process governed by a dialectical law: antithesis exists within every thesis, as does the resolution, or synthesis, of the conflict, which in turn gives rise to a new antithesis, in an endless progression. Such a dialectic, examined historically, reveals the progressive growth and self-realization of reason and freedom. Hegel's philosophy imbued Whitman with hope: the thought that a better society would emerge from the Civil War.

Whitman's optimism as to America's future, however, did not sustain him through another, although understandable, blow: the termination of his services in Washington in 1874, for cost-cutting reasons. Without a steady income, the articles and poems written at this time were not sufficient to fill the coffers. Moreover, now that he lived in Camden and no longer in Washington, fewer friends visited him. "I get desperate at staying in — not a human soul for cheer, or sociability or fun, and this continued week after week and month after month," he wrote to Doyle in the winter of 1875. Yet, despite his growing despair, he was planning a new edition of *Leaves of Grass* and a new volume, *Two Rivulets.* His preface to the latter work, set forth his deepest concerns and desires.

I would make a full confession. I also sent out *Leaves of Grass* to arouse and set flowing in men's and women's hearts, young and old, (my present and future readers,) endless streams of living, pulsating love and friendship, directly from them to myself, now and ever. To this terrible, irrepressible yearning, (surely more or less down underneath in most human souls,) — this never-satisfied appetite for sympathy, and this boundless offering of sympathy — this universal democratic comradeship — this old, eternal, yet ever-new interchange of adhesiveness, so fitly emblematic of America — I have given in that book undisguisedly, declaredly, the openest expression.

Many male admirers throughout the world, drawn most particularly to Whitman's *Calamus* poems, began writing him. John Addington Symonds, the author of *The Renaissance in Italy,* a basic work on cultural history, had first read Whitman's poetry when a student at Trinity College, Cambridge. "It revolutionized my previous conceptions," he wrote, "and made another man of me." Encouraged by Whitman, Symonds proceeded to write openly in his poetry of his "passionate friendship," and of his visits to "soldiers' barracks and male brothels." In time, he married an upper-class lady and fathered three children (Harold Blodgett, *Walt Whitman in England,* 59). Bram Stoker, the author of *Dracula,* also wrote to Whitman; as did the literary scholar Charles Warren Stoddard. Nor should the recognition and financial support Whitman received from English subscribers to the Centennial Edition ("Author's Edition") of his works be minimized. Among the illustrious names appearing on the list were Tennyson, the Rossettis, Edmund Gosse, George Saintsbury, and Mrs. Gilchrist.

Whitman had not heard the last of Mrs. Gilchrist. By 1875, her passion for him had erupted unchecked. Still, she was not completely to blame for what occurred. Whitman's letters to her had grown increasingly warmer in tone. That he had sent her his mother's ring as a token of his affection might, quite naturally, have been misconstrued by her as a kind of engagement gift. When, on January 18, 1876, she announced in a letter her projected arrival in the United States with her three children, Whitman took fright. Silence on his part ensued. Nevertheless, she kept writing: "Hold on but a little longer for me, my Walt — I am straining every nerve to hasten the day — I have enough for us all (with the simple, unpretentious ways we both love best)" (Allen, 473). When finally Whitman replied, he attempted to dissuade her from making the voyage, using his poor health as an excuse. Instead, he would visit her in London as soon as he was stronger. Mrs. Gilchrist had a mind of her own. She made the trip. Only when she finally met the poet, in the fall of 1876, did she realize that her dreams of love and passion were delusions. Theirs would be a nonsexual friendship. He helped her find a house in Philadelphia. She, on her part, told him that a room in her new home would always be at his disposal when he felt inclined to visit. Their conversations, revolving around literary subjects, such as Whitman's favorite novelist, George Sand, were lively. Grace, one of Gilchrist's daughters, depicted a visit by Whitman to her mother as follows:

The poet sat in our midst, in a large bamboo rocking-chair, and we listened as he talked, on many subjects — human and literary. Walt Whitman was at this time fifty-eight, but he looked seventy. His beard and hair were snow-white, his complexion a fine colour, and unwrinkled. He had still, though stricken in 1873 by paralysis a most majestic presence. He was over six feet, but he walked lame, dragging the left leg, and leaning heavily on a stick. He was dressed always in a complete suit of grey clothes with a large spotless white linen collar, his flowing white beard filling in the gap at his sunburnt throat. He possessed a full-toned, rather high, baritone voice, a little harsh and lacking in the finer modulations for sustained recitation; having an excellent memory, he declaimed many scenes from Shakespeare, poems by Tennyson, and occasionally his own. The "Mystic Trumpeter" was a favorite with him. (Allen, 476)

Now somewhat sturdier on his feet, Whitman decided to spend some months at the farm of Mr. and Mrs. Stafford, not far from Camden. He had met and become friendly with their son, Harry, employed by the printer who set Whitman's books. His long stays at the farm, including the summer of 1876, and his deepening friendship with Harry brought the poet untold happiness. So improved had his health become in this new and loving environment that he found himself able to walk to Timber Creek, around four hundred yards from the Stafford home. His slow pace had the advantage of allowing him, in the manner of Rousseau and Thoreau, to study plant, animal, and bird life at close range. The notes Whitman took at the time were later incorporated into his *Specimen Days.*

So pleased was Whitman in his new environment that he even set up a routine for himself, as had been his habit in the good old days. He hoped that the day-to-day physical disciplines would relieve some of his remaining lameness and renew his old-time vigor. Because the area was isolated, he took what he believed to be healing mud baths, after which he would wash himself down with a hard brush, then bathe in the cool stream, and finally sun himself. Refreshed and reinvigorated, and despite the slurring of some of his words, he started, as he had when a youth, to sing operatic arias and popular songs, and declaim passages from Shakespeare, Homer, Tennyson — or his own works.

Life was returning to Whitman. His increasing mobility allowed him to visit New York to give some lectures, most notably on Lincoln's death. In autumn 1879, after dreaming for years of traveling West, he was invited as guest of honor and visiting poet to the Kansas Quarter Centennial Celebration. Lectures, poem recitations, and interviews kept him busy while also buoying his spirits. His trip was also satisfying on a more personal note: it furnished him the opportunity of seeing his brother Jeff and his nieces, settled in St. Louis, Missouri. He also traveled to Denver, went to the Great Plains and the valley of the Mississippi, and finally, took the famous Atchison, Topeka & Santa Fe railroad. Although exhausted when he arrived home, in January 1880, Whitman was infinitely pleased. Everything about his trip had captivated him: rock formations, trees, cacti, grasses of all types, animals such as prairie dogs and antelopes, cowboys — even the strange names of the towns he visited. What an irony it was to think that Whitman, who had written about Manifest Destiny in his early poems, who had pointed to the heroism of the Americans venturing across the continent, overcoming all the dangers and even settling in the most remote areas, had himself never before, made the trip to his country's heartland.

Whitman, vigorous in spirit if not always in body, was not to be stopped. On June 3, 1880, he was off on another trip to visit Dr. Richard Maurice Bucke, the superintendent of a mental institution in London, Ontario, and a great admirer of *Leaves of Grass*. Bucke considered Whitman as a kind of god figure, a "preterhuman" individual. Together the two men traveled to the St. Lawrence, up the Saguenay River, to Montreal, Quebec, the Thousand Islands, and other beautiful places. All the while, Whitman was taking notes for future magazine articles and lectures — as was Dr. Bucke, for his projected critical study, *Walt Whitman* (1883).

Unfortunately, Whitman would now be confronted with another hurdle in the series that had plagued him throughout his life. All seemed well and good when the 1881 edition of *Leaves of Grass*, published in Boston by Osgood & Co., began receiving fine reviews and was enjoying fairly good sales. On March 1, 1882, the city's district attorney notified the publisher that because Whitman's poems had been classified as obscene literature, they were banned. Deletions would have to be made if the ban were to be lifted. Since Whitman was agreeable to only certain minor alterations and not the vast ones demanded by the district attorney — the omission of such poems as "A Woman Waits for Me" and "Ode to a Common Prostitute" — the ban remained. Osgood & Co. prepared a settlement. The poet's future publisher would be Rees Welsh & Co., of Philadelphia, after which David McKay, also of Philadelphia, was to take over Whitman's titles and publish both *Leaves of Grass* and *Specimen Days and Collect*.

O'Connor, with whom Whitman had had a serious disagreement over the suffrage issue, suddenly came to the poet's defense, interpreting the Boston ban on *Leaves of Grass* as an infringement of freedom of the press. His letters to the newspapers must have been efficacious because the press, as a body, labeled the directors of Osgood & Co. timorous for not having taken the issue to court. Whitman was more than grateful for the outcry against censorship. Throughout his life he had felt that anything that even smacked of intellectual or artistic constraint was not only anathema to him, but contrary to the American way.

Meanwhile, Whitman's following in England had continued to increase rapidly among both illustrious and notorious authors. When Oscar Wilde visited Whitman during one of his trips to the States, he was so impressed with the "grand old man" that he drank the elderberry wine Whitman's sister-in-law had made with the greatest of pleasure, stating that "if it had been vinegar, I would have drunk it all the same, for I have an admiration for that man which I can hardly express." Whitman did not accept all of Wilde's aesthetic theories, and they had a heated conversation. Nevertheless, Whitman was fascinated by Wilde: "He seemed to me like a great big, splendid boy. He is so frank, and outspoken, and manly. I don't see why such mocking things are written of him" (Allen, 502).

By 1882 the literary climate in America had changed. Some of the most revered poets, such as Longfellow and Emerson, had died. Although Whitman and Longfellow had never been close, the latter's visit to the ailing poet at Camden was so deeply appreciated that it may explain Whitman's highly complimentary memorial to him. As for Emerson, Whitman praised his "master's" personality, his "conscience, simplicity, culture, humanity's attributes at their best," but he did not extol the literary accomplishments of a man who had done so much to help him when he needed it the most. Was this omission due to the fact that Emerson had not included a single poem from *Leaves of Grass* in his anthology *Parnassus?*

When Whitman's brother George and his wife, Lou, with whom he had been living since his mother's death in May 1873, moved to a farm near Burlington, Whitman decided to buy a house on Mickle Street in Camden. Although it needed a great deal of repair — it did not even have a furnace — it had the advantage, for Whitman, of being near the noisy railroad tracks and a block from the streetcar, which could take him to the Manhattan-bound ferry. Whitman's style of living in his new house, purchased in 1884, did not change. His needs had been and still were very few. Life, however, was made a bit easier for the aged poet when a kindhearted widow, Mrs. Davis, agreed to become his housekeeper.

Among the many admirers who visited Whitman in 1884 were the famed British actor Henry Irving and his manager, Bram Stoker. Edmund Gosse, a lecturer at Cambridge, a poet, and an acquaintance of Swinburne and the Pre-Raphaelites, also came. Friends invited the poet to dinner; others, aware of his diminished finances, gave him money directly or collected sums for him to tide him over difficult periods: William Rossetti, Mrs. Gilchrist, Henry James, Robert Louis Stevenson, Havelock Ellis, George Saintsbury, and many unknowns. Artists, including the then-well-known J. W. Alexander, painted him — as did the famed Thomas Eakins.

At the home of a new friend, Thomas B. Harned, a Camden lawyer, with whom Whitman took dinner each Sunday, the poet renewed his acquaintance with his host's brother-in-law, a bank clerk, Horace Traubel. He had met Traubel, the son of a cultured German immigrant, years back, when Traubel was only fifteen. Now, a friendship ensued, and Traubel became Whitman's steady visitor.

When friends saw that Whitman was growing increasingly lame, it was suggested that ten dollars be contributed to the purchase of a horse and phaeton to help him get around. Mark Twain, Whittier, Holmes, Edwin Booth, and others gave. More than delighted with the purchase, Whitman took advantage of the increased independence it gave him. He drove about himself for the next three years. By 1888, the ailing and semi-invalided Whitman had to put a stop to his pleasurable jaunts. Because he was in need of constant attention, his friends hired a male nurse to care for him. Traubel went to Whitman's home daily, recording the conversations between them, even those uttered when the poet was semidelirious. It was at this time that the poet told Traubel that he had a great secret, but he never revealed its nature. Eventually, the transcripts taken down with such care turned into Traubel's five-volume *With Walt Whitman in Camden.*

It was Traubel who, during these dismal days, was there to help Whitman publish "Good-Bye My Fancy" and the last edition — the so-called deathbed edition — of *Leaves of Grass* (1891). It was also thanks to his assistance that Whitman completed a new volume of prose and poetry, *November Boughs,* which his disciple brought to the printer. Included in this brief volume was an important preface, "A Backward Glance o'er Travel'd Roads," as well as reminiscences. In a spirit of acceptance and friendliness, and without malice to any of his detractors, Whitman outlined briefly what he had meditated upon for years: his aesthetic theories.

So here I sit gossiping in the early candle light of old age — I and my book — casting backward glances over our travel'd road. After completing, as it were, the journey.... After completing my poems, I am curious to review them in the light of their own (at the time unconscious, or mostly unconscious) intentions, with certain unfoldings of the thirty years they seek to embody.

That I have not gain'd the acceptance of my own time, but have fallen back on fond dreams of the future — anticipations.... That from a worldly and business point of view *Leaves of Grass* has been worse than a failure — that public criticism on the book and myself as author of it yet shows mark'd anger and contempt more than anything else....

I consider *Leaves of Grass* and its theory experimental — as, in the deepest sense, I consider our American republic itself to be, with its theory. (I think I have at least enough philosophy not to be too absolutely certain of any thing, or any results.)

After reviewing the purpose of his poetry and his reasons for abandoning traditional themes, Whitman compared his ideas on poetics with those of other nineteenth-century writers, intent, even to the last, on setting the record straight for posterity.

Leaves of Grass indeed (I cannot too often reiterate) has mainly been the outcropping of my own emotional and other personal nature — an attempt, from first to last, to put a Person, a human being (myself, in the latter half of the Nineteenth Century, in America,) freely, fully and truly on record....

I say no land or people or circumstances ever existed so needing a race of singers and poems differing from all others, and rigidly their own, as the land and people and circumstances of our United States need such singers and poems to-day, and for the future. Still further, as long as the States continue to absorb and be dominated by the poetry of the Old World, and remain unsupplied with autochthonous song, to express, vitalize and give color to and define their material and political success, and minister to them distinctively, so long will they stop short of first-class Nationality and remain defective.

Deeply saddened by the death of his favorite brother, Jeff, in 1890, Whitman finally made his will, leaving whatever money he had to his two sisters, Mary and Hannah, and to his housekeeper, Mrs. Davis. His sister-in-law, Mrs. George Whitman, became ex-ecutrix of his property, the necessary funds to be used to support Edward. His gold watch was given to Harry Stafford and a silver one to Peter Doyle. In an 1892 codicil, Whitman gave his gold watch to Traubel and the silver one to Harry Stafford. Nothing was bequeathed to Doyle, from whom he had not heard for several years. What was surprising to some, in view of the fact that his needs had always been so Spartan — but was actually in keeping with his love for his family — was his request that a mausoleum be built. He asked that the remains of his parents and those of members of his immediate family be exhumed and buried with him. Evidently, Whitman, an agnostic, believed in the immortality of the soul and therefore wanted those he loved to be together in death.

On December 17, 1891, Whitman had a chill. The following day he developed a congestion in the right lung. Although the pain was intense, he never complained. He died on March 26, 1892. An autopsy was performed and the cause of death was given as "pleurisy of the left side, consumption of the right lung, general miliary tuberculosis and parenchymatous nephritis. There was also found a fatty liver, gallstone, a cyst in the adrenal, tubercular abscesses, involving the bones, and pachymeningitis" (Allen, 543).

The funeral took place on March 30. Thousands of people went to Whitman's house to look at the coffin. One of them was Peter Doyle. Although no minister officiated at Harleigh Cemetery, friends spoke instead. Texts by Confucius, Buddha, and Jesus; sections from the Koran, Isaiah, St. John, the *Zend-Avesta,* and Plato were read. "Out of the Cradle Endlessly Rocking" was intoned.

> O you singer solitary, singing by yourself, projecting me,
> O solitary me listening, nevermore shall I cease perpetuating you,
> Never more shall I escape, never more the reverberations....
>
> My own songs awaked from that hour,
> And with them the key, the word up from the waves,
> The word of the sweetest song and all songs,
> That strong and delicious word which, creeping to my feet....
> The sea whisper'd me.

Whitman had succeeded in changing the direction of American and world poetry.

Part 2

The Work

A perfect writer would make words sing, dance, kiss, do the male and female act, bear children, weep, bleed, rage, stab, steal, fire cannon, steer ships, sack cities, charge with cavalry or infantry or do any thing that man or woman or the natural powers can do.

— *Daybooks and Notebooks,* III, 742

POETRY

Many trouble themselves about conforming to laws. A great poet is followed by laws — they conform to him.

— CW, VI, 39

2

"And Have Distanced What Is Behind Me"

Whitman declared his courageously independent and innovative stand as poet in "Song of Myself," one of his most celebrated works. "And have distanced what is behind me for good reasons, / But call any thing back again when I desire it" (31). Indeed, his writings were significantly at variance with those of other Americans of his time. Common denominators, nevertheless, also existed between them.

Like Thoreau, Whitman felt a sense of oneness with nature in all its manifestations, particularly in its wild, fertile state. Moreover, he and Thoreau were both do-it-yourself men, especially Thoreau, a citizen of Concord, who had built himself a cabin on a tract of land owned by Emerson, where he had actually lived full-time *in* nature for at least two years. Thoreau and Whitman both believed that most people of their day were leading — as Thoreau put it — lives of "quiet desperation," so committed to earning a living that they had divested themselves of their potential for silence, receptivity, and wonderment at nature. Unlike Thoreau, however, Whitman had rejected puritanical idealism, calling himself "the equalizer of his age and land": one who gave uniform importance to body and to soul. Both men, each in his own way, were socially committed individuals. Thoreau had spent a night in jail for refusing to pay a required poll tax, which was to help finance the Mexican War. An abolitionist, he had spoken publicly against the Fugitive Slave Law — which enjoined citizens to help federal officials capture escaped slaves — going so far as to defend John Brown after his capture at Harpers Ferry, West Virginia, where he had seized a U.S. arsenal in his continuing attempt to promote slave insurrections. As for Whitman, we have already seen how he devoted many years of his life caring for hospitalized stagecoach drivers and Civil War soldiers.

Whitman and Ralph Waldo Emerson had also shared many an

idea. Both believed in spiritual and intellectual freedom, whatever the person's class, race, or economic condition. Unlike the passionate and affective Whitman, however, Emerson was a thinking type. Yet he, too, had rejected discursive reasoning, proclaiming direct intuition as the valid guide. Emerson considered "wholeness," which could even be gleaned from a dream, to be one of the best guides to a more profound sense of Self and Deity, reasoning that it "may let us deeper into the secret of nature than a hundred concerted experiments." The poet, although perceived differently by Whitman and Emerson, was seen by both as a liberating force; it was the poet's role to probe his own hidden spiritual and imaginative world "by unlocking, at all risks," the Boston sage stated, "his human doors." While Whitman, as we know, considered himself emancipated from inherited modes of behavior, championing visceral and sexual experiences of all kinds, Emerson had always felt uneasy with sensuality and passion. A wise man should remain detached and distance himself from the empirical world, he believed; focusing instead on the real world within: the "Over-Soul" (God) — the infinite. Antipodal to Whitman's unconstrained personality, and his rejection of conventional themes and syntax, were Emerson's relatively traditional manner of expression, his ordered living habits, and his balanced temperament. Yet, like the Bostonian philosopher, Whitman was a *seer*, intuiting elements existing in a dimension beyond the pragmatic world.

Although Whitman never met Nathaniel Hawthorne, the patrician poet James Russell Lowell claimed erroneously that his short stories were like Hawthorne's. Both men were concerned with questions of morality: the New Englander's *Scarlet Letter* revealed an intense inner struggle between his need to understand himself and his fear of peering into his darker side. A sense of urgency and conflict permeated Hawthorne's works: a war between faith and skepticism, as well as between a need to love and an inherent coldness. Although Whitman was also clearly at war with himself, inner struggle being evident in such short stories as "Bervance," his agony was made manifest most poignantly in his poetry: a battle waged between his yearning to liberate himself from his gnawing secret and his fear of earning society's stigma should he do so. Like Hawthorne, who lived in his own mysterious realm, Whitman's so-called openness masked the tragic sexual tensions that were forever corroding his being. An analogy may be made between Whitman's fundamental fear of disclosure and the storyteller's reply in Hawthorne's "The Antique Ring" — when he was asked the meaning of the ring: "You know that I can never separate the idea from the symbol in which it manifests itself." The same may be said of Whitman's poetry: his veiled but clashing feelings give great energy to his verbal orchestrations.

A man of the earth, Whitman had an approach to life that was diametrically opposed to that of the restrained and aristocratic Edgar Allan Poe. The hallucinatory, macabre, and fantastic visions in, for example, Poe's "The Fall of the House of Usher" or "The Raven" were just as alien to Whitman as nature was to Poe, who with few exceptions, considered this fertile realm as a mental construct. In keeping with the Romantics, Whitman felt nature to be embedded within soul and psyche. So strong a force was it, that it had the power both to release him from torment and to endow him with serenity. Affinities, nevertheless, did exist between these two great writers: their restless minds were forever seeking, inquiring, and questioning. Moreover, they were mystics, exploring spheres transcending the visible world, dimensions lying beyond the time–space continuum — searching for spiritual rather than material answers to life's circumstances. Whitman, for whom tonal rhythms and consonances were of primal importance, seconded, to some extent, Poe's statements to the effect that "Music is the perfection of the soul, or idea, of Poetry," in which he looked upon music as being essential to the creative process. Poe, however, was a theoretician, Whitman was not. He lived his song — powerfully, empathetically.

Sharp differences existed between the works of Whitman and those of William Cullen Bryant, whose eighteenth-century approach to nature and poetry yielded him his masterpiece, "Thanatopsis." Although he was a Romantic, who considered nature to be a consoling force, he nevertheless stood outside of it, lending moral meanings to the flower or rivulet he etched, but only after the event. Unlike Wordsworth's "Poems of the Imagination," for example, where identification between the object named and its meaning are *one,* no such unity exists in Bryant's lines. A derivative poet, Bryant, unlike Whitman, was rooted in European poetics, his meter-and-rhyme-bound verses being predictable. Nor did he possess the imaginative, passionate, and perceptive power of the author of "Song of Myself."

John Greenleaf Whittier, a Quaker motivated by social causes, and author of the popular and sentimental autobiographical poem *Snow-Bound,* had cast, so Whitman had heard, his copy of *Leaves of Grass* into the flames. Judging such writings to be morally offensive, this New England poet of nature, cut himself off from any possible association with the Brooklyn poet. Unlike Whitman, Whittier stated (and was proud of it) that he wrote "good Yankee rhymes." Other critics suggested that he lacked the technical ability and variety to be an exceptional poet. Nevertheless, many of his images — for example, his verbal visualization of domestic tranquility in *Snow-Bound,* particularly the blanket of whiteness left after the New England storm — endowed the atmosphere of his works with a deeply moving sense of enchantment.

When editor of the Brooklyn *Eagle* (1846), Whitman had reprinted some poems by Henry Wadsworth Longfellow, one of America's most celebrated poets. At Longfellow's insistence, the Brooklyn poet spent several uncomfortable evenings at his home, most aware of the fact that he did not belong to his intellectual circle. Longfellow, like Whitman, was the creator of an American mythology revolving around cities, waterways, and country spaces, but this author of *Evangeline* and *Hiawatha* also verbalized a vision of the New World that was, unlike the Brooklyn bard's, sentimental, traditional, uncritical, and historically inaccurate. While *Leaves of Grass* was disturbing, rebellious in essence, and rooted to life, Longfellow's poems were nostalgic, relatively aloof, and cerebrally oriented. Although Longfellow also had a sense of the lyrical, neither his technique nor his language was original — nor did he possess that brilliant resonance, that tonal and deeply syncopated rhythmic quality, that imbued Whitman's lines.

"I never read his Book," wrote Emily Dickinson in a letter (April 25, 1862), referring to *Leaves of Grass,* "but was told he was disgraceful." Although a spirit of contest, inquiry, and continuous transformation prevailed in her search for true form, meaning, and faith, and her analytical, probing mind helped her create some of the greatest poems of all time, unlike Whitman, she was a hermetic poet. Esoteric in nature, poetry was her lifeline to the world: "She ate and drank the precious words," endowing them with a fresh life culled from her private lexicon of signs, symbols, and totems. Rather than meld with the crowd as was Whitman's habit, she cut herself off from social intercourse, withdrawing into her room, and dressing exclusively in white, the color of Druids. Yet, like Whitman, she reveled in nature. Unlike him, she was unable to cope with seasonal changes, experiencing summer's end as a divestiture, that left her depressed and overcome with feelings of loss. For Whitman, nature, in all its forms, was a catalyst, an energizer, a powerfully positive force.

Revolutionary in his poetry, Whitman refused to follow what he considered to be the staid rules of prosody: the iambic pentameter of the traditional English poets. Partial to free verse, to cadenced lines, responding with stressed or unstressed syllables to the mood and feeling of the moment, he rejected anything that smacked of mechanical and artificial alternation of accented and nonaccented stanzaic structures. To emphasize the energy implicit in some of his lines, he would sometimes even interchange conventional meter with free verse.

The poet of America and of democracy, Whitman was sympathetic and compassionate in his feelings toward human beings, whatever their class or inclinations. He believed in the brotherhood of people, in social justice, and in freedom, and he viewed the Union, particularly during the Civil War, as something sacred. "I am the man, I suffer'd, I was there." He conveyed his feelings of equality in his poems imagistically, by pairing a prostitute ("The prostitute draggles her shawl, her bonnet bobs on her tipsy and pimpled neck") with a head of state ("The President holding a cabinet council"). As "Wound-dresser," he knew love and grief, and therefore could empathize with others.

Satiric at times, Whitman decried the hypocritical piety of men of the cloth and worshipers who were more interested in material comforts than spiritual well-being; he denounced the vulgarity and materialism of the Gilded Age in general. Nevertheless, Whitman is remembered as a major force in American literature not for his negative preaching, but for his generosity, expansiveness, and largeness of spirit that overflowed into all nature and sought to penetrate the cosmos itself.

Whitman the visionary emerges full-blown in "Crossing Brooklyn Ferry." In it, he conveys feelings of cosmic oneness by fusing in his mind's eye the flow of the water with his own poetic consciousness; the natural and human world, with the constructed mechanical sphere. Microcosm becomes macrocosm as image upon image catapults forth in an ever-expanding universe, a world of dilating feelings — and of a revelatory exploration of the ineffable.

3

"I Am the Poet of the Body and I Am the Poet of the Soul"

A work of art with epic quality, "Song of Myself" (1855, 1881) has the broad sweep and symbolic impact that *Beowulf, The Song of Roland,* and *The Nibelungenlied* had for medieval societies. Like these lyrical works, "Song of Myself," encompasses religious, social, economic, and political elements. Nothing was too minute nor too gigantic for Whitman to absorb in his poem; nor too peripheral to excite and fulfill his visions and prophecies; nor too constricting to liberate his "barbaric yawp." Uncrafted, perhaps, in its lack of reserve, its hungering for the new and the different, what emerges is nature — human and nonhuman — as filtered through the poet's feelings in all of their intense viscerality.

When Whitman first published "Song of Myself," in 1855, America was in the throes of one of its cyclical national crises. Conflict revolved around the rapid growth in technology, communication, transportation, manufacturing — and unemployment — resulting from the Industrial Revolution. Immigration was also a concern: five hundred thousand foreigners arrived in America between 1820 and 1830. More than five times that number were to come to these shores in the next two decades. According to the figures of the day, by 1850 12 percent of the population was foreign-born. Forces identified with social progress were also being established, including cooperative communities such as Robert Owen's New Harmony, founded in 1824 in Indiana, and Charles Fourier's so-called phalanxes, the best known being Brook Farm. Equality, territorial expansion, individualism, agrarianism, collectivism, and antislavery movements were all being discussed, as well as problems relating to crime, suicide, illness, and sexuality. Not harmony, but disunity prevailed.

Whitman's "Song of Myself," utopian in vision, alludes to some of the above-mentioned themes, but never didactically. Extolling freedom of spirit and purpose, laissez-faire liberalism, and a class-less, egalitarian society, it strongly repudiates what the poet considered America's growing commercialism and acquisitiveness. While questioning, castigating, and satirizing these negative characteristics, the poet's jubilant song in fifty-two parts also awakens in readers a deep love for their native land, as well as for nature and for humankind in general. A spirit of Eros binds rather than separates people. The poet's exuberant sequences of powerful images, repetitive salvos, synecdoches, alliterations, elliptical phrases, and symbols of universal magnitude are celebrations of life; canticles of love, shoutings, aimed at awakening Americans to a new world based on joy, fearlessness, and sexual and spiritual ardor.

"I Have Said That the Soul Is Not More Than the Body, / and I Have Said That the Body Is Not More Than the Soul" (48:1269)

Soul and body are one for Whitman. No longer is the former to be divinized and the latter reviled and labeled the "animal" in humankind, as had been done by Platonists, Gnostics, and Christians. In Plato's dialogue "Phaedrus," reason was identified with the head, the rational, and divine part of the human being — in opposition to the body, which was likened to the animal, or the irrational sphere. The cleavage between body and soul became a burden born by humankind throughout the ages. One should recall that Plato had banned the poet from his *Republic*.

For Whitman, the dynamics of body and soul — inseparable, indeed one and the same — exist in a continuous interplay, each working with the other throughout the life process. Together they teach individuals and societies how to deal with life's adversities as well as with its joys. The pleasure principle is not unalloyed by the intrusion of pain.

> The pleasures of heaven are with me and the pains of hell with me,
> The first I graft and increase upon myself, the latter I translate into
>   a new tongue. (21:423–24)

Like Job, whose faith in God was all-powerful, yet who also retained his identity — "but I will maintain mine own ways before him" (Job 13:15) — Whitman celebrated the fulfillment of an organically *whole* being. His physical and spiritual sides having melded together, at least temporarily, he reveled in the happiness accruing to each in its togetherness. He neither accepted chastisement for the body, nor proclaimed excesses in the opposite extreme: "I

believe in you my soul, the other I am must not abase itself to you, /
And you must not be abased to the other" (5:82).

For Whitman, love of the body/soul complex stood above all
else during life's trajectory. A pre-Nietzschean, he maintained that
Christianity taught humankind not how to live, but how to die; that
it cut people off from the joys of earthly existence so as to better save
their treasures for heaven. Did the Sermon on the Mount not advise
the accumulation of good deeds on earth so as to assure entrée into
heavenly spheres?

Lay not up for yourselves treasures upon earth, where moth and rust doth
corrupt, and where thieves break through and steal: But lay up for yourselves treasures in heaven, where neither moth nor rust doth corrupt, and
where thieves do not break through nor steal (Matt. 6:19–20).

Whitman could not condone advice that taught human beings
to reject the present in favor of the Hereafter. To denigrate one
part of being while lauding the other is not only to divide what is
whole, but to encourage dissension, rather than harmony, within
the personality.

Whitman's hymnal sequences in "Song of Myself" spread a gospel of wholeness and of passionate love born from the *total* person:
the body/soul complex.

Earth of shine and dark mottling the tide of the river!
Earth of the limpid gray of clouds brighter and clearer for my sake!
Far-swooping elbow'd earth — rich apple-blossom'd earth!
Smile, for your lover comes.

Prodigal, you have given me love — therefore I to you give love!
O unspeakable passionate love. (21:442)

Nor could life exist, Whitman contended, without the dual forces
of good and evil. Unlike Saint Augustine, who rejected the existence
of evil in a God-created world, referring to it as a *privatio boni*,
Whitman believed that just as both factors live inchoate in the Godhead, so they do in humankind. In this regard, he shared the belief
of the German mystic, Jakob Boehme, who contended that since
the Godhead was a *totality*, light existed within him alongside darkness. "I am not the poet of goodness only," Whitman wrote, "I do
not decline to be the poet of wickedness also" (22:463).

In that Whitman lived in the present — considered by him, and by
mystics in general as an eternal present — he was very much aware

of the disparities implicit in the world of contingencies. Because he lived both good and evil within his personality, he attempted to deal with these powers empirically, as well as poetically. He was forever searching for ways to break down society's masks, its unshakable beliefs, its rigid thought processes, most frequently used by groups and individuals as defense mechanisms to protect them from the "dangers" awaiting those who open their minds to untrodden paths. While Whitman's verbal shock techniques sometimes thrust his readers into fearful abysses, they also made them aware of their shadowy characteristics, thus shaking them out of their lethargy — their deadly regressive conventional existences.

> Evil propels me and reform of evil propels me, I stand indifferent...
> I moisten the roots of all that has grown. (22:465)

Earth and Heaven, high and low, credos and ideas of all sorts, allowed the poet the freedom and abandon he needed to reap the joys of this earth — to experience life's fullness, an expression for Whitman of Divine immanence.

When experiencing moments of transcendence, prior to or during the creative process, Whitman, like Divinity, and like such visionary poets as William Wordsworth, John Keats, Percy Bysshe Shelley, or Charles Baudelaire, leaped into a fourth dimension (the nonrational sphere, or, in psychological terms, collective unconscious), thereby cutting himself off, albeit temporarily, from the differentiated or earthly realm, with all of its struggle and pain. When actually transcribing his hallucinatory experience — that is, struggling to find the right words to convey idea, meaning, rhythm, sensation, and tone, Whitman returned to the three-dimensional world (rational) and all of its dichotomies — including the pull of good and evil.

Never harassed or dominated by a compulsive need for programmed activity or a work ethic, Whitman, as *vates,* saw himself as the prophet of a new world. He loafed, journeyed, rested, splashed in the clear and muddied waters, gathered up pebbles and rocks, filled his lungs with pure country air as well as with the pollutants of urban areas. Because sensuality and spirituality cohabited within him, so, too, did sin and damnation coexist with beatitude. But mortification of the flesh never became part of his credo. On the contrary, Whitman celebrated "every atom of my blood"; his mouth, tongue, lungs, breath, heart, semen, the "loveroot," and "crotch." Everything intoxicated him — all was food for life and poetry. A distillation of opposites generated rapture, as colors, textures, aromas, transparencies, opacities, vocalizations, awakened his creative urge.

> Sea if stretch'd ground swells,
> Sea breathing broad and convulsive breaths,
> Sea of the brine of life and of unshovell'd yet always-ready graves,
> Howler and scooper of storms, capricious and dainty sea,
> I am integral with you, I too am one phase and all phases." (22:454)

Like the psychopomp of old, Whitman leads his readers on a journey to a temporal realm of his own creation, via a vigorously fresh transpersonal language divested of guilt and devoid of retribution: "Not an inch nor a particle of an inch is vile, and none shall be less familiar than the rest" (3:58).

"Stop This Day and Night with Me and You Shall Possess the Origin of All Poems" (2:33)

The poet, like the shaman, medium, and hero, is the transmitter of a mystery. Although endowed with supernatural powers and inhabiting both temporal and atemporal spheres, he is not divinized, nor does he acquire immortality, except in his poetry.

The poet/hero symbolizes an evolving being whose essential desire is to rectify conflictual situations within himself and society; to combat those monsters that seek to pervert idealism and purity. Psychologically, the hero is a manifestation of primordial energy, of *libido* (psychic and physical powers): a virtually superhuman force who can probe and then disclose nature's secrets.

Not only does the poet/hero/shaman/medium ritualize while solemnizing what he intones, but his poetic voice takes on oracular qualities. Like Orpheus, he awakens the dormant into life, thrusts the living into a world of contingencies, thereby opening the door onto what lies beyond the discernible.

Whitman's poet/hero enjoys good health; he is exuberant, his comportment is in harmony with his vision of life, and he empathizes with the world at large. As "atom," he transforms the invisible into the visible, the transparent into the opaque, the abstract into the concrete. Thus may the reader penetrate and finally become an inhabitor of the poet/hero's civilization. In that the poet/hero is astride both the third and fourth dimensions, past and present are synonymous, as are inner and outer worlds. He is at one with the earth and its millions of suns.

> Stop this day and night with me and you shall possess the origin of
>   all poems,
> You shall possess the good of the earth and sun, (there are millions
>   of suns left,)
> You shall no longer take things at second or third hand, nor look
>   through the eyes of the dead, nor feed on the spectres in books,
> You shall not look through my eyes either, nor take things from me,
> You shall listen to all sides and filter them from your self. (2:33)

Because of the intensity of the poet's perceptions and his lust for
life, he, like Brahma, the Hindu creator of the universe, is both the
material and the immediate cause of his creation. Like Brahma, the
poet emanates his poem out of his substance and reenters it as its
indwelling spirit.

That Whitman used the word *Song* in "Song of Myself" is no co-
incidence. To be sure, it indicates a metrical composition for singing
with accelerating and slackening rhythms, a variety of diapasons
and tonal harmonies, and cacophonies capable of activating nerve
and flesh as well as electrifying the atmosphere. We know, too, that
Whitman was very drawn to the opera form and that stanzas in
"Song of Myself" and other of his works feature sequences of arias
and recitatives.

Other affinities exist between the "song" motif in Whitman's
poem and Hindu scripture, to which the poet became increasingly drawn. Since fine singing requires great breath control, it
may be suggested that Whitman was alluding to Brahman (the
neuter form of the masculine name Brahma) and Brahman (a member of the highest, or priestly caste of Hindus), identified with
the breath of life (*prana=spiritus*, "breath") or with infinite space.
Like the Hindu Deity, the poet sings or breathes his poem into
existence from himself — in timelessness and spacelessness. As
is stated in the "Chandogya Upanishad" (VIII), he has the freedom of entering the fourth dimension at will when creating his
poem.

The two syllables in the word *Myself,* of the poem's title, bring to
mind the coexistence of the poet's supernatural and natural sides.
The *My* is identified with his ability to live in the ego-oriented rational world of everyday reality; and the *Self* relates to his ability to
transcend the empirical domain, to perceive the beyond, while divesting himself of his recognizable individual aspect. Like Brahma,
he is an all-enfolding Consciousness, part of the Void or universal
sphere, from which everything emanates and into which, accord-

ing to the Upanishads, all returns. "Divine am I inside and out," Whitman writes, "and I make holy whatever I touch or am touch'd from" (24:524).

The poet, like Brahma, is the incantator, communicating to humankind the infinite in finite terms: in images, sonorities, and ideas. Not only are the words *logos* (intelligence, activity, or will), but also *phallos* (instinct, viscerality, libido) yielded to mortals. In the beginning, Vedic texts tell us, Brahma's thought flowed forth through Vak, the Goddess of discourse, voice, and speech, thereby giving birth to the universe in song. So, the poet/creator reveals to humankind what has been lost to consciousness, a solar or lunar language, similar in nature perhaps to Pythagoras's language of the spheres, or the single language spoken by humanity prior to the erection of the Tower of Babel. Mystics believe that in archaic times communication between humans and animals, material and non-material matter, existed. Poets, like shamans and oracles, having reached certain spiritual levels were given the gift of languages — an ability to return to synthetic modalities: total expression.

> Now I will do nothing but listen,
> To accrue what I hear into this song, to let sounds contribute toward
>   it. . . .
> I hear all sounds running together, combined, fused or following. . . .
>   (26:582)

As revelator, the poet promises the reader to pull aside the curtain masking reality.

> Dazzling and tremendous how quick the sun-rise would kill me,
> If I could not now and always send sun-rise out of me.
>
> We also ascend dazzling and tremendous as the sun,
> We found our own O my soul in the calm and cool of daybreak.
>
> My voice goes after what my eyes cannot reach,
> With the twirl of my tongue I encompass worlds and volumes of worlds.
>
> Speech is the twin of my vision, it is unequal to measure itself,
> It provokes me forever, it says sarcastically,
> *Walt you contain enough, why don't you let it out then?* (25:560)

The poet, like Vak, will be *voice* and *song*: giver and not taker in the

Endless unfolding of words of ages!
And mine a word of the modern, the word En-Masse.

A word of the faith that never balks,
Here or henceforward it is all the same to me, I accept Time absolutely.

It alone is without flaw, it alone rounds and completes all,
That mystic baffling wonder alone completes all. (23:477)

In his *Poetic Principle,* Poe indicated that the work of art is grasped intuitively by the poet during moments of pure ecstasy, when expanded consciousness opens him up to rapture. During these glimmerings, the unconscious, in some inexplicable way, seems to be receptive to cosmic vibrations that then filter into the conscious sphere, which, in turn, grasps, blends, sorts, and rearranges the new riches into images, feelings, and sounds. Thus do the conglomerates of infinite particles pave the way for fresh awareness.

For Whitman, as was true for Poe, intuition was the great unifying principle that not only nourished but also reoriented the psyche. Once logical and rational realms were abandoned, obstructions leading to unknown heights were also removed, inviting the traveler to experience extraterrestrial spheres outside of the three-dimensional world. When the journey into a land of enchantment had ended, the poet returned to mundane existence and attempted to transform the newly discovered feelings and sensations into multiple rhythms and tonal harmonies.

Poe had also noted that once the intensity of the poetic vision flagged, as it was fated to do, the sublime, as of necessity, became reduced to the paltry and banal. Be it the *Iliad* or *Paradise Lost,* he considered the poem to be made up of a "succession of brief" intuitive forays and not one single ecstatic experience. The same may be said of the fifty-two sequences of the "Song of Myself," a transliteration of Whitman's apocalyptic fantasms into a language comprehensible to humankind. Analogies, metaphors, symbols, and other figures of speech, the means by which he communicated his revelations, are experienced by readers according to the depth of their feelings and understanding: "You shall listen to all sides and filter them from yourself" (2:37).

"The Smallest Sprout Shows There Is Really No Death" (6:126)

Rejecting linear concepts of time — that is, the notion of a beginning and an end, as is implicit in the Bible's seven days of creation and as forwarded in the notion of Christ's birth and death — the poet sings of these and other events in *myth time,* that is, in an *eternal present.*

Understood as a primordial experience, not necessarily personal but rather transcendental, myth, to Whitman, is a living and burning reality. As such, it deals with both the existential and archetypal worlds: present, past, and future embedded within its structure. In that the myth in general and Whitman's in particular lives outside of temporal time, it knows no bounds, flowing in cyclical, sacred, and eternal dimensions. When, therefore, Whitman sings his credo in lusty song, conflating tenses and times, merging the smallest atom with the infinite Almighty, energy mounts as dynamism accelerates. "Urge and urge and urge, / Always the procreant urge of the world" (3:44).

As the poet drives out the minimal domain, he pushes forward, flowing into the flux and reflux outside of the empirical world: from the many, therefore, into oneness: "Out of the dimness opposite equals advance" (3:45). As he is fired with flame, like the shamans of old, "electrical" charges build, currents interact, power infiltrates the poet's being: "Stout as a horse, affectionate, haughty, electrical," like the winged horse Pegasus who flew to heaven, symbolically conflating the world of impetuous desire and creative imagination into poetic inspiration (3:50). Not through books or cerebrality are leaps into the unknown to be effected. To be touched by sparks and flames triggers heightened consciousness, allowing Whitman to say: "I and this mystery here we stand" (3:51).

That electricity should have played such a large role in Whitman's poetry is not surprising. The Austrian physician Franz Anton Mesmer, who had established his clinic in Paris in 1778, had treated patients all over Europe by hypnosis. He attributed his success to "animal magnetism," a magnetic power that existed throughout the universe and that he knew how to concentrate in his own person and direct to others.

The very concept of magnetism, Whitman believed, not only brought people together, but when coursing through the cosmos in the form of lightning or animal magnetism, also accounted for negative changes: "The sickness of one of my folks or of myself, or ill doing or loss or lack of money, or depressions or exaltations" (4:71). Likewise, Whitman wrote, this phenomenon could engender family feuds, battles, anguish, but could not cleave "Me and myself" (4:71).

Let me also note in this connection that experimentation in

things electric had been going on for centuries. Robert Boyle discovered that attraction and repulsion were mutual and that such forces were transmitted through a vacuum; Benjamin Franklin, the inventor of the lightning rod, and Ebenezer Kinnersley of Philadelphia identified charges as positive and negative; Charles A. Colomb started a quantitative study of electricity. The names of those associated with the further investigation of electricity are many: Hans Christian Oersted discovered that a magnetic field surrounds a wire carrying current; André-Marie Ampère worked in electrodynamics while also confirming the relationship of electricity to magnetism; Dominique F. Arago, researching the field of optics, was also known for his discoveries in magnetism; Michael Faraday who developed the first dynamo, discovered electromagnetic induction.

The topic of electricity, which led to exciting scientific speculations in Whitman's day, inspired him to convert these catalytic notions into words. Like those binding and separating currents flowing throughout the universe, the poet's imagination and feelings traveled in time and space in renewing and/or slackening vigor. The multiple electrical charges he experienced opened him up to mat or colorful visual frames of Manhattan or of Long Island, West or North, wealthy or impoverished countrysides. Flash-forward sequences or receding strips leaped into his mind's eye. While observing these elements, from a distance as well as in closeups, the poet-as-artist alters their negative and positive consistencies and potencies in his own special language — or "hieroglyphs." Either repelled or attracted to each other, each word used was designed to stir, excite, or incite its opposite, by pacifying or deactivating elementary particles inherent in the soul/body complex.

In that Whitman is dealing with electric verbality, as well as with mythical concepts, archaic lands and peoples come to life again and again in "Song of Myself." Past, present, and future are invited to cohabit in an electrically charged atmosphere:

> They are alive and well somewhere,
> The smallest sprout shows there is really no death,
> And if ever there was it led forward life, and does not wait at the
>   end to arrest it,
> And ceas'd the moment life appear'd. (6:125)

Everything in the manifest world has become a sign of another reality for Whitman: an indication of an existing, although invisible, form of a highly active life. Implicit in such a point of view are the scientific theories of the popular French naturalist J. B. Lamarck, who believed that organisms react to new or changing environments by means of acquired characteristics.

In Whitman's world of symbols and analogies, death is nonexistent. Such attitudes suggest a belief in metempsychosis and reincarnation. Not only drawn from Hindu and Buddhist beliefs, Whitman's view may also be regarded as a restatement of a whole Neoplatonic tradition, which had been in the air for centuries and with which he was conversant: the beliefs of Paracelsus, Nicholas of Cusa, Giordano Bruno, Johannes Kepler, Johann Wolfgang von Goethe, Emerson, and others. Neoplatonists considered everything in the universe to be linked, everything in the differentiated world to be an emanation of the *All*. As such, universal sympathies acted and reacted upon each other, whether visible or not, organic or not, conscious or not. The isolated pulsation, thought, sensation, simply did not exist. In that each particle reverberated in its own way upon another, human feelings, like chemical substances or electric charges, also influenced their courses.

The human being possesses an identity, a unity, and adheres to various laws, but since the individual's universe is a microcosm of the macrocosm, this universe is interconnected through analogy with that of others in indefinable ways. Although one might not know the general direction of one's life course, nature is not blind. Whitman, like Goethe, believed that every aspect of being is in search of its own completion. Nature, therefore, has its own process of becoming, its own orienting and directing devices, its own unity. The ability to apperceive these paths, to understand an infinitesimal part of one's destiny, may be gained through mystical encounters: each person peers into his or her own depths in search of that inner flame or electric spark. Such probing does not rule out conflict, abrasion, attraction, ambivalence, indeed, it encourages it, since everything is part of the life/death experience that is renewed ad infinitum. Immortality is fathomless in that everything in the universe feeds on and is nourished by the other, be it physically or psychologically: "All goes onward and outward, nothing collapses, / And to die is different from what any one supposed, and luckier" (6:129).

Life and death are one and the same: to be born into life is to be born into death.

I hasten to inform him or her it is just as lucky to die, and I know it.

I pass death with the dying and birth with the new-wash'd babe, and
    am not contain'd between my hat and boots,
And peruse manifold objects, no two alike and every one good,
The earth good and the stars good, and their adjuncts all good.

I am not an earth nor an adjunct of an earth,
I am the mate and companion of people, all just as immortal and
    fathomless as myself.
(They do not know how immortal, but I know.) (7:132)

Immortality, Whitman indicates, does not preclude earthly suffering. The strain and pain of being "slighted" is deeply felt, as are
the "stings" he must endure from those who are unable to understand his way and seek to destroy him. The gratification that comes
with the afterflow of the creative process serves to alter his dismal thoughts, transporting them — and him by extension — from
human to nonhuman spheres. Nor should the poet, or anyone else,
feel guilt at being rejected or derided. Everything in the *chain of
being,* from stone to Deity, experiences the duality of the workaday world: without pain, joy remains unknown. Courageously, but
inconclusively, Whitman claims he will show himself plain and
remove the mask:

Undrape! you are not guilty to me, nor stale nor discarded,
I see through the broadcloth and gingham whether or no,
And am around, tenacious, acquisitive, tireless, and cannot be
    shaken away. (7:145)

Everything within him vibrates, resonates, howls as his poetic eye
filters his creation. He knows that rhythms, sonorities, and words
gestate within him, in the form of wild animals hunted down, or
"fresh-killed game," or "boatman and clam-diggers," flatlands and
mountains, all reinvigorating the process that links disparities into
union in the life/death cycles.

As poet/prophet/teacher, Whitman exists within and outside time.
Time, for the poet, is experienced in a continuous unfolding of
words that has the power to awaken the slumbering and reviv-
ify the dormant, thus enabling him to feel connected with the
universe: "The clock indicates the moment — but what does eternity indicate?" (44:1137). Unlike Samuel Beckett's concept of time,
viewed as a "Double-headed Monster" forever gorging itself on the
living, Whitman's is more like Victor Hugo's, who felt strengthened

and emboldened by his acute sense of relatedness to an infinite universe. Whitman also felt inhabited by an increase of electric charges, enabling him to break out of an imprisoning three-dimensional reality.

> Magnifying and applying come I,
> Outbidding at the start the old cautious hucksters,
> Taking myself the exact dimensions of Jehovah,
> Lithographing Kronos, Zeus his son, and Hercules his grandson,
> Buying drafts of Osiris, Isis, Belus, Brahma, Buddha,
> In my portfolio placing Manito loose, Allah on a leaf, the crucifix
>   engraved.... (41:1026)

Identifying and cohabiting with divinities from time immemorial enabled Whitman to glimpse eternality — to peer into the depths of his superhuman nature. Standing, paradoxically, as if from afar yet within the melee, he felt in a position to reveal social injustices in the earthly sphere, as well as to rise beyond it. Like the Neoplatonists and alchemists, partisans of perpetual transmutations, Whitman indicated that nothing within the cosmos disappeared; it merely altered in form and texture.

In keeping with the views of Xenophanes, Whitman believed that everything coming from the ground, be it animal, mineral, or vegetable, was composed of and emerged from the *prima materia*. Such a view gives credence not only to the notion of universality, but also, as previously discussed, to the suggestion of an undifferentiated state, thus blending the pure and the impure. After an earthly trajectory in the world of contingencies, all things return to this state: incarnation is necessarily followed by obliteration into mass. "Afar down I see the huge first Nothing, I know I was even there" (44:1153).

Since nothing is permanent or impermanent in the cosmos, the death/rebirth sequence is as much of a process as all else. Forms of life are distinguished only by their modalities and stages of evolution. So involved are the series of transformations — from the minutest particles to the largest of entities — that continuity and contiguity are implicit within the *One*.

> I waited unseen and always, and slept through the lethargic mist...
>
> Long I was hugg'd close — long and long.
>
> Immense have been the preparations for me,
> Faithful and friendly the arms that have help'd me.

Cycles ferried my cradle, rowing and rowing like cheerful boatmen,
For room to me stars kept aside in their own rings,
They sent influences to look after what was to hold me. (44:1154).

The poet swings into the life/death cycles, unaware of positive or negative influences; Good or Evil; Heaven or Hell; Joy or Sorrow. While following the ancient Egyptians' credo of death and resurrection, as well as the ceremonies involved in ancient and modern fertility rituals, he ejaculates burgeoning feelings of eternality and relatedness in jubilant song: "I chant the chant of dilation or pride" (21:428).

"Why Should I Pray?
Why Should I Venerate and Be Ceremonious?" (20:398)

The poet rejects organized religions with their crushing dogmas and fear-inspiring rituals, promises of Heaven and threats of Hell, demands on worshipers to bow, scrape, and kiss sacerdotal rings. "Not one kneels to another, nor to his kind that lived thousands of years ago" (32:689). To prove his love for the Divine, Whitman needs neither to flagellate himself nor deprive himself of life's joys in an *imitatio Christi*. To experience the transpersonal requires him to give full sway to his senses, be it in his love for the Divine or for things of the earth.

The poet's God is a totality: one that includes light and darkness and that inhabits a universe of eternal becoming. Gods old and new, be they worshiped by polytheists or monotheists, givers or takers, sowers or reapers, creators or destroyers — or all of these combined — are unfathomable. Only may their fruits be experienced.

As the poet journeys on through life's course, he seeks to love and not to fear, to understand and not to shudder. Relieved of burdensome dogmas, he is not a victim of metaphysical anguish, as was, for example, the scientist and religious philosopher Blaise Pascal when facing the infinite, thus the unknowable. Whitman wrote:

And nothing, not God, is greater to one than one's self is...
And I say to mankind, Be not curious about God,
For I who am curious about each am not curious about God...
(No array of terms can say how much I am at peace about God and
    about death.)

> I hear and behold God in every object, yet understand God not in
>   the least,
> Nor do I understand who there can be more wonderful than myself.
>   (48:1271)

The poet's feelings dilate until a moment when he knows himself
to be in communion with the universe. Rather than restricting his
thoughts, compartmentalizing them into a variety of creeds, each
inspiring fear and trembling, and castigating the beliefs of others,
his mind and senses are receptive to them all: "The big doors of the
country barn stand open and ready" (9:167). Nothing impedes his
lust and love for God; nothing fossilizes his mobile ideas of worship
nor paralyzes the gyrating rhythms inhabiting them; nor does any
factor prevent passivity from transforming into wildness, nor stop
the hunter from hunting; nor stay the passage from cradle to bier.
The poet feeds on change; on love and not hate:

> I do not despise your priests, all time, the world over,
> My faith is the greatest of faiths and the least of faiths,
> Enclosing worship ancient and modern and all between ancient and
>   modern,
> Believing I shall come again upon the earth after five thousand years,
> Waiting responses from oracles, honoring the gods, saluting the sun,
> Making a fetish of the first rock or stump, powowing with sticks in
>   the circle of obis,
> Helping the llama or brahmin as he trims the lamps of the idols,
> Dancing yet through the streets in a phallic procession, rapt and
>   austere in the woods a gymnosophist.... (43:1096)

All forms of worship are acceptable to the poet; all faiths and all
deities; all "sermons, creeds, theology." Nor are atheists or skep-
tics excluded from Whitman's embrace: "I know every one of you,
I know the sea of torment, doubt, despair and unbelief" (43:1114).
Sun and moon worship and whatever incites awe in humankind ex-
cites the poet's interest: "There is no stoppage and never can be
stoppage" (45:1190). As he peers electrified, into space and time,
"quadrillions of eras, a few octillions of cubic leagues" (43:1194),
and "What is known I strip away." Able to "See ever so far, there
is limitless space outside of that, / Count ever so much, there is
limitless time around that" (44:1135; 45:1196).

Tramping on and on in his perpetual quest, the poet listens to
signs, experiences sensations, peers every now and then into the infinite, unwilling to accept curtailment or stratification in any domain:

"I have no chair, no church, no philosophy" (46:1205). The experience of living, coupled with the discovery of one's own path, which the individual alone can accomplish, is crucial not only to the poet, but to every human being. In direct address, Whitman says: "Not I, not any one else can travel that road for you, / You must travel it for yourself" (46:1210). He further exhorts his readers:

> Long enough have you dream'd contemptible dreams,
> Now I wash the gum from your eyes,
> You must habit yourself to the dazzle of the light and of every
>   moment of your life.
>
> Long have you timidly waded holding a plank by the shore,
> Now I will you to be a bold swimmer,
> To jump off in the midst of the sea, rise again, nod to me, shout, and
>   laughingly dash with your hair. (46:1228)

Friedrich Nietzsche was of like mind when he launched his criticism of Christian civilization — in such writings as *Origin of Tragedy, Thus Spake Zarathustra,* and *Beyond Good and Evil* — for having encouraged a "slave mentality." Just as Nietzsche looked forward to the birth of the hero who would consciously affirm life, so Whitman believed in the Poet-Superman. For Whitman, such a being represented the highest form of passion and creativity; he was endowed with the energy to lift people outside of conventional attitudes, inviting them to penetrate beyond the rational world, with its systematic schemes, into irrational and unlimited spheres — into a metaworld *Beyond Good and Evil,* to use Nietzsche's title. Whitman like Nietzsche rejected Christianity for all of its don'ts, its credos that teach people how to die but not how to live. And also like Nietzsche, Whitman encouraged "dancing and laughing," so that humanity would be able to better partake of the lust for life in *this* world.

Courage was a must for Whitman's Poet-Superman, and for all those who aspired to follow his credo, seeking to journey forth in the time-space continuum — independently, isolated, and unprotected by dogma and the restrictive religious institutions enclothing it.

"This Is the Touch of My Lips to Yours, This the Murmur of Yearning" (19:379)

Since Whitman preaches a lust for life and believes soul and body are one, it follows that mystical communion may occur in a state

of erotic ecstasy. The joy of feeling *one* with the cosmos, thus of
being part of a larger plan, inspires him with feelings of love. The
sexual act and its consummation, whether interpreted in the "Song
of Myself" on a physical or spiritual plane, serves to reaffirm the
poet's feelings of fullness and fulfillment.

The raw imagery in some of Whitman's erotic passages is similar in many ways to the phallic visualizations in the *Interior Castle*
by Saint Teresa of Ávila. Her passionate yearning for Christ's visi-
tation so heightened her senses as to allow her to better experience
the intensity of Divine ecstasy. Compare the power and viscerality
of Whitman's visualizations in "Song of Myself," which serve him
so effectively in the release he feels after the consummation of the
sexual act.

> How you settled your head athwart my hips and gently turn'd over
>   upon me,
> And parted the shirt from my bosom-bone, and plunged your tongue
>   to my bare-stript heart,
> And reach'd till you felt my beard, and reach'd till you held my feet
>   (5:88).

The enactment of the fellatio and the ensuing orgasm, as critics have interpreted the following lines, parallel God's love for
humankind.

> And I know that the hand of God is the promise of my own,
> And I know that the spirit of God is the brother of my own,
> And that all the men ever born are also my brothers, and the women
>   my sisters and lovers,
> And that a kelson of the creation is love,
> And limitless are leaves stiff or drooping in the fields. (5:92)

Whitman's concretization of spirit and flesh in the sexual act is,
then, a humanization of the Divine experience. Orgiastic sensations
are not only identified with sexual intercourse, but are analogized
in images of grass, water, trees, flowers, clouds, lightning, and other
natural manifestations. The images of trees and grass, especially,
phallic for the most part, spell fertility and rebirth.

One of the most ambiguous of sequences in "Song of Myself"
deals with the poet's tactile description of twenty-eight joyful young
men bathing on the seashore. As the author's eye (I, eye) shifts, a
second image is brought into the action: a woman is seen hiding
behind the window of a house. She yearns to join the handsome

young men, but because of her guilt-ridden feelings and fearful attitude, refrains from doing so. Only as a voyeur does she live out her autoerotic fantasies, libidinizing in her imagination the pleasures of physical contact with the twenty-eight young men on the beach.

The number twenty-eight, identified so frequently with the lunar cycle of fertility and renewal, suggests the androgynous nature of the young men on the beach. When the twenty-ninth bather, the lady (perhaps a mask for the I-poet), now envisages herself "dancing and laughing" at the thought of the love fest she could enjoy were she to join the young men in the water, her fantasies emerge, and she sees herself passing her hand over the young men's glistening bodies.

> Dancing and laughing along the beach came the twenty-ninth bather,
> The rest did not see her, but she saw them and loved them.

> The beards of the young men glisten'd with wet, it ran from their
>   long hair,
> Little streams pass'd all over their bodies.
> An unseen hand also pass'd over their bodies,
> It descended tremblingly from their temples and ribs.

> The young men float on their backs, their white bellies bulge to the
>   sun, they do not ask who seizes fast to them,
> They do not know who puffs and declines with pendant and bending
>   arch,
> They do not think whom they souse with spray. (11:208).

Is it the woman who fondles the young men's bodies? the woman who emerges to link what is disparate? Is she Eros? Does she play and interplay in group sex? Is she the one taking the risk of being overwhelmed by the gratification experienced? Is the twenty-ninth bather really a woman who lives out the drama in her dreamworld? Or is it the poet imagining himself a woman, actively making love to the group of young men? Or is he the man who longs to play the passive role in a love relationship?

> I have instant conductors all over me whether I pass or stop....
> I merely stir, press, feel with my fingers, and am happy,
> To touch my person to some one else's is about as much as I can
>   stand. (27:615)

Important is the intent and extent of the love experience which, for Whitman, requires that one love one's body as a beautiful unity. Only then may one partake in the raptures of the world body in heterosexual or homosexual love. Caring is also of utmost import, for it encourages the poet to touch his lips to those of others around him, as voyeur or in reality. Whatever the form of the sexual act — with one or many, with men or women — individuals are free to experience Eros, that binding principle in nature, as they wish. "I wear my hat as I please indoors or out" (20:397). No God can punish the poet; no church can destroy the immensity of his feelings of communion through sex.

In such lines as "Through me the afflatus surging and surging, through me the current and index" (24:504), Whitman equates the poetic urge with the phallus. Logocentrism and phallocentrism become one, each endowing the other with meaning, each allowing the other to see, hear, feel, smell, the miracle unfolding before him.

> I do not press my fingers cross my mouth,
> I keep as delicate around the bowels as around the head and heart,
> Copulation is no more rank to me than death is. (24:519)

As the erotic sequence proceeds, masks and veils are removed while phallic metaphors abound: the farmer penetrating the bowels of the earth with his "Firm masculine colter"; blood, milky stream, "Root of wash'd sweet-flag! timorous pond-snipe! nest of guarded duplicate eggs!" An image of semen like "Trickling sap of maple, fibre of manly wheat, it shall be you!" is followed by a conflation of sexual and spiritual powers in the image of "Winds whose soft-tickling genitals rub against me it shall be you!" (24:532). Touching, probing, licking, feeling, heighten the poet's autoerotic fantasies, bringing him to that moment of intense gratification. Elements of air and wind, as well as the entire personified landscape, become eatable, drinkable — like the ambrosia and nectar of the Gods.

> You sweaty brooks and dews it shall be you!
> Winds whose soft-tickling genitals rub against me it shall be you!
> Broad muscular fields, branches of live oak, loving lounger in my
>   winding paths, it shall be you!
> Hands I have taken, face I have kiss'd, mortal I have ever touch'd, it
>   shall be you. (24:540)

Whether indulging in onanism, single or group sex, body contact, or touching, the poet is brought to a climax: "Unclench your floodgates, you are too much for me" (28:641). Ejaculation conveyed metaphorically as "Rich showering rain, and recompense richer afterward" (28:645) releases love swells as well as the creative instinct in the form of flashes of illumination in a world of eternal becoming.

For Whitman, genitals not only have sexual meaning, but like linga, in the cult of Shiva, they stand for fertility, both on an earthly and heavenly plane. Traceable to pre-Vedic societies in the Indus Valley civilization (2000 B.C.), the root of the word *linga* is *langala,* meaning plow, an implement with clear phallic symbolism. Whitman's phallic images serve to catalyze his sexual but also his creative urge, and in this regard may be considered archetypal organs for regeneration.

Vocal images also enter Whitman's verbally orchestrated composition. Some barely audible tones, like the inhalation and exhalation of cosmic or earthly breath, or whispers in raspy but also mellifluous diapasons, disclose their nuanced messages in vocalizations intoned by a medley of sounds ranging from human voices to birdcalls. A cataloging of instruments — violoncello, cornet, alarm bells — sound traditional in their harmonies but also modern in their jarring cacophonies and sequences of what could be alluded to as concrete music. Vocal pitches also enter Whitman's tonal choruses and operatic arias sung by tenors and sopranos. Even planets chime as "The orchestra whirls me wider than Uranus flies" (26:603). Swept out of earthly spheres, the poet reaches into galaxies. That Uranus is named is significant not only because it was considered the most distant of planets at the time, but more importantly, it was named after the Greek's Father God, who had been castrated by his son Cronus. The introduction of the father/son antagonism brings to mind Whitman's still-brewing rage against his own father.

Rapidly, however, the poet pursues his course as a universal soul, continuing his visionary journey into dizzying heights. Still the earth, with all of its antagonistic polarities — master, slave; jailed, free; weak, strong; sick, healthy; beggar, rich man; sea captain, farmer — seems not only within his grasp, but desirable. Included as well in Whitman's cataloged sequences is his embrace of people the world over: in C[K]anada, Oregon, California, Texas, and other lands. Energized to the limit, the poet now loves and feels loved, and flies into space: "I sound my barbaric yawp over the roofs of the world" (52:1333).

Whitman's rejection of society's controls — be they religious, sexual, ideational, or aesthetic — is set forth in the strongest of terms in "Song of Myself." Like Cronos, he will go against the status quo, that is, the Uranus-like patriarchal notions of his day, and fly the banner of freedom and democracy. As the poet of a new world, he spreads the gospel of love and fellowship. Unlike the English philosopher Thomas Hobbes, who wrote in his *Leviathan* that man by nature is a selfishly individualistic animal at war with other men as well as with himself, Whitman sided with another English philosopher, Anthony Ashley Cooper, the third earl of Shaftesbury, in reacting negatively toward rationalism as an ethical basis for society, and claiming that human beings are innately equipped with spontaneous instincts that promote harmony.

Yet, underlying all of Whitman's bravura, the questions posed in his long and melodious recitative, "What is a man anyhow? what am I? what are you?" (20:391) — remain unanswered.

4

"Singing the Phallus"

Because of their eroticism, Emerson had tried to persuade Whitman to omit certain poems from the *Children of Adam* cluster. The poet was adamant: sexually explicit or not, the collection would remain as is. Moral considerations, Emerson claimed, did not motivate his suggestion. He wanted the book to sell well and believed the reverse would happen were the poems in question included.

Not unaware of the prevailing puritanical consciousness ruling the United States at the time, Whitman may not have realized that poems praising prostitution, masturbation, and by inference homosexuality would not be judged objectively. In any case, keenly interested as he was in acquiring readers, he nevertheless felt it more important to stand his ground than to sell his book. Although he respected and even revered Emerson, he was not convinced that the New England philosopher had *really* understood his point of view. As representative of a new American society, Whitman wanted it known that he was not a traditionalist, not a follower of American puritanism. Rather, he was prepared to defy it. In his letter to Emerson, used as preface to the 1856 edition of *Leaves of Grass,* Whitman wrote:

This tepid wash, this diluted deferential love, as in songs, fictions, and so forth, is enough to make a man vomit; as to manly friendship, everywere [sic] observed in The States, there is not the first breath of it to be observed in print. I say that the body of a man or woman, the main matter, is so far quite unexpressed in poems; but that the body is to be expressed, and sex is.

Children of Adam (1860, 1867)

That Whitman's original title for *Children of Adam* was *Enfants d'Adam* suggests his strong adherence to France's tradition of sexual freedom. Since youth Whitman had been reading the works of Voltaire, Diderot, Volney, Rousseau, and other eighteenth-century men of the Enlightenment. He identified with their spirit of free thought and their courage; and was impressed by their strength of character when faced with exile and the humiliation of having their writings condemned by parliament and/or burned. These ground-breakers had not yielded to expediency. Hadn't the French Revolution, which Whitman regarded as one of the great turning points of history, been fostered by the men of the Enlightenment?

Children of Adam, comprising sixteen poems, sings of God's creation. Not only exalting sexuality, the poems also pay tribute to Whitman's credo of body/soul unity. Celebrations of "the eternal decency of the amativeness of Nature, the motherhood of all," Whitman writes in his letter to Emerson, his poems do not follow the path of timorous adherence to "the fashionable delusion of the inherent nastiness of sex, and of the feeble and querulous modesty of deprivation." On the contrary, the prophetic American bard is ready to prove his "faith in sex" and his disdain for "concession."

Although the Garden of Eden is the locus of *Children of Adam,* this paradisaic realm is not to be confused with the patriarchal domain depicted in Genesis. The latter, well ordered and well reasoned, is dominated by spirit alone and a mode of behavior based on complete adherence to "higher principles." Because such regulations were disregarded by Adam and Eve, they were cast out from Heaven. Whitman's Eden, although serene and beautiful, precludes the concept of the Fall, as well as the Christian notion of Heaven and Hell.

That a condition of perfection, divested of conflict and pain, exists in Whitman's Eden may be regarded to some extent as a mirror image of certain aspects of nineteenth-century utopianism and its concomitant evolutionary theories. The poet's conviction that the development of physically and mentally superior people was possible through regulation of the environment and regimens of exercise and diet led to a kind of sanctification of the body. Such improvements in the human species are in keeping with the views of the French naturalist, Jean Lamarck, a proponent of organic evolution based on the notion of acquired characteristics: the development of new and hereditary traits in an organism are triggered by environment. Lamarck's theory of evolution could not help but appeal to the eugenicist Whitman. To control the environment and breeding would pave the way for the perfectibility of the human race in America and throughout the world. Whitman must have had his family in mind when forwarding his theory: to prevent hereditary and environmental abnormalities through science would improve humanity's lot.

"To the Garden the World" (1860, 1867)

In the single-stanza poem "To the Garden the World," which opens the *Children of Adam* cycle, Whitman's Edenic population, having freely ascended to a Divine world, adheres to a philosophy of bodily joy and sexual fulfillment. Sex has not only become a liberating force, but a democratizing one as well.

The rhythmic sweep of Whitman's lines, their caesuras, enumerations, repetitions, and wavelike pulsations, entice the reader to follow him into his realm of supernatural beatitude — his Garden of Heavenly Delights. The physicality of his utterances and the diapason of his song were, and still are, unique in American poetry.

> To the garden the world anew ascending,
> Potent mates, daughters, sons, preluding,
> The love, the life of their bodies, meaning and being....
> Amorous, mature, all beautiful to me, all wondrous,
> My limbs and the quivering fire that ever plays through them, for
> reasons, most wondrous....

The Poet/Adam is strong, vigorous, and endowed with such democratic ideas as equality between men and women. Adam is not a defiler. Nor is Eve. On the contrary, they no longer need to hide their private parts with fig leaves as the Church had ordered placed on the works of Cranach, Dürer, Michelangelo, and other artists. The body, God's creation, is as beautiful as the soul.

"From Pent-up Aching Rivers!" (1860, 1881)

The protagonists in "From Pent-up Aching Rivers" look upon themselves with trancelike rapture, the corrosive sense of sin being nonexistent.

> From what I am determin'd to make illustrious, even if I stand sole
> among men,
> From my own voice resonant, singing the phallus,
> Singing the song of procreation,
> Singing the need of superb children and therein superb grown people,
> Singing the muscular urge and the blending,
> Singing the bedfellow's song (O resistless yearning!
> O for any and each the body correlative attracting!

O for you whoever you are your correlative body! O it, more than all
   else, you delighting!)

Adam's offspring, perfect in body, soul, and mind, will fulfill the
poet's utopian dream for a better America — an earthly Eden —
where all classes of people and all forms of love will be given status.
Thus will a new mentality and ruling consciousness come into being,
not based on bourgeois ethics, but rather on a hedonism founded on
truth and beauty.

Whitman's Eden may be associated not only with Lamarckian theories, but with the German tradition of *Walpurgisnacht* (Witches'
Sabbath). Legend tells us that the orgiastic interludes taking place
every first day of May on the Brocken, the highest peak of the Harz
Mountains in Germany, celebrated the witches' rendezvous with the
Devil, and hence the outset of their own increase in activity. While
Goethe's hero, Faust, entered this chaotic magical realm in a spirit
of abandon, Richard Wagner's thirteenth-century hero, Tannhauser,
a minnesinger, was punished for having enjoyed the pleasures of the
flesh, and died. For Whitman's protagonists such sensuality is a celebration of the divine act that opens them up to the "true song of
the soul."

"I Sing the Body Electric" (1855, 1881)

The visceral cantos of "I Sing the Body Electric," one of the most
resonant in *Children of Adam,* spring from Whitman's elemental
depths. While exalting love — amativeness and adhesiveness — he
induces his readers to indulge in such experiences for the sheer joy of
being alive. Each part of the body/soul complex takes on physicality
as love object: when touched, joints, hips, limbs, wrists, neck, shoulders, undulate and thrill. The "play of masculine muscle" (2:28)
sways in rhythmic encounters at the sight of "love-flesh swelling and
deliciously aching" (5:58). So charged is the atmosphere and so titillating is it to the senses that Thomas Mann alluded to this poem as
an "anatomical hymn."

Not only does Whitman develop in the poem his brand of morality revolving around the body/soul mystery, but he uses body
language to accomplish his goal. The narrator depicting the happenings is no voyeur, any more than Adam had been a corrupter.
His legions of revelers, to the contrary, are there to "discorrupt" the
inhabitants; to "charge them full with the charge of the soul" (1:4).

The poet's slings and arrows were aimed not only at the hypocrisy
permeating so-called polite society, but at preachers of temperance

such as Sylvester Graham (eponym of the cracker), who bran-
dished their credos of purity without any medical evidence to back
them up. Graham stated, for example, that overindulgence in sex
(once a month being sufficient) led to such illnesses as tuberculosis and imbecilism he condemned masturbation, which he declared
was instrumental in the progressive deterioration of a man's mental faculties. According to Graham and others of his ilk, the mere
mention of the body, much less sex, was not a fit subject for
conversation.

Because the fashion of covering one's body from head to toe was
also one of Whitman's bêtes noires, he enjoins his readers in "I Sing
the Body Electric" not to hide their bodies: God's handiwork. To do
so serves no purpose since he, the poet, sees through men's heavy
broadcloth suits: "It is in his walk, the carriage of his neck, the flex
of his waist and knees, dress does not hide him" (2:13).

Nor do clothes screen a woman's form: "The sprawl and fulness of
babes, the bosoms and heads of women, the folds of their dress, their
style as we pass in the street, the contour of their shape downwards"
(2:17).

Alluding to the body/soul complex in a rhetorical question, Whitman cajoles his readers to bring the subject out into the open: "And
if the body were not the soul, what is the soul?" (1:8). In one of
his well-known parallelisms, he associates the body with Divine attributes: "The man's body is sacred and the woman's body is sacred"
(6:83). Neither men nor women should be ashamed of their bodies;
the sexes are equated. "That of the male is perfect, and that of the female is perfect" (2:10). Pursuing his direct discourse, the poet states
categorically: "You are the gates of the body, and you are the gates
of the soul" (5:67).

Because there was no gender bias against women in Whitman's
egalitarian society — both sexes "are just the same" — certain critics
have considered him a proponent of feminism. And, to a certain extent, Whitman was indeed farseeing in his understanding of woman.
Until the eighteenth century classes in anatomy were based on the
teachings of Aristotle, Galen, and Paracelsus. An androcentric vision of life was presented to students of medicine, philosophers,
and any others interested in the subject. Species, from the lowest
to the highest on the ladder, were hierarchized according to a "one-
sex," or androgynous model. In keeping with this system, woman
was considered to be a potential, or "inverted," man. Thomas
Laqueur writes in *Making Sex: Body and Gender from the Greeks
to Freud:*

In the one-sex model, dominant in anatomical thinking for two thousand years, woman was understood as man-inverted: the uterus was the female scrotum, the ovaries were testicles, the vulva was a foreskin, and *the vagina was a penis.*

Cultural history changed with the coming into being of dimorphism or the notion of biological differences. Even the two-sex theory, proclaiming a dissimilarity between men and women, did little to remedy the prevailing inequality. In Victorian times, women were considered passionless, the difference in their organs accounting for the variety of their behavioral patterns.

In the one-sex world, females would be depicted as *more* passionate than males (often dangerously so, in a theme underlying many witchcraft trials and autos-da-fés). Females are inferior males and males, by general refinement of their perfection, have tempered passion with intellect and judgment. Therefore, females must be more passionate. (Stephen J. Gould, "The Birth of the Two-Sex World," *New York Review of Books,* June 13, 1991)

That Whitman believed in the equality of the sexes was not only a leap forward with regard to feminism, but an equally progressive notion aimed at furthering his goal of establishing an egalitarian society. Sexual liberation as he saw it was also aimed at dignifying human labor. Rather than hierarchizing different types of jobs, the work accomplished by firemen, omnibus drivers, farmers, housekeepers, wrestlers, swimmers, and others was equally beautiful and important in his new democracy.

So, too, did Whitman march forward in "procession" against the antidemocratic institution of slavery. Onerous was the sight of "A man's body at auction" (7:95) or "A woman's body at auction" (8:118). Such auctions were on a par with the Salem witch trials and other forms of persecution. For Whitman, everything that smacked of cruelty and deprivation was true corruption — a profanation of God's Creation.

In what could be labeled an operatic recitative, the poet apostrophizes the body, cries out to it in rapturous tones:

> O my body! I dare not desert the likes of you in other men and
>   women, nor the likes of the parts of you,
> I believe that the likes of you are to stand or fall with the likes of the
>   soul (and that they are the soul). (9:128)

While cataloging body parts in giant sweeps, Whitman verbally palpates each of them. His personifications and metaphorizations of eyes, head, mouth, tongue, lips, teeth, cheeks, temples, forehead, wrist, strong shoulders, upper arm, breast, ribs, backbone, hips, womb, nipples, and other parts, in a variety of rhapsodic interludes, serve to endow each one with *livingness*. Like the infant discovering his body (the genitals most importantly) via touch, odor, taste, and sight, the poet finds excitement in each part of the Divinity's work. If a person cannot love his or her own body, Whitman suggests, he or she cannot love that of others.

Love and sex bring on the epiphany, or climax, in "I Sing the Body Electric," thereby liberating the participants from whatever their inhibitions may be. Only then may Whitman's new world order come into being and invite men and women, body and soul, to cohabit in harmony.

"A Woman Waits for Me" (1856, 1871)

Seemingly, it was "A Woman Waits for Me" (originally entitled "The Poem of Procreation") that Emerson asked Whitman to delete from the Adam cluster. Considered by many to be ithyphallic, it contained images and a message that were antipodal to the standard sexist views of the time. As has been seen, Whitman looked forward to the creation of a race of women who would be the equals of men. Indeed, in this same vein is his "Poem of Remembrances," in which he wrote, "I say an unnumbered new race of hardy and well-defined women are to spread through all These States, / I say a girl fit for These States must be free, capable, dauntless, just the same as a boy" (16).

Such lines as those declaring that a woman "contains all, nothing is lacking" (1) serve not only to discredit many sexists in Whitman's day, but those of later times, particularly believers of theories enunciated by Freud, who maintained that females were born lacking a penis, thus suffered from "penis envy."

In a similar vein, Whitman rejects any identification between sex and sin, maintaining that sex is a pleasurable experience and not merely to be indulged in for procreative purposes alone. Since "Sex contains all, bodies, souls" (3), the body/soul complex not only functions as a superb unit, but also enriches the act of lovemaking and by extension life itself.

Despite such positive statements concerning the feminine, contradictions in Whitman's thinking exist, as in "Yet all were lacking

if sex were lacking, or if the moisture of the right man were lacking" (2). The inference suggests that when the right man is absent,
a woman is incomplete. Had he been evenhanded on the subject,
he would have included the idea that without the right woman, the
man is also incomplete.

Whitman's ideal women are strong, athletic, independent, courageous, intelligent, and energetic — and not simpering, weak, and
passive ladies as portrayed by the Romantics.

> They know how to swim, row, ride, wrestle, shoot, run, strike,
> retreat, advance, resist, defend themselves,
> They are ultimate in their own right — they are calm, clear, well
> possess'd of themselves. (18)

Because women are his equals socially, politically, and poetically,
they "are not one jot less than I am" (15). Whitman seems here
to be reiterating the notions of Mary Wollstonecraft, as enunciated in her *Vindication of the Rights of Woman* (1792). Not only
did she believe in women's education, but in structured exercise for
them as a means of building the strength of their bodies. So, too,
did Frances Wright, the author of *Views of Society and Manners
in America* (1821), advocate racing, swimming, and other forms of
vigorous exercise for women in order to make them proud of their
bodies, thereby encouraging them to become psychologically as well
as physically independent. Whitman, along with Wollstonecraft and
Wright, believed women's obligations transcended cooking, bringing up children, and saving souls. The sexually and intellectually
liberated woman would not only be capable of working alone or
alongside her husband, but would also be the fittest of mothers for
her children.

> I shall demand perfect men and women out of my love-spendings,
> I shall expect them to interpenetrate with others, as I and you
> interpenetrate now,
> I shall count on the fruits of the gushing showers of them, as I count
> on the fruits of the gushing showers I give now,
> I shall look for loving crops from the birth, life, death, immortality,
> plant so lovingly now. (36)

Whitman's new race of women were to be sexually aware, as well
as physically robust, and intellectually prepared to enter the political, economic, and artistic marketplace, thus to follow whatever
endeavor they chose. Such a possibility must have sent chills up

and down the spines of many nineteenth-century women and men. More would be expected of the former in every way. To maintain the dominant patriarchal scheme of things for the latter meant to keep women under control, harnessed to their traditional religious and moral activities.

Although, theoretically, Whitman believed that women should no longer be dominated by men, that husbands or fathers should not dictate their reading matter, the emphasis in his verses is on procreation: women of the future will be the creators of a superhuman race capable of becoming superb mothers and superb career women. Since Whitman was focused on America's well-being as he saw it, he was more interested in delineating an ideal type of woman whose function would enhance democracy than in exploring the needs and well-being of individual women.

Elizabeth Cady Stanton, a feminist pleased with Whitman's egalitarian stand toward women, included some reservations about his poem in her 1883 diary:

He speaks as if the female must be forced to the creative act, apparently ignorant of the fact that a healthy woman has as much passion as a man, that she needs nothing stronger than the law of attraction to draw her to the male. (Killingsworth, 69)

No matter how profeminist Whitman's stand, his preference went to the "deliciousness of his sex." And, rather than probing female/male relationships, breeding seems to be the dominant theme in "A Woman Waits for Me." In this manner, the eugenicist Whitman succeeded in linking sexuality with politics. Nevertheless, his statements, brazen for the time, made inroads on his and future generations.

Whether or not Whitman was the unqualified proponent of sexual equality, he never veered from considering the poet as the Great Inseminator, the Ithyphallic Deity whose semen flows forward, thereby participating in the gestation of a new and beautiful race. Parallels between physical fertility and poetic creativity are for him a reality.

I pour the stuff to start sons and daughters fit for these States,
I press with slow rude muscle,
I brace myself effectually, I listen to no entreaties,
I dare not withdraw till I deposit what has so long accumulated
within me. (28)

"Spontaneous Me" (1856, 1867)

Added to the conflation of sexuality and poetic creativity in "Spontaneous Me" is the proviso of poetry's visceral beginnings. Without body contact and the gamut of private sensual nuances thus incited, neither images, nor colorations, nor sense awareness would blossom.

> The real poems (what we call poems being merely pictures),
> The poems of the privacy of the night, and of men like me,
> This poem drooping shy and unseen that I always carry, and that all
>   men carry,
> (Know once for all, avow'd on purpose, wherever are men like me,
>   are our lusty lurking masculine poems,)
> Love-thoughts, love-juice, love-odor, love-climbers, and the climbing
>   sap,
> Arms and hands of love, lips of love, phallic thumb of love, breasts
>   of love, bellies press'd and glued together with love. (8)

Nature, be it human or nonhuman, as viewed by the poet, is physical. As such, it must first be observed as is the body, tactilely, from the outside and in images: then, affectively, when the intensity of the moments is re-created in verbal form. Thus does the poet eternalize what is, and reveal what has heretofore lived in secreted inner realms.

As the following image comes into focus — "The wet of woods through the early hours" — Whitman's gaze centers on two sleepers: a boy and an older man, lying close to each other, "one with an arm slanting down across and below the waist of the other" (18). Not only does the poet meld old and young in spontaneous embrace, but he frames them against, and thus identifies them with a natural background of grass, flowers, pools of water, bees, leaves — imaging humans participating in an inhuman feast.

By considering sexuality as an inspirational force that brings on activity, excitement, and the ejaculation of semen/word, Whitman parallels human reproduction with the birth of the poem. Interpenetration (to use his language) of body and word creates a dialectic between subject and object: the eye of the poet and nature's eye looking at each other, feeding on each other, each invigorating the other in a hymn and celebration, in this case, of homosexual love.

> The limpid liquid within the young man,
> The vex'd corrosion so pensive and so painful....

The young man that wakes deep at night, the hot hand seeking to repress what would master him,
The mystic amorous night, the strange half-welcome pangs, visions, sweats,
The pulse pounding through palms and trembling encircling fingers, the young man all color'd red, ashamed, angry;
The souse upon me of my lover the sea, as I lie willing and naked.
(27)

A fascinating, but strange role change occurs during the orgasmic process: the old man becomes the autoerotic youth. Although fear intrudes with the thought that sexual and/or masturbatory acts could be felt afterward as having been sinful, the release afforded by the experience, in a personified impassable, objective, and serene nature, has a healing effect on the narrator. Ambiguity is, nevertheless, present. The poet, still unwilling to reveal the true nature of his act, masks it by emphasizing the excitement of fulfillment brought on by the orgasm, rather than by explaining its motivation. A synecdoche for the poet's creative power, the orgasm, with oceanic force, blurs all tensions, while also bathing the participants in its regenerative spray. The flood of feelings and the wildness of the poet's nature, once set down in the poem, brings "wholesome relief, repose," and contentment to its creator. In a rather cavalier manner, he says at the end, "I toss it carelessly to fall where it may," until the next experience inflates and triggers another poetic segment (44).

"We Two, How Long We Were Fool'd" (1860, 1881)

Again Whitman proclaims uninhibited sexuality — between "We Two," believed to be two men. Now the narrator, interchanging roles, plays both father and mother to a youth identified as insecure and lost.

Nature, in its wildness and instinctiveness, encourages feelings of joy and abandon in the narrator and his lover, who are analogized with "fishes swimming in the sea together," with plants, trunks, foliage, roots, and bark. No longer do they belong strictly to the human sphere. Rather, like the animists of old, they *are* nature, living within the very bark of the oak or in the locust blossoms. "We are the coarse smut of beasts, vegetables, minerals," and like "predatory hawks," soaring far above empirical domains, they look down upon horizontal lands, verticalizing and verbalizing, thus fulfilling their species' highest aspirations. Universal in stature and cosmic in power, they *know* immanence: "We have circled and circled till we have arrived home again, we too," and have completed the gamut from birth to death in the sexual act (18).

Calamus (1860, 1871)

Although Whitman described *Children of Adam* as being "full of animal fire," he considered the *Calamus* cluster both "ethereal" and "athletic." Not to be viewed as contradictory, these terms refer to the phrenologists' definitions of love: amativeness and adhesiveness, the latter more spiritual in nature* (*CW,* IX, 150).

Calamus may be considered a meditation on the mysticality of friendship, love, and the sexual act. While Whitman calls for the creation of a secret camaraderie, by inference, among homosexuals, bonding is also to be effected on a larger scale, universally and politically — thus helping to democratize society the world over. Songs of loneliness, urgings for long-lasting and solid relationships between men, the *Calamus* poems leave the reader with a yearning for connectedness, not only between couples, but between the poet and the society of which he is a part.

The "calamus" (Greek, *kalamos*) is a plant, stalk, or grass with long, narrow leaves and a phallic-looking root resembling the penis and testes. Because it grows near ponds and marshes, that is, in secluded areas — "in paths untrodden" — it is identified with the poet in general and Whitman in particular: a man who felt alienated from society because of his outspokenness on sexual matters. On the other hand, because of the calamus's shape, it becomes a metaphor for Eros, love and relatedness, a way of life the poet felt was crucial to his vision of democratic America.

In that *calamus* (Arabic, *qalam*) also means the quill of a feather, used as a pen in the West until the fifteenth century, such an image may also suggest the metier of the writer. In Islamic tradition, it is believed that Allah created the qalam out of light a thousand years before he brought anything else into being. When he ordered the qalam to write, it shuddered and asked: "What must I write?" Allah answered: "Destiny." As a symbol of universal intelligence, light then flowed from its point as ink from a pen and it began inscribing onto sacred tablets all that was to happen until the Resurrection.

---

*When Whitman wrote to Emerson about "manly friendship, everywhere observed in the United States," and stated that "there is not the first breath of it to be observed in print," he looked upon himself as being the first to write overtly about homosexual love. Although such an assertion may be correct, one should not omit the celebration of male friendships, by Melville and Thoreau, albeit in a different way.

Thus was a new world order ushered in via the word — for Islam and for Whitman.

Since *calamus*, symbolized by the pen, conflated spirituality and mentation, as well as physicality, in that it also represented the phallus, Whitman's title indicated a generative force within the universe. It linked essentials — the sexual with the sacred — thus substituting earthly multiplicity (and frequently discord), for spiritual and physical oneness during the period of gestation: prior to the birth of the poem.

Idealistic, even simplistic, Whitman, a true utopian, failed in his grand scheme of things to take human nature into account. Since time immemorial, prophets, philosophers, man-gods, and saviors have planted their credo into the hearts and minds of humanity with little or no resulting amelioration of earthly tragedies. Still, no diminution of attempts to find an answer to life's dilemmas was forthcoming in Whitman's day. Economists and political scientists had been busy creating societies that would, they hoped, bring financial and spiritual stability into being, basing their ideas on the fundamental principle of love and camaraderie.

Had not the French writer George Sand and the reformer Charles Fourier believed that connectedness existed between man and God and that a "harmonious" society could be developed given the proper economic conditions? Albert Brisbane, Horace Greeley, and Parke Godwin, who introduced and developed Fourierism in the United States, were instrumental in the establishment of Brook Farm, the North American Phalanx, and a colony founded in Texas by the Frenchman's disciple, Victor Considérant. Brook Farm (West Roxbury, Massachusetts, 1841–46), founded by the transcendentalists, sought to encourage human endeavor and brotherly cooperation that would lead to the highest form of physical, intellectual, and moral education. Because such impressive individuals — Theodore Parker, Henry Channing, Nathaniel Hawthorne, Margaret Fuller, Emerson — were associated with the community, optimism reigned high among many of its members. The more realistic Emerson, however, considered the experiment with skepticism. Hawthorne expressed serious doubts about communal living and the notion of human progress in *The Blithedale Romance* (1852). Nor must Robert Owen, the pioneer of British socialism, be omitted from the roster. His society, the New Harmony Community, was to be based on small, cooperative units. Because of poor economic planning, his group, founded in southern Indiana in 1825, lasted for only two years.

Whitman's ideal society existed in his mind alone — as a dream, an illusion enshrouded in maya's veil. Not a philosopher per se, although he loved to philosophize, Whitman was above all a poet. And, in *Calamus,* he was a deeply poignant poet of homosexual love. The *Calamus* cluster reveals not only a restless and anguished psyche, but a condition of ambivalence concerning his "secret." Despite his courageous proclamation to Emerson that he would speak the truth about his sexual proclivities, he did so only in veiled, ambiguous, and illusive terms. Understandably, perhaps. Had he not felt the stigma of being marginalized in a heterosexual society?

Love between men in *Calamus,* and elsewhere in *Leaves of Grass,* is most frequently presented under a disguise: via symbols, allusions, conceits, role-playing (substituting a female for a male lover), equivocal metaphors, coded language. Other strategies are also used by Whitman as a means of obfuscation: by alternating highly lyrical and/or cacophonous sonorities, he sweeps the reader into his *feeling* realm, thereby submerging any kind of objective understanding of the true nature of his sexual inclinations.

Whitman must have been cognizant of the reasons for his use of poetic strategies. Mention is made in his *Notebooks* of Plato's dialogue *Phaedrus:*

Phaedrus (Plato) purports to be a dialogue between Socrates & Phaedrus — the latter a young man, who, coming to Socrates, is full of a discourse by Lysias on *Love* — he reads it to S. — who finally proceeds to give a discourse on the same theme — by love he evidently means the passion inspired in one man by another man, more particularly a beautiful youth. The talk seems to hinge on the question whether such a youth should bestow his "favors" more profitably on a declared "lover," or on one not specially so.... His whole treatment assumes the illustration of Love, by the attachment a man has for another man, (a beautiful youth as aforementioned, more especially) — (it is astounding to modern ideas). (Miller, *Walt Whitman's Poetry: A Psychological Journey,* 146)

Homosexual love is also referred to in the *Notebooks* in such statements as "They 'lie down together' 'kiss' & fondle each other &c &c" (5, 1881–83).

In Whitman's previous poems, but even more explicitly in *Calamus,* he identifies the types to which he is drawn. Although, as already discussed, he preferred barely literate young men from problematic working-class homes, they had to be strong, rowdy, athletic, and virile to meet his requirements. Refinement, wealth, and physical weakness were in no way exciting to him. Indeed, Whitman kept learned people at a distance. Did he think they would see through his mask? Or was it because he sought to be a guiding spirit, to dominate, and feared intellectual competition? Perhaps he sought to become a surrogate father and shower young men with the affection and tenderness he and they had never known as children. Such role-playing allowed him to become what his father had failed to be: thus transforming a negative, destructive, and choleric figure into a positive and helping force. As such, he would be rectifying his own early divestiture and filling a once-aching void. If the occasion warranted, Whitman could, and also did become a mother figure for these naive young men. His feminine, soft, and tender side saw to their sheltering, feeding, and nurturing.

The sense of being needed and loved by someone endowed Whitman's weakly structured ego with strength, for he suddenly saw himself as a dominant power in the lives of others. His loving letters to Peter Doyle and Harry Stafford, both insecure young men, unable to cope with the vagaries of the everyday world, revealed their need of paternal guidance to help them through emotionally traumatic periods. They also revealed other interesting details.

Weren't Peter Doyle and/or Harry Stafford, and the many other young men whom Whitman had loved and befriended, walking duplicates of aspects of his own adolescent psyche? The son of an irascible father and a domineering — even castrating — mother, who was forever leaning on her son, be it for financial reasons or simply to help care for the sickly members of the family, Whitman became an emotionally deprived man. Indeed, he had not enjoyed his youth — except on those occasions when he wandered away from his home into nature's embrace. It could be conjectured that Peter Doyle and Harry Stafford were projections of that aspect of Whitman that was, psychologically speaking, a *puer aeternus*. Many Romantic poets, namely, Shelley, Keats, Wordsworth, Lamartine, Vigny, Byron — were also eternal adolescents, but unlike Whitman, they were not loners. Although Whitman befriended young men, as far as is known he never lived with them, even during his ten-year stay in Washington, D.C. Nevertheless, he always yearned for a permanent relationship that would lend stability to his life, thereby to fill the gaping maw within his psyche.

Emotionally spent at times, hence frequently subject to periods of despondency, Whitman also frequently underwent a numinous experience: moments of religious ecstasy. Bursting with excitement, filled with a sense of liberation, he yielded during these privileged instances to his impulses, which blossomed into what seemed like endless verbal permutations and constructs.

Although the *Calamus* poems have no dramatic continuity and Whitman was forever changing and reordering them for new editions, a prevailing need is evident in all of them: the desire to bind himself to another — *to love* and *be loved*. Confessional to a certain extent, although this tone was probably a poetic strategy to deceive his readers further by masking his real intent, some of his *Calamus* poems remind one of conversations with a dear friend — or even of seductions. Similar dialogues in prose are inscribed in his *Notebooks:* they were his means of explaining himself to his audiences, of revealing his sorrows, as well as his spiritual and physical needs.

"In Paths Untrodden" (1860, 1867)

Whitman invites his readers "In Paths Untrodden" to follow him on a journey defined as a search for adhesiveness — a higher form of male love. As leader and guiding power of a new society and religious approach to life, the poet takes his disciples on mysterious walks into unknown areas. Although the verb *to tread* means to walk, dance, step, beat, crush, trample, or subdue, it also refers to copulation with regard to male birds. Since Cro-Magnon times, birds have been identified with the soul, as attested to in the Lascaux cave paintings and in later religious and literary texts, including Plato's *Dialogues*. Whitman's linkage between soul, walking, and population suggests a need for that potent connecting cosmic principle — love.

> In paths untrodden,
> In the growth by margins of pond-waters,
> Escaped from the life that exhibits itself,
> From all the standards hitherto publish'd, from the pleasures, profits, conformities.

As the prophet of a new society and father figure for male youth, the poet will lead/lure and tread with them — and the reader as well — into unknown dimensions: those marshy lands where the phallic calamus plants grow. There they will be awakened, enlightened, spiritualized — initiated into a new world. In isolation, like the initiates of old — the word *initiate* is derived from the Latin *initium,* "going within," meaning "to enter" — the poet's followers will penetrate into fresh territories: open the door onto a different way of viewing life. Only by experiencing deeper insights into the life process may initiates pass from a so-called inferior or superficial state of understanding to a superior one. Only then may they begin to realize their potential.

In the all-male environment into which the poet lures the reader, the initiate finds himself in a position to receive secrets that would have otherwise been denied him, thus paving the way for him to be reborn into another domain. Perils, nevertheless, are implicit in the renunciation of the world. So are inexpressible joys.

> That the soul of the man I speak for rejoices in comrades,
> Here by myself away from the clank of the world,
> Tallying and talk'd to here by tongues aromatic,
> No longer abash'd (for in this secluded spot I can respond as I would
> not dare elsewhere.)

That he feels free to convey his feelings in a *temenos,* or sacred space, far from society, yields the poet ineffable pleasure. Yet, the experience of polarities is crucial in the learning and love experience. Were he to remain far from the madding crowd and live out an ideal relationship with a partner for a protracted period of time without the application of judgmental faculties, stasis, aridity, or a mechanical quality in the love experience could ensue. The same is true of the individuals who refuse to follow the poet into "paths untrodden": their daily activities become rote. To fracture and fragment the known, to venture into untapped areas, paves the way for deepening relationships, while also opening the door onto greater riches.

What Whitman offers his reader in dazzling arrays of images, powerful rhythms, and visceral tonalities are revelations of a whole secreted shadowy realm. The new insights gleaned, he hopes, will serve to overthrow society's restrictive "standards," which he considers deleterious to the individual and thus to society as a whole. To his readers, he offers pleasure and not sorrow, freedom and not constriction. Yet, in Whitman's use of harsh, unpleasant guttural and palatal sounds, as in the word *clank* ("Here by myself away from the clank of the world") and *abash* ("No longer abash'd"), he is also warning those who seek to follow him that strength, perseverance, even heroism, are needed to "dare" cut free from the crowd and live out one's existence in a "secluded" world — perhaps as a pariah.

Among the calamus, and far from social reproach and oppression, the poet sings out his song — born from his needs and cast from his desire for "manly attachment." Far from the world of deceptions and difficulties, his *temenos* has yielded him nutritive and gestating powers, which he now realizes have extended and completed himself in "this delicious Ninth-month in my forty-first year." Ready for rebirth, he sings the purity of each new love episode.

> To tell the secret of my night and days,
> To celebrate the need of comrades.

Is the poet really free, as he claims to be? Or does he seek a protective male environment into which to withdraw — there to live out his isolated love experience, as well as to compose his new poetics based on the verbalization of sexual episodes?

"Scented Herbage of My Breast" (1860, 1881)

Focusing on the death motif in "Scented Herbage of My Breast," the poet makes us privy to a *Liebestod* experience. Having been initiated into the male sexual order, he dies to the heterosexual one, to be reborn into a sphere where "perennial roots, tall leaves" will always be available to him. Such phallic images, as well as mystical soliloquies, threnodies, and apostrophes, reoccur throughout the poem: coded references to a world beyond.

> O slender leaves! O blossoms of my blood! I permit you to tell in your own way of the heart that is under you,
> O I do not know what you mean there underneath yourselves, you are not happiness.

The genital analogies in the above and other passages have spiritual as well as creative applications. Identifiable with the Osiris and Christ myths, they tell of the ordeals of those who seek to bring forth a new way or world order, including dismemberment and crucifixion. Only after Osiris and Christ descended into an underworld were both made privy to larger knowledge, followed by rebirth and deification.

Whitman experiences a similar ascesis when writing. After his ascension/descent (for the mystic these are the same), or period of withdrawal into himself, the timeless/spaceless regions he has spanned open him up to revelation: "Yet you are beautiful to me you faint tinged roots, you make me think of death." Emerging into light again, he is reborn into the "calm" beatitude that comes with fulfillment.

The imagery of leaves, running through the poem, draws upon a primitive vegetal world, signifying both sexual and spiritual fertility. In keeping with Whitman's coded language, leaves as well as other vegetative images include both phallic and vaginal elements. The passage from vegetal to animal to human may be associated with the evolution of a latent idea dwelling inchoate in the poet's collective unconscious: its passage into consciousness; its leap into the poem — its life eternal as a biocosmic symbol.

In that vegetation symbolizes the development of a world of possibilities — as seed, sperm, or word — that will become actualized into differentiated matter, the root plunged deep into the earth or the idea embedded in the mind may be said to be endowed with infra-human nature. In Genesis we read: "God made you be born from the earth as a plant." Leaves, whether growing from the calamus plant or understood as *qalam,* identified with the quill or pen, or as leaves of paper, are to be used by the poet to engrave his sacred experience.

> Grow up taller sweet leaves that I may see! grow up out of my
>   breast! . . .
> Do not fold yourself so in your pink-tinged roots timid leaves!
> Do not remain down there so ashamed, herbage of my breast!
> Come I am determin'd to unbare this broad breast of mine, I have
>   long enough stifled and choked;
> Emblematic and capricious blades I leave you, now you serve me not.

The mere mention of genital metaphors floods the narrator with desire, once again conflating sexuality with poetics. The poet will set the example and become guide to the uninitiated disciple and reader, leading those who have patiently waited for someone to "take control of all." Not only will their yearning for man-to-man love be fulfilled, thereby liberating them from society and its "entire show of appearance," but the experience will enable them to reconnect with their own depths — their own roots — by living out the death and resurrection ritual.

Poetic inspiration follows the same pattern as nature's cyclicality: birth, death, and resurrection. Like Charles Baudelaire and J. K. Huysmans, particularly in the latter's novel *Against the Grain* — in which the protagonist suffers inordinately from stimulus of the senses, most specifically of touch — so Whitman has recourse to tactile sensations to arouse his readers.

"Whoever You Are Holding Me Now in Hand" (1860–1881)

More dramatic and perhaps more aggressive than the previous poems, "Whoever You Are Holding Me Now in Hand," addresses the reader overtly, enticing him to become a follower, to interpenetrate with the author, and become "a candidate for my affections." On the other hand, one may ask, Is the poet really addressing the reader or is he talking to his lover? The poem's title, which is also its opening line — "Whoever you are holding me now in hand" — may reveal the author's need to give himself to the reader as is, without his mask.

The poet warns the reader that he is not what he purports to be and that there may be grounds for suspicion and fear on the part of those hearing his song.

> I give you fair warning before you attempt me further,
> I am not what you supposed, but far different.

That the reader may seek to immerse himself in the poet's world might prove to be "destructive": lead to doubt and uncertainty; to rejection of previous moral standards that had once meant security and calm. Furthermore, the initiation period into this new way would be demanding: "Your novitiate would even then be long and exhausting." Yet, without making any promises, the poet entices the stranger to follow his way. The use of indirection and misdirection serves to confuse the reader, to tease him into participation, offering him a glimpse into his garden of sensual delights.

> Here to put your lips upon mine I permit you,
> With the comrade's long-dwelling kiss or the new husband's kiss,
> For I am the new husband and I am the comrade.

The reader or stranger, now the object of the poet's seduction, is induced to leave the world of conformity, to abandon the material domain, to separate himself from society, and to experience a rite of passage that would prepare him for the trials of the *real* world: endow him with faith in himself, with strength to pursue his vision, and with the ability to carve out his own independent path.

The road, the poet warns again, is not easy. The reader is again told that if he is not prepared to sacrifice everything he has in life, as so many other creative spirits have done before, "Put me down and depart on your way."

Then the poet makes a fascinating about-face, changing his tactics most subtly to more provocative, yet more passive, attitudes. The androgynous poet entices the stranger to his fold: the paradisaic soul/body complex.

Or if you will, thrusting me beneath your clothing,
Where I may feel the throbs of your heart or rest upon your hip,
Carry me when you go forth overland or sea;
For thus merely touching you is enough, is best,
And thus touching you would I silently sleep and be carried eternally.

Sensitive and loving, the androgynous poet, responding as male and female to the joys of tactile encounters, fondles, touches, palpates, and rubs parts of the body. In so doing, he is flooded with, paradoxically, sensations of serenity and of tantalizing excitement. In either case, the ambiguity of the feelings experienced may be likened to the orgasmic experience: as pleasure principle or as the intense sense of fulfillment and liberation following the creative poetic act.

Intellectual and abstract theories are arid fabrications of the mind, Whitman declares. Even his own "leaves" (he is referring to the calamus, but also to the leaves in a book) are empty without life's succulent energy.

But these leaves conning you con at peril,
For these leaves and me you will not understand,
They will elude you at first and still more afterward, I will certainly
    elude you,
Even while you should think you had unquestionably caught me,
    behold!
Already you see I have escaped from you.

Reading teaches nothing. Only the experience *itself* has the capacity to titillate and activate emotion — thereby bringing the poem to birth. Nor can the experience be possessed or contained in a word or line. It may only be sensed or intuited.

The poem, like lovemaking, becomes a verbal replica of the privileged moments known to the participants. As an artistic construct, the poem remains an artifice: a concretization of ecstasy, a mirror image of higher truths that exist in a metasphere. And if the illusion the poet seeks to realize for the reader cannot provoke him into participation, he has failed in his intent. If such is the case, he asks him directly and in no uncertain terms, to "release me and depart on your way" (37).

"For You O Democracy" (1860, 1881)

Whitman now offers his reader a radiant scene depicted with the objectivity and detail of such paintings by Thomas Eakins as "Max

Schmitt in a Single Scull" or "The Swimming Hole." Both poem and
paintings feature young men in a variety of activities: sporting on the
grass, rowing in shells on the Schuylkill, shooting in marshes, and
sailing before the winds. Whitman had always admired the candor
and uncompromising reality of Eakins's paintings. "I never knew
but one artist, and that's Tom Eakins," he said, "who could resist the temptation to see what they think ought to be rather than
what is" (Russell Lynes, *The Art-Makers of Nineteenth-Century
America*, 367).

In "For You O Democracy," Whitman sings of companionship in
a landscape "thick as trees," of good fun "along the rivers of America," of watching and joining his friends as they swim, row, race, and
wander about from the great lakes to the prairies and mountains,
"With the love of comrades, / With the life-long love of comrades."

Objectivity but also symbolism mark Whitman's verbal canvas,
studded as it is with phallic images of trees reaching up to the heavens and metaphors of the womb, in the waters flowing along the
byways of the New World. Just as the poet requires insemination,
then periods of gestation, to foster his work, so, too, does America
in order to fulfill its potential.

> Come, I will make the continent indissoluble,
> I will make the most splendid race the sun ever shone upon,
> I will make divine magnetic lands....

The plethora of Whitman's water images introduces a whole
subliminal sphere of prenatal and preconscious existence: the undifferentiated realm of nonknowing, of unconcern, shorn of all
problems. Since water dissolves hard matter, it may be looked upon,
psychologically, as a liquefying agent, making solid and problematic
conditions — be they sexual or intellectual — more malleable.

Why, one may ask, does the author entitle his poem "For You
O Democracy"? Because democracy not only represents the ideal
form of government for the poet, but because he conceives of it as
a mother figure. By conflating the ideal and the real, he is also pay-
ing homage to his own mother. Although he occasionally smarted
from her subtly dictatorial ways and sought to evade the burdens
she had placed upon him, Whitman adored her. Understandably,
compassionate and loving mother figures prevail in many of Whitman's poems, including "These I Sing in Spring" from *Calamus*. In
the latter poem, Mother Earth and the Water Mother figure promi-
nently in a fertile atmosphere of wild flowers, trees, and grasses of

all sorts. Democracy is identified with the mother; camaraderie with males, who are children of sorts, bounding about gleefully in natural surroundings.

"Of the Terrible Doubt of Appearances" (1860, 1867)

Love, a disastrous experience, no doubt, has brought the poet to the brink of despair. Fear is intense and traumatic. Questions, nevertheless, arise in the reader's mind. Were the love experiences undergone and then depicted in the poem *real?* Or were they fantasy? illusion? dream? masturbatory sequences? Or, perhaps, in keeping with Platonic tradition, emanations from a cosmic metamind, from the realm of Idea?

> Of the terrible doubt of appearances,
> Of the uncertainty after all, that we may be deluded,
> That may-be reliance and hope are but speculations after all,
> That may-be identity beyond the grave is a beautiful fable only....

Whitman is haunted by the thought that what he has taken to be truth, be it in the love experience or in the creation of a poem, might merely have been a stratagem. For the Hindu, illusion and/or deception is symbolized as maya's veil, a power that serves to halt humankind's vision, allowing them to perceive only the world of multiplicity and not that of primordial unity. For the Judeo-Christian, Satan is tempter, adversary, and obstructor, a psychological image of inner opposition. Although this cosmic force is considered a negative power by the religious, others look upon it as a positive element. In this view, the satanic entity in humankind is that force that catalyzes people into thinking, acting, and uprooting staid and regressive notions in individuals and societies. For the mathematician and philosopher René Descartes, the satanic principle or, as he called it, *le malin génie,* was called into being by the mind to stimulate the thinking process, to initiate questioning so as to expand one's approach to a situation. Because the *malin génie* was a creation of the intellect, he affirmed, once the problem of the moment was solved, it disappeared.

For Whitman, however, who was not a thinking type, but highly emotional in his encounters and in his relationships with people, as well as in his work, "doubt" left him in a state of turmoil. For him, in his poem, the satanic principle is alive and well. If, as he fears in the poem, "reliance and hope are but speculations," then everything comes into question: his own identity as well as cosmic powers.

> The skies of day and night, colors, densities, forms, may-be these are
> (as doubtless they are) only apparitions, and the real something
> has yet to be known....

Most painful are his doubts concerning his talent, his needs, and his sexual proclivities. The intensity of his anguish, the fearsomeness of the mockery leveled at him by others, fill him with a sense of failure — and dread. Should he have followed in the well-worn tracks of a Longfellow or a Tennyson? Or is his anguish merely a mirage or fantasy?

And what of his love experiences? Has he really read the hearts and thoughts of his love objects clearly? Or has he been deceived by his feelings toward them? Whitman, who has always *felt* into relationships rather than reason them out or question the motivations of himself or others, decides to probe no longer. To enjoy the love of the moment will be sufficient. "When he whom I love travels with me or sits a long while holding me by the hand."

Whether his loves are just a memory or even an illusion, they have brought him momentary satisfaction. He, therefore, has no need of engaging in philosophical discourse or speculations, or probing into the world of Ideas, Forms, or Intellect.

> I cannot answer the question of appearances or that of identity
>   beyond the grave,
> But I walk or sit indifferent, I am satisfied,
> He ahold of my hand has completely satisfied me.

Doubt remains, nevertheless, as to whether Whitman was or was not satisfied with his chance encounters or momentary relationships. That he had to define his attitude in "Of the Terrible Doubt of Appearances" leads one to believe that although he longed to function as a detached and objective creature, he never really succeeded in accomplishing this feat.

"The Base of All Metaphysics" (1871)

Whitman takes to task not only the word *metaphysics,* but the arid world of the professor and his students — the latter, forever listening with rapt attention to so-called words of wisdom. Enumerating the names of such German philosophers as Kant, Fichte, Schelling, and Hegel, and the Idealist systems they concocted, Whitman also adds Socrates, Plato, and Christ to the list. Love and camaraderie are Whitman's only values and only truths.

See philosophies all, Christian churches and tenets see....
Yet underneath Socrates clearly see, and underneath Christ the divine
    I see,
The dear love of man for his comrade, the attraction of friend to
    friend.

"Recorders Ages Hence" (1860, 1867)

Because the fear of being unloved as man and poet again corrodes
the author's sense of well-being, he admonishes his followers to
"Publish my name and hang up my picture as the tenderest lover."
Anguish mounts within him when aloneness prevails, and the poet
probes the depths and reality of his love experiences. Encountering
an abyss within himself, and within others, he dwells in the dread
of torment. "Who knew too well the sick, sick dread lest the one he
lov'd might secretly be indifferent to him...."

The gutturals and sibilants in the above line, in addition to the
repetition of such words as *sick, sick,* serve once again to point up
Whitman's powerful sense of inadequacy, his fear of loneliness —
and his contradictory nature, since he needed to live away from
others so as to better indwell. The particularly acute sense of distress
inhabiting "Recorders Ages Hence" stems to a great extent from the
cruel criticisms meted out to him by his detractors.

"Trickle Drops" (1860, 1867)

One of the most audacious of Whitman's poems, "Trickle Drops"
depicts the actual sexual experience: from fondling, to penetration,
to ejaculation. It may also be interpreted as the steps taken by the
poet in the creation of his work: the caressing of the idea its insertion
or infusion into the mind, and its ejection as poem.

> Trickle drops! my blue veins leaving!
> O drops of me! trickle, slow drops,
> Candid from me falling, drip, bleeding drops. (1)

The "drops" and the "bleeding drops" may symbolize the seat
of the hurt: the pain his rejection of contemporary moral standards
caused him both sexually and as a poet. The image may also refer to
an identification with Christ in an *imitatio Christi.* In Luke (22:44)
one reads about Jesus going to pray in the Garden of Gethsemane
on the western slope of the Mount of Olives (the subsequent scene
of his betrayal): "And being in an agony he prayed more earnestly:

and his sweat was as it were great drops of blood falling down to the ground."

Whitman's wounds also bleed: "Stain every page, stain every song I sing, every word I say, bloody drops." Nevertheless, he is ready to face the world, to reveal his secret, to sing his song of sublimated homosexual love. Shame, to be sure, will be his, as will suffering — as it had been Christ's, who bled because he, too, had brought a new message into the world, uprooting the standards of his day.

The poet is inspired to take courage from Christ and his disciples, who fought valiantly and suffered deeply in order to reveal their credo to the world. Similarly, Whitman, whose religion revolves around the highest form of love, is ready to know supreme sacrifice:

> Let them know your scarlet heat, let them glisten,
> Saturate them with yourself all ashamed and wet,
> Glow upon all I have written or shall write, bleeding drops,
> Let it all be seen in your light, blushing drops.

"City Of Orgies" (1860, 1867)

In "City of Orgies," Whitman discloses his passion for the anonymity large cities afford him. There, amid the multitude, he is free to indulge in orgies, to cruise, to court young bus drivers, soldiers, sailors, thieves, priests, and any others that strike his fancy.

On the other hand, like Paris for Baudelaire, Whitman's Manhattan makes him more keenly aware of his isolation. Observer and voyeur, he accepts the fact that he will never quite succeed in losing himself in the multitude, in divesting himself of that deeply rooted sadness that permeates the world of one who lives on the fringes of society.

Moods, however, alternate swiftly in "City of Orgies," in rhythm with the urban landscape as viewed by the observing poet. All seems mobile, floating — houses, windows, streets, the shifting crowd of lads he meets during his days and/or evenings devoted to gay cruising and to playing male games.

> Offering response to my own — these repay me,
> Lovers, continual lovers, only repay me.

"That Shadow My Likeness" (1860, 1881)

Reminiscent of Plato's allegory of the cave (described in his *Republic*), the poet sees himself as double. One part of him, like the uninstructed beings enchained in a cave in the bowels of the earth, lives the life of a pariah, in bleakness and blackness. The other side of him, yearns to move up from the world of shadows into a sun-drenched world — where Idea and Reality dwell.

> That shadow my likeness that goes to and fro seeking a livelihood,
>   chattering, chaffering.
> How often I question and doubt whether that is really me.

The shadow, understood psychologically, is a group of personal characteristics that the individual in question considers inferior or weak and that his ego's self-esteem will not allow him to recognize. Because he can neither assimilate nor accept these qualities in himself, his conscious considers them negative. Should Whitman reject his shadow, the darker and more problematic side of his personality, he would not only be joining the status quo in repudiating what he considered his "baser" side, but more importantly, he would be repudiating a part of himself — his own chaotic elements. To do so would be to destroy any possibility of facing his contradictions and thus dealing with what he and society considered destructive.

Whitman needed courage to overcome the vilifications *Leaves of Grass* elicited, as is made clear by the following example from Rufus Griswold, one of his most outspoken detractors, wrote:

In our allusions to this book [*Leaves of Grass*] we have found it impossible to convey any, even the most faint idea of its style and contents, and of our disgust and detestation of them, without employing language that cannot be pleasing to ears polite; but it does seem that some one should, under circumstances like these, undertake a most disagreeable, yet stern duty. The records of crime show that many monsters have gone on in impunity, because the exposure of their vileness was attended with too great indelicacy. *Peccatum illud horribile, inter christianos non nominandum* [that horrible sin not to be mentioned among Christians]. (Woodress, *Critical Essays,* 26).

Bitter rejection is not an uncommon fate for revolutionaries, especially in their lifetime, and *Children of Adam* and *Calamus* are indeed revolutionary: thematically, for their brazen approach to sex; visually, for the poet's painterly prose, colorful panoramas, and explicit visions; rhythmically, for the bodily vibrations and undulations the subtext triggers in its attempt to replicate copulation; sonorously, for the flow of the poem-songs, which, when voiced, are as lyrical as operatic sequences.

5

"Within Me Latitude Widens, Longitude Lengthens"

Whitman had disclosed his ideas concerning the poet's role as guiding spirit and spokesperson for the New World's pluralistic society in his 1855 preface to *Leaves of Grass*.

The greatest poet hardly knows pettiness or triviality. If he breathes into any thing that was before thought small it dilates with the grandeur and life of the universe. He is a seer.... He is individual.... He is complete in himself.... The others are as good as he, only he sees it and they do not. He is not one of the chorus.... He does not stop for any regulation.... He is the president of regulation. What the eyesight does to the rest he does to the rest. Who knows the curious mystery of the eyesight?

The poet's vision, like that of Prometheus and Columbus, was revolutionary. All-encompassing, it retained neither a national point of view nor a single ideology. Transcending physical, intellectual, and emotional boundaries, it embraced the world as a whole. Whitman's newly acquired inner strength, born from the powerful nutritive currents flowing through him at this time, encouraged him to speak his ideas and feelings in "Salut au Monde!" and "Song of the Open Road."

"Salut au Monde!" (1856, 1881)

Whitman's galvanic poem "Salut au Monde!" enumerates, among other elements, the multiple functions of the American bard. The title "Salut au Monde!" suggests his admiration for the French in general, and for the eighteenth-century Enlightenment in particular.

Why should Whitman have been so drawn to the philosophes, generators of the Enlightenment? Considered dangerous by the old guard, these revolutionary thinkers used a critical approach to systems and beliefs, accepting no ideology — be it scientific, religious, political, economic, or philosophical — without first evaluating its worth and impact. The philosophes believed in the notion of progress, in the use of experimental methods, and in the application of reason in Divine as well as in human affairs.

An admirer of Voltaire, one of the Enlightenment's most outspoken free thinkers, Whitman had been nurtured on his works, most importantly, his *Philosophical Dictionary* (1765). A call to arms, it cajoled its readers to "dare to think." Condemning fanaticism, superstition, and almost all the rituals practiced in the Roman Catholic Church, Voltaire, the Deist, maintained that revealed religions were the cause of intolerance, discord, and bloodshed. Although others of the Enlightenment also attacked Christianity, it was Voltaire's succinct statement on the subject, "Crush the infamous" — referring to superstition, but interpreted as an injunction to crush the Catholic Church — that resonated in everyone's ears.

Like Voltaire, Whitman believed in free thought and in the value of applying reason to empirical as well as to Divine matters. Not only did he own the *Philosophical Dictionary,* but he described its author in his "Voltaire: A Fragment by Walt Whitman" (1856) as having "a clear head, never to be cheated by the traditions, quibbles, shams, and tyrannies of those who made a good thing out of churches and courts. He loved to expose the old shysters. He also loved knowledge in itself."

Whitman also admired Count Constantin F. Volney's *Ruins; or, Meditations on the Revolution of Empires* (1791). Like Voltaire, but using a different approach, Volney conveyed his belief in reason, science, natural law, tolerance, and progress. His scholarly explorations of a philosophy of history, in addition to his religious skepticism at a time when fanaticism was the rule of the day, impressed thoughtful readers in France, England, and the United States. He was a traveler as well, his accounts of journeys to Syria, Egypt, and Turkey being helpful to Napoleon in his Egyptian campaign. A utopist of sorts, Volney, like Fourier and Owen, envisaged the establishment of a worldwide community in which greed and possessiveness, corruption, and dissolute ways would have no place.

Both Voltaire and Volney saw the world, its wars and politics, not as God-directed, but in human and international terms. Not only was history, but contemporary foreign and internal influences as well, instrumental in building and dissolving societies. Voltaire's and Volney's ideas served to broaden Whitman's own notions concerning history, humankind, and such concepts as good and evil.

He, like Voltaire and Volney, attempted to understand the reasons for hierarchies in societies, the origins of wars, the principles of growth in economic systems. Most importantly, these two thinkers, and other spokespersons of the French Enlightenment, opened Whitman up to the world at large, to a more objective awareness of self: as an individual who was also part of the interaction of a group.

The very use of the word *salut* in the title of Whitman's poem conveys the poet's unbounded admiration and awe for the world. Understood in religious terms, *salut* may indicate his heartfelt wishes that all humanity know salvation, felicity, and fraternity.

Like a dramatic performance or an operatic spectacle, "Salut Au Monde" opens with an introductory stanza featuring Whitman being led by the hand and guided around the earth.

> O take my hand Walt Whitman!
> Such gliding wonders! such sights and sounds!
> Such join'd unended links, each hook'd to the next,
> Each answering all, each sharing the earth with all. (I, 1)

Whitman's world journey is reminiscent in some ways of Voltaire's philosophical tale *Micromegas* (1752). Here, two giants traversing interplanetary spheres see the earth from a distance and admire people's scientific and mathematical discoveries and their ability to use reason as arbiter of their views. So, too, will Whitman's guide invite him not only to penetrate vast expanses of land throughout the world, but a space-time continuum as well. Just as Voltaire's creatures questioned everything in the manifest world, the poet's guide asks him for his reactions to the marvels he encounters, empowering him to think and to broaden his understanding of existence.

The quite extraordinary second stanza of "Salut au Monde!" triggers the poet's gigantic need to see, feel, hear, discover, and absorb everything he encounters. Nothing seems to assuage his infinite appetite for knowledge, as his insatiable mind peers into every sphere of activity, be it geological, geographical, historical, philosophical, or aesthetic. The poet *actually* feels himself growing, physically, intellectually, spiritually, and psychologically, conveying such expansion in abstract terms.

> Within me latitude widens, longitude lengthens,
> Asia, Africa, Europe, are to the east — America is provided for in the west.

Within me is the longest day, the sun wheels in slanting rings, it does
    not set for months,
Stretch'd in due time within me the midnight sun just rises above the
    horizon and sinks again. (2:14)

As the poet's dramatic intake pursues its course, seeking, seeing,
and absorbing all the while, Whitman appeals more and more directly to the sense of sound. So reactive was he to sound that tones,
in and of themselves, had a powerful — and creative — effect on his
nervous system. Nor must Whitman's propensity to sonance be considered unusual, in view of the fact that he was a reader of Hindu
texts and the Bible. In the *Rig-Veda,* for example, sound (as in the
word *yak,* an active power in Brahma), resulting from rhythmic vibrations of primordial tone *(nada),* was considered the originator
of the cosmos. Whitman's knowledge of the Bible led him to understand that the very sound of *word* had divine and creative import. In
Deuteronomy, one reads: "Man doth not live by bread only, but by
every *word* that proceedeth out of the mouth of the Lord doth man
live" (8:3). In John, one finds: "In the beginning was the Word, and
the Word was with God, and the Word was God" (1:1). Pythagoras
spoke of the "music of the spheres." Knowledge, then, does not appear as vision alone, but as auditive perception also, as in mantras,
for example, echoings of divine primordial vibrations.

    When the poet's guide asks him: "What do you hear Walt Whit-
man?" his response is representational, but when read aloud, it may
be experienced as radiant tones:

I hear the workman singing and the farmer's wife singing,
I hear in the distance the sounds of children and of animals early in
    the day,
I hear emulous shouts of Australians pursuing the wild horse,
I hear the Spanish dance with castanets in the chestnut shade, to the
    rebeck and guitar....
I hear fierce French liberty songs,
I hear of the Italian boat-sculler the musical recitative of old poems.
    (3:22)

Tones of all ranges reach Whitman's ears: the bells of Mexican
muleteers, the muezzin calling the Arabs to prayer, the bass and so-
prano vocalizations of Christian choirs, the cry of the Cossack, the
sailor's voice when going out to sea, the intoning of Hebrew psalms,
the rhythmic relatings of Greek myths, and "I hear the tale of the di-

vine life and bloody death of the beautiful God the Christ," and the "Hindoo teaching his favorite pupil" (3:38).

As the sense of sight is called into participation in the fourth sequence, the poet's perspective shifts. The eye, which is to the human world what the sun is to the cosmic domain, endows him with an increase in confidence. Indeed, he at times takes on the stature of a giant, able and willing to observe as well as to command global happenings from some point in outer space. At other times he seems reduced to earthly size, involving himself in terrestrial dramas. The poet's continuous displacements not only alter his point of view, they also change the magnitude of the objects upon which he focuses: from a distance, these diminish in size; at close range, they appear gigantic.

Once the poet's perceptive and intuitive eye peers into cosmic vastness, it invites spiritual light to flow into mind and psyche, radiating its particles of experience throughout the visible world, but also within the poet's private inner domain. Like Shiva's third or frontal eye, indicating spiritual light, or Plato's organ of sight, understood as mirror to the soul, the eye of the poet provides with the means of both observing and participating in the excitement of creation. Thus will his new self be born, generating in the process a frenetic desire to broaden, and deepen his life experience without closure.

> I see a great round wonder rolling through space,
> I see diminute farms, hamlets, ruins, graveyards, jails, factories, palaces, hovels, huts of barbarians, tents of nomads upon the surface.... (4:41)

Not only does this giant poetic power that Whitman now experiences enable him to see into empirical reality, but it authorizes him to observe "the curious rapid change of the light and shade" — to see the far and wide of things (4:45). Like God, the creator of the world, he, its energizer, observes the "plenteous waters" — the *prima materia* — the multitude of mountain peaks and their verticalities, as these transcend earthly configurations and peer into the divine world (4:48). The poet's newly acquired giant stature allows him to span space and view ranges from the Andes to the Himalayas, Elbruz to the Karnac Alps, the Pyrénées to the Carpathians. Volcanos, such as Vesuvius and Etna, containers of the elements (earth, fire, water, and air) within their depths, intermingle, and erupt when nature's primary energies feel stifled. Deserts, parched and sterile lands upon which the sun beats down, are seen mythically, as undifferentiated space where caravans wandered, as had those men of God in ancient times: Moses, Jesus, St. Anthony — in search of Divinity's word. Antithetical to the heat of the sun-baked deserts are the congealed spaces, next conjured up by the poet, of stationary and floating icebergs in the Arctic and Antarctic. Bodies of water the world over now spiral forth in catalog style — from the White and Greenland seas to those rounding Cape Horn and the Gulf of Mexico, from the Niger River to the Indus. Stormy and calm bodies of water, identified with cosmic and human temperaments, are also indications of the author's mood swings.

As the poet's eye spans cultures and civilizations in a time-space continuum, images of ancient galley ships juxtaposed to those of modern trains filter into view. Whitman's infinite desire for life allows him to leap with joy when observing the fruits of modern technology. Such advances in communication as the telegraph have invited culturally different continents to trade and converse with one another, thereby bringing togetherness to diversity. On a negative note, however, the poet sees the rapid increase of modern technology, if not organized or functioning in an orderly manner, as inviting turmoil and even chaos to the world. Machine-driven cultures, as foreseen by Whitman, are symptomatic of a new and ever-expanding mechanistic and inflexible order.

Contemporary civilizations, as opposed to ancient ones, flash into the poet's eye, as they had in Goethe's *Faust* (part II), after the mystery of matter had been solved, and Helen and Paris, reborn from death, became visible once again as *eidola* (lower souls). The excitement generated by Whitman's continuous catalogings of "I see . . . " when alluding to ancient empires — Assyria, Persia, India — spirals forth with cumulative intensity. Place names and God figures, accompanied at times with images, vignettes, and epithets, catapult forth: Christ, Hercules, Bacchus, Hermes, and many more well-loved who have vanished from the earth and are still missed by some. Parallelisms are drawn as the poet eyes Death, when tramping through certain ancient battlefields, or as recalled in the names of conquerors and heroes peppering so many sagas, or commemorated in granite boulders, cliffs, and cairns. Each culture follows its own religious rituals when mourning its dead, some burying them in the sea and others under tumuli or gravestones; some transforming them into dust by incineration. "I see them raised high with stones by the marge of restless oceans, that the dead men's spirits when they wearied of their quiet graves might rise up through the mounds and gaze on the tossing billows, and be refresh'd by storms, immensity, liberty, action (7:111).

As images and sonorities heighten in volume and density, Whitman pursues his effective poetic strategy, namely, his telegraph style, juxtaposing long and short words in staccato rhythmic patternings. In so doing, he captures the frenetic mood he sought to impose during the course of his whirlwind tour, taking readers from the steppes of Asia to the Brazilian vaquero, the Samoyede and Finn to the Hottentot "with clicking palate," and to the world of the Parisians and Viennese. All classes, all races, all continents, all types — murderers, betrayers, idiots, barbarians, philosophers — are embraced by the poet in his salute to "the inhabitants of the earth" (10:162).

Love, that Eros quality, is the catalyst in the poet's desire to bind himself to others, to be with others, to relate to others. From one to all; the individual to the universal: "My spirit has pass'd in compassion and determination around the whole earth" (13:212). Warmed by the cities he has absorbed unto himself, the islands whose birds he has heard and seen, to all earthly life in all spheres, the poet extends his arms:

> Toward you all, in America's name,
> I raise high the perpendicular hand, I make the signal,
> To remain after me in sight forever,
> For all the haunts and homes of men. (13:223)

"Song of the Open Road" (1856, 1881)

In "Salut au Monde" Whitman sang of the vastness of life's spectacle while eying, inhaling, and palpating the globe both from outer space and from earthly regions. In "Song of the Open Road" the Bard/Narrator also relates his venture and adventure on the open road with unabashed joy: "light-hearted," "healthy," "free," and unimpeded. Whitman's use of *open* in the title is significant in that it emphasizes his need for unlimited expanse — spaces divested of closures and restrictions, be they physical or moral. To tramp along the open road without goal or destination is to fulfill a deep-seated need in the poet. A great admirer of George Sand's writings in general, Whitman must have been particularly struck by the following statement appearing in her novel, *Consuelo:* "What is there more beautiful than a road? It is the symbol and the image of an active and varied life.... And then that road is the passage of Humanity, the route of the universe.... So far as the sight can read, the road is a land of liberty."

On the open road, the poet finds himself energized, free to "inhale great draughts of space" for the sheer pleasure of filling his being with a whole world of imponderables (5:58). Although his attitude suggests an unwillingness on his part to commit himself to any belief, place, or person, it also discloses an unconscious fear and resentment of physical and psychological entrapment.

Life for Whitman, as it was for André Gide in *Fruits of the Earth* (1897), is a hymn to joy and self-liberation. Only after rejecting society with its traditions, family structures, and guilt-laden views, is the poet able to sing his credo: "From this hour I ordain myself loos'd of limits and imaginary lines" (5:53). The use of the word *ordain* indicates a religious approach to the poet's act, and therefore, one that is not to be taken lightly. To free himself of the torments of a shackled existence, although anguish-provoking, is tremulously exciting, as attested to by such phrases as "delicious burdens," referring to his personal torments vis-à-vis his family and his career as a writer, but also aimed at his readers, whose presences remain embedded in his mind (1:12).

The narrator's exploration of the world's roads and byroads, and the continuous displacements such motility entails, enable him to discover new directions. The search or quest implied not only endows him with the courage necessary to fulfill his mission, but also gives his life an inner orientation; thereby fomenting the onset of his much-needed rehabilitation: the process of understanding his own self-worth. "I am larger, better than I thought" (5:60). No longer will the poet deny his ways, despite the harsh criticisms leveled at him. Rather, he will open himself up to the world. Unlike Christ — who said, "But whosoever shall deny me before men, him will I also deny before my Father which is in heaven" (Matt. 10:33) — Whitman spoke words of love and acceptance to his fellow creatures: "Whoever denies me it shall not trouble me, / Whoever accepts me he or she shall be blessed and shall bless me" (5:68).

Because "Song of the Open Road" is a journey or pilgrimage that will lead the poet to his center, thereby bringing balance and harmony where chaos might have prevailed, it may be considered a *rite de passage*. If the trials and tribulations met with en route are successfully passed, the poet will gain access to a wider understanding of himself and his place in society, thereby depleting his profound sense of inadequacy. Traveling, for Whitman, implied a purification, a shearing off of the social laws aimed at crushing the energies of whoever rebelled against their constrictions. To hide, to secrete, to bury what "others" consider evil, and pursue these practices clandestinely, has become increasingly distasteful to Whitman.

Voyages and quests for truth and self-discovery have been many and fruitful in all literatures throughout history. Odysseus, Aeneas, Dante, Gargantua and Pantagruel, Gulliver, to mention but a few, all quested for some form of fulfillment, some form of liberation from an all-encroaching sense of constriction. Will Whitman's search bring him the independence of spirit for which he yearned?

Petulance, even arrogance, to a certain extent, at least superficially, are unconscious masks worn by the poet to hide his sense of inferiority. Why the necessity for dissimulation? The poet begins his self-interrogation by assessing himself and his needs at the outset of his journey. He is determined to tell his story as it is. When venturing forth, he claims to ask little from the world: not even "good-fortune" — since "I myself am good-fortune." Adamant now, he is "Done with indoor complaints, libraries, querulous criticisms." Strong in body and in mind, he merely wants to "travel the open road" (1:6). Clues inserted here and there, however, suggest that the narrator is not the liberated man he would like to be, but rather a deeply entrapped individual whose burdens — be these enjoyable and/or painful — are with him always:

(Still here I carry my old delicious burdens,
I carry them, men and women, I carry them with me wherever I go,
I swear it is impossible for me to get rid of them,
I am fill'd with them, and I will fill them in return.) (1:12)

Because his burdens are "delicious," they inspire him with pleasure, with regard to his poetic talents; but also with anguish, when caused by his unresolved sexual identity, and the stifling effect on him of his family's economic and psychological needs. To reach a modus vivendi is crucial. It alone is going to enable him to accept himself and his obligations, thereby freeing him from those turmoils that obstruct his capacity to enjoy life in its vastness and its excitement.

Openness and freedom, when applied to his creative domain, mean his decision not to follow the well-worn poetic modes and stanzaic patterns with their metered beats. Nor will he adhere to classical vocabularies. His search revolves around the discovery of a language emerging from and accessible to the people — *all* people. The new paths traversed on the "open road" encourage him to continue experimenting with new forms and images, and hazardous themes. He seeks to "reach" out and to "pass" others, but his route is paradoxical, since it invites him to "merge" with them as well. To accomplish such antithetical goals requires a poetic discourse suitable to the author's hedonistic ideology, a vocabulary suitable to his newfound temerity. Because the pleasure principle is to prevail in his new aesthetics, it will bring to birth a new sense of jubilation in humankind the world over.

In sharp contrast are Whitman's enumerations of sad times — "The early market-man, the hearse, the moving furniture into the town" (2:22) — referring perhaps to his father's death (July 11, 1855) and to his subsequent guilt feelings for not having been present when it occurred. Was this incident instrumental in triggering his wanderings and thus affording him release from the affliction of culpability?

> The earth expanding right hand and left hand,
> The picture alive, every part in its best light,
> The music falling in where it is wanted, and stopping where it is not
>   wanted,
> The cheerful voice of the public road, the gay fresh sentiment of the
>   road. (4:39)

Perhaps Whitman might also have incurred a sense of guilt because he felt such relief after his father's passing. Gone was the irritable, domineering, and reproachful figure, who was forever condemning him for his desultory ways. On a positive note, Whitman could have taken comfort in the fact that he had always been a dutiful son, particularly in 1853 and 1854, when the family was under enormous financial pressure and he had seen to the well-being of them all. At certain times in his life, his conscious mind might have reasoned that if he were to turn himself into the poet he wanted to become, he would have to break out of the vicious cycle of disease, depression, and distress imposed upon him by his family. Only then would he succeed in paving the way for real independence. Subliminally, however, it must have been another story. Still, the increased awareness his struggle brought him endowed him with the certitude necessary to function both as an individual and as part of the collective to which he belonged.

Along the way, he keeps his eye peeled for tiny details and immense spannings, for everything novel but also for the valuable elements ancient ways might bring. While looking about, he discovers the mysteries of a world "unseen"; glimpses and discerns types: "the rich person's carriage, the fop, the eloping couple." Heteroclite

objects parade before the poet/traveler as if projected onto a screen
in sequences of positive and negative film strips. While pursuing
his journey, he creates a dialectic between objective and subjective
worlds: between the visible, forever ejaculating into livingness and
"unseen existences."

Wandering expands the bard's universe: triggering his imagination to "think heroic deeds" and inspiring him to create freely in the
open air (4:48). Like Shelley's hero, the great Ozymandias, Whitman, standing before vast horizons, feels empowered to perform
deeds of grandeur. At times his tone conveys inflation: "I think
I could stop here myself and do miracles" (4:50); "I inhale great
draughts of space" (5:58). Feelings of arrogance heighten: "The east
and west are mine and the north and the south are mine" (5:59).
Giddy with power, the poet bellows: "I am larger, better than I
thought, / I did not know I held so much goodness" (5:60).

Unlike the overconfident Icarus — who refused to follow his father's warnings not to fly too close to the sun, and fell into the
sea because the sun's heat melted the wax holding his wings to his
body — Whitman leaves the earthly "long brown path" and ascends
to untold heights. Divested of roads or markings of any kind, but
infused with a limitless idea of himself, he peers into cosmic regions.

> Now I see the secret of the making of the best persons,
> It is to grow in the open air and to eat and sleep with the earth. (6:71)

So brazen has the poet become, so saturated is he with his
self-importance, that he feels empowered to transcend empirical
roadways and glide into aerated spheres, where beauty alone is en-
countered. Not only will "I scatter myself among men and women
as I go," but will "re-examine philosophies and religions" (6:83).
Theoretical teachings are not sufficient to bring harmony to a
human being: "They may prove well in lecture-rooms, yet not prove
at all under the spacious clouds and along the landscape and flowing
currents" (6:83).

Whitman agreed with certain of Jean-Jacques Rousseau's ideas as
expressed in his *Emile* or *Education* (1762): namely, that children
should learn through the life experience and not via books alone.
The free development of natural faculties and joy in play are pre-
requisites for a successful instructional process. To limit education
to book learning is to constrict a child, thereby encouraging in him a
negative and rebellious reaction. Nor was corporal punishment for
children acceptable to Whitman or Rousseau, any more than rig-

orous taskmasters imposing their rigid curricula on students. Such destructive techniques cannot help someone carve out a future in the workaday world. Nor should intellectuals, living in their cluttered rooms, removed from reality, from "the efflux of the soul" (7:94) instruct the young — or anyone.

Yet, paradoxically, the higher the poet of life experience flies, the more cut off he is from the world of reality. Identifying with prophets and messiahs, himself becoming the people's helper, he chants: "I will toss a new gladness and roughness among them" (5:66). Never will Whitman preach sacrifice as Christ had commanded: "If any man will come after me, let him deny himself, and take up his cross, and follow me" (Matt. 16:24). Neither threatening his followers nor seeking self-mutilation to earn redemption, Whitman intends to give, and receive, love on a grand scale.

The element air, emphasized by Whitman in his ascensionary stanzas (5–9), may be associated with wind and breath, thereby symbolizing subtle and intermediate spheres between Heaven and Earth. Such climes bring soul forces to mind: "And [God] breathed into his nostrils the breath of life; and man became a living soul" (Gen. 2:7). In Hindu philosophy, with which Whitman was familiar, the God called Vayu represents "vital breath" as well as cosmic creative breath, identified with the verb *breathe,* itself breath. Such symbols may indicate a dematerialization of Whitman's world of concretion (or earth): the coarse becoming refined, the liquid, distilled. Although such sublimation usually implies spiritual growth, in Whitman's case it indicates a condition of inflation. As a world of wishful thinking and of dream is taking precedence, a concomitant unwillingness on his part to deal with the material world was also becoming apparent. He prefers wafting in his fantasy spheres, blending in limitless aerated domains, uncommitted, and therefore far from stress and distress.

Yet, paradoxically, he conflates Earth and Heaven:

Toward the fluid and attaching character exudes the sweat of the
    love of young and old,
From it falls distill'd the charm that mocks beauty and attainments,
Toward it heaves the shuddering longing ache of contact. (8:111)

Love, the unifier of polarities, arouses the joy of elation as well as the "ache of contact" in the fleeting love experience. While linking the pleasures of physical and emotional union, Whitman as always elicits their opposites in pain.

Intent upon sweeping the reader into his fold, there to hold him, he begins the next six of the seven remaining stanzas with *allons,* the French imperative for "let us go." Although "inducements" are offered his readers — "We will sail pathless and wild seas" (10:125) — the requirements imposed by the bard for entry into his group make it difficult to join. Courage and imagination, a physically fit body, and a fine character are demanded of those who wish to probe life's infinite possibilities with the eugenicist narrator.

> Allons! with power, liberty, the earth, the elements,
> Health, defiance, gayety, self-esteem, curiosity....
>
> He traveling with me needs the best blood, thews, endurance,
> None may come to the trial till he or she bring courage and health,
> Come not here if you have already spent the best of yourself,
> Only those may come who come in sweet and determin'd bodies,
> No diseas'd person, no rum-drinker or venereal taint is permitted
>   here. (10:127)

Love, in this male-oriented group of "great Companions," will mark these "swift and majestic men" who "are the greatest women" (11:150). Gender differences vanish when building a new race: some men play aggressors, others, passive women. A Superman comes into being as an accumulation of sexual energy charges the atmosphere and is released through the poem.

> To take your lovers on the road with you, for all that you leave them
>   behind you,
> To know the universe itself as a road, as many roads, as roads for
>   traveling souls. (13:178)

Never a moment of rest for the narrator. Each second must be spent in living and seeing to the "progress of the souls," taking them "on the grand roads of the universe," preaching a call to battle and "active rebellion" (14:211, 13:181). Each member of the poet's group "must go well arm'd" (14:212), not passive but vitally alive, as, for good or for evil, they all push ahead together.

The poet's zest for life enables him, but only ephemerally, to transcend his ever-recurring despair. When peering deeply into himself through the lenses of the external world, he glimpses *plain.* "Behold through you as bad as the rest." Buried within him is despondency, hurt, and shame. "Behold a secret silent loathing and despair" (13:196). His goal of self-liberation has not been achieved. He does, however, know how to hide his anguish under the guise of laughter and dancing, when supping with friends and strangers. His various masks are always ready to suit the occasion.

Never will he allow himself to be overcome with despair. His song — with its repetitions of *allons,* reminiscent of the first word of *La Marseillaise,* the French national anthem that commemorated the end of the monarchy — encourages people to pursue their individual struggle for self-affirmation. Offering himself to humanity, he sings, "Camerado, I give you my hand!" ready to guide others as he had been led by the hand in "Salut au monde!" No longer the disciple, he has become a leader, engaging the world to follow him in dance, pleasure, bodily contact, love, and freedom of spirit. As momentum increases, the poet sweeps his partners into a thrilling complex of spiraling rhythms and tonalities. Grateful to his readers, he confesses that without them his voice would have remained interiorized and silence would have prevailed. Once again he exhorts them to join him in his quest.

> I give you my love more precious than money,
> I give you myself before preaching or law;
> Will you give me yourself? will you come travel with me?
> Shall we stick by each other as long as we live? (15:220)

Strengthened by his determination to endow a new generation with a fresh vision of life, the bard feels fulfilled — flooded with a raison d'être to pursue his arduous and perilous journey.

I will take each man and woman of you to the window and open the shutters and the sash, and my left arm shall hook you around the waist, and my right shall point you to the endless and beginningless road along whose sides are crowded the rich cities of all living philosophy, and oval gates that pass you in to fields of clover and landscapes clumped with sassafras, and orchards of good apples, and every breath through your mouth shall be of a new perfumed and elastic air, which is love. — Not I — not God — can travel this road for you. (*UPP,* II, 66)

6

"I See You Face to Face!"

While "Song of the Open Road" celebrated Whitman's search for personal liberation and free access to the world, "Crossing Brooklyn Ferry" awakens him to a curiously complex and ambiguous inner topography that invites him to say, "I see you face to face!" In "The Song of the Broad-Axe," also treated in this chapter, Whitman focuses on a tool to explore humanity's constructive and destructive sides. Eruptive and electric in its kinetic effect, "A Song for Occupations," draws attention to working people in a growing industrial society.

"Crossing Brooklyn Ferry" (1856, 1881)

Rather than ambulating with feet firmly implanted on earth or inviting the reader to follow the poet into untried territories, as in "Salut au Monde!" and "Song of the Open Road," Whitman uses the machine — the ferry — in "Crossing Brooklyn Ferry" to trigger activity. Such a device allows the poet to guide his readers into the modern age and also to express his ambivalent feelings toward these changing times.

"Crossing Brooklyn Ferry" limits Whitman's frame of vision to one specific area — the daily ferry ride from Brooklyn across the river to Manhattan. In that the machine is programmed to pursue its routine of repetitious voyages, it may be viewed as a metaphor endowed with a calming effect. Well-regulated and relatively secure in its construction, as is a house, the ferry, by its very limitations, encourages greater introspection than the extroverted vision of "Song of the Open Road."

Whitman had ambivalent feelings about machines. Certainly he looked back with pride at a great historical event, Robert Fulton's launching of the steamboat *Clermont* (1807), which took passengers from New York City to Albany. A frequent traveler to Manhattan, he valued the ferry's capacity to link Brooklyn with

New York City. Nevertheless, he sorrowed at the future ramifications of this and other mechanical inventions. He feared an overly mechanized and industrialized nation.

Aside from these practical matters, Whitman's ferry, viewed symbolically, invited the reader's eye to travel in both empirical and spiritual realms. Since Whitman had for years been fascinated by ancient Egyptian beliefs and rituals, analogies between his ferry ride and the Egyptian myth of the "solar bark" are in order. One of the many artistic depictions of the Egyptians' sacred boat, which took the deceased into the twelve regions of the underworld, featured the sun-god, Ra, standing on its deck during the course of the trajectory. In "Crossing Brooklyn Ferry" the sun not only sheds its light on the boat per se, but in so doing, illuminates the narrator, who also stands on board. Indeed, the entire landscape is clothed in orchestrated luminosities, opacities, and densities. Glare and muted rays fluctuate, depending on time schemes and atmospheric conditions. The enfolding dimming of the scene during the course of the ferry's trajectory, indicating the oncoming of evening, may also suggest a withdrawal of light from the narrator's rational, or outside, domain and its descent into his subliminal spheres, or, as in the Egyptian myth, into the underworld. By associating the narrator's journey with that of the sun, the poet conflates astral, spatial, and maritime navigation in his verbal canvas. A parallel between Whitman's ferry ride and the voyage of the compassionate Amida Buddha, known as the Great Boatman, may also be made. Just as the Buddha guided the deceased beyond the world of pain and attachment into the next, so Whitman entices his readers to opt for broader values and scapes during their life/death process.

Whitman's expert use of mobile light rays likens his verbal canvas to the works of American "luminist" painters: Thomas Cole, Asher B. Durand, Thomas Doughty, John Frederick Kensett, and Frederick E. Church, who introduced fresh and bold but also sober and contemplative views of American scenery. Their translucent mists and radiant colorations imbued their canvases with a melancholy underlay as well as a new approach to nature in its infinite atmospheric personalities. That a new fascination with landscape painting had been born in America may be attributed in part to Emerson, for he had informed his readers that real emancipation of being is to be found in nature. Whitman furthers this view.

Whitman uses the technique of multiple luminosities in "Crossing Brooklyn Ferry" both for its aesthetic value and as an ideological strategy: to diffuse paradoxically and/or concentrate light. Such a

feat is effected by an expert interplay and linkage of ferry and water images. The continuous movement of the river and the ship,
each traveling at different speeds, as well as the interaction between
the clouds and the sun's rays and the ensuing complex of shadings,
results in moments of high drama.

That the ship travels both in space and in time promotes feelings
of transcendence in the narrator and the reader, thereby activating the dream meditation. Understood as a metonymy for cosmic
motion, the ensuing reveries serve to take the narrator and reader
out of the human sphere and place them in transpersonal dimensions. Mood swings also parallel changing luminosities: the sun's
dazzling radiance may spell joy; its hiddenness at nightfall, dismal
foreboding. When the moon's secret glow or when sinister darkness
permeates the atmosphere, it may inspire latent sensations of both
fear and pleasure.

An intimate meditation, "Crossing Brooklyn Ferry" opens with
the narrator standing on deck looking down at the "Flood-tide below." Verticality of focus changes to horizontality as the poet's eye
looks outward — to vast expanses.

> Flood-tide below me! I see you face to face!
> Clouds of the west — sun there half an hour high — I see you also
>   face to face. (1:1)

The implications of the narrator stating, "I see you face to face!"
while staring at the water below, are multiple and ambiguous. Has
the water been transformed into a mirror enabling the narrator to
observe his face below? Does the "you" refer to the reader he is addressing and with whom he would like to come into contact? If the
latter, Whitman would be availing himself of the popular technique
used in confessional poetry: a ritual discourse that not only compels the reader to face the author and vice versa, but that leads to
an emotional and intellectual interchange between the two. If, on
the other hand, the narrator observes a mirror image of himself in
the waters below, he may be probing his motivations in a kind of
Orphic descent into his subliminal depths.

The narrator's gaze is not stationary, but ascends rapidly from
maritime to supernal levels. Just as the water had mirrored his face
below, so his eyes now reflect as well, alternating cloud formations
and the sun's radiance. The poet's fluctuating imagery paralleling
the density and extent of the transforming masses of vapor, is
depicted in horizontal and vertical visual frames, as well as in cir-

cular and centrifugal designs, each instrumental in modifying the narrator's mood swings. The day's changes from brilliance to shadowiness also act as annunciators of atmospheric change: prophets of storms, rain, obscurity, gloom.

From subjective and personal spheres he now turns his attention to impersonal and faceless people on board the ferry.

> Crowds of men and women attired in the usual costumes, how
> curious you are to me!
> On the ferry-boats the hundreds and hundreds that cross, returning
> home, are more curious to me than you suppose.... (1:3)

Although the passengers come from different social classes, there is nothing unique about any of them. Whitman's introduction of the collective image allows him to mingle high and low in keeping with his democratic beliefs. His egalitarian image, however, includes both the mask of conformity (the "usual costumes") and a hint of mystery: the suggestion that there is something "curious" about the scene. That the word *curious* is again repeated in the following line (1:4), gives one pause. *Curious* implies inquisitiveness as well as the presence of some strange thought or pulsation that seems to be agitating or troubling the poet. Suspense mounts in this otherwise serene panoramic view. What is this "curious" factor to which the poet is alluding? Abstractions follow.

> The impalpable sustenance of me from all things at all hours of the
> day,
> The simple, compact, well-joined scheme, myself disintegrated, every
> one disintegrated yet part of the scheme,
> The similitudes of the past and those of the future,
> The glories strung like beads on my smallest sights and hearings, on
> the walk in the street and the passage over the river.... (2:6)

The "impalpable sustenance" refers not only to food taken in orally, but to spiritual and philosophical regimens dating back to history's beginnings. Each culture attempts to explain the ineffable and the infinite in finite terms. The pre-Socratic atomists, Democritus and Leucippus; the Roman poet Lucretius, in his *On the Nature of Things;* the seventeenth-century Descartes, in *Discourse of the Method;* Isaac Newton in *Principia* — all produced a rational "well-joined scheme," integrating each element or thought into its proper niche. However, the ferry-riding narrator ("myself disintegrated") questions the various schemes. At best, answers are problematic.

The poet's meditation pursues its rhythmic course in keeping with the watery currents below, the pace of the clouds above, and the interlacing of solar luminosities. Such a space/time continuum serves to link linear and cyclical orders. Past, present, and future converge, and all generations are connected.

> The glories strung like beads on my smallest sights and hearings, on
>   the walk in the street and the passage over the river,
> The current rushing so swiftly and swimming with me far away,
> The others that are to follow me, the ties between me and them,
> The certainty of others, the life, love, sight, hearing of others. (2:9)

The "beads" may refer to ritualistic rosaries or prayer beads used by the devout; or to the monads, elementary units, as defined by Gottfried W. Leibniz in his *Monadologie*. This German philosopher believed in the existence of a preestablished and hierarchized harmony in the universe: a "chain of beings" made up of an infinite number of monads, ranging from the smallest to the greatest — God. Having delved into the philosophical and religious works of the time, Whitman could have derived sustenance for a while from many of their fixed and secure concepts with their organized rituals and ideologies. However, to accept such panaceas permanently was not in Whitman's makeup. No longer a child living in his mother's orbit, although still tied to her umbilical cord/"beads," he could neither see the world through her eyes nor anyone else's. Nor adhere to fads or to popular "currents," which changed with the tides of the generations:

> Others will enter the gates of the ferry and cross from shore to shore,
> Others will watch the run of the flood-tide. (2:13)

As the narrator looks at "others" coming on the ferry, he ponders that each approaches life in a different way, with love and rapture but also with disbelief and anger. Theories and faiths, he muses, will alter: "Fifty years hence.... / A hundred years hence, or ever so many hundred years hence (2:16). But the narrator, still leaning on the rail, gazes into a world beyond contingencies:

> It avails not, time nor place — distance avails not,
> I am with you, you men and women of a generation, or ever so many
>   generations hence. (3:20)

Very much the observer as well as the participant, his dual meditations meld into one: the ferry — or myriad ferries in years to come — moving from one shore to the other is associated with the larger question of one generation and the following. Although the length of the ferry ride may shorten in keeping with technological improvements, the narrator rationalizes that atmospheric influences, such as accelerating or decreasing currents, will also play their part in determining the vehicle's speed. That both factors are at variance, as is all else in the cosmos, may also be understood as metonymies for the days and years during the course of a life: "numberless masts of ships and the thick-stemm'd pipes of steam-boats" (3:25). Here again, the *multiple* merges into *oneness*. So important a concept was oneness for Whitman, so crucial a role did it play as a mediating power in balancing the heights and depths of his mood swings and the interplay between his extroverted and introverted natures, that it could be counted upon to rectify his tendency toward excesses.

Diminishing light values accompany the poet's anticipated intrusion of a cold winter: the "Twelfth-month" migration of the sea gulls to warmer southern spheres. Their journey, like that of the ferry and like the mechanics of the Cartesian and Newtonian universe, is programmed — thus emphasizing sameness. The narrator observes the sea gulls "floating with motionless wings," their "oscillating" bodies flying in "slow-wheeling circles." The images of the wheel and the circle may be understood as symbols of eternity, and also of the sun, a source of light in the empirical world. When associated with Buddha's Wheel of Time, the "slow-wheeling circles" also refer to spiritual illumination.

As the narrator looks at the "reflection of the summer sky in water," his entire vista seems to be built on a mobile network of analogies: each entity reflecting itself in and being a reflection of the other in a never-ending unfathomable universe (3:31).

> Had my eyes dazzled by the shimmering track of beams,
> Look'd at the fine centrifugal spokes of light round the shape of my
>   head in the sunlit water,
> Look'd on the haze on the hills southward and south-westward,
> Look'd on the vapor as it flew in fleeces tinged with violet,
> Look'd toward the lower bay to notice the vessels arriving. (3:32)

The "fine centrifugal spokes...of light round the shape of my head in the sun-lit water," never-ending, expanding and diminishing circular patterns, are strangely reminiscent of some of Van Gogh's later paintings, and these patterns encapsulate the myriad factors involved in the poet's visual frames. From the summer sky with its vaporous violet-tinged clouds, to the sloops, schooners, steam tugs, vessels, and the "white wake left by the passage, the quick tremulous whirl of the wheels," alternating time sequences issue forth in prismatic clusters, adding to the stanza's glittering and benumbing quality (3:42).

Centrifugal, a term created by Newton, that the poet uses to describe the "spokes of light," indicates an object moving or tending to move away from the center. So, too, does the poet's radiance, like the sun's flame, increase in dimension as it spreads over the hazy hills in vaporlike waves, inviting the narrator to observe a metaphorized universe in terms of the flight of sea gulls. Like these ascending birds, so the narrator's thoughts and sensations move in hazy climes, pursuing their dramatic course "in fleeces tinged with violet." The poet is also riveted by the more mundane flux of discordant happenings occurring, most particularly, in the "lower bay": he sees the approaching vessels transporting their cargoes from one bank to another in an increasingly industrialized world. Cacophonies also strike hard at the narrator as he hears the noise and activity of the ferries and the workers loading and unloading cargoes. Excitement peaks as the reader is told of the soot of "fires from the foundry chimneys burning high and glaringly into the night," and "casting their flicker of black contrasted with wild red and yellow light over the tops of houses, and down into the clefts of the streets" (3:48). The agitation and commotion on the waterways, as well as the previously mentioned animation generated by the various religious and scientific theories, serves to emphasize the passage from one generation to another. The tensions evoked prepare the reader and narrator for the journey inward: a sinister path that must be traversed by all people on Ra's solar bark. Only via such a descent, can the discovery of one's *real* identity occur. In the world of myths and legends, journeys and quests can be effective only if questions are posed and answers probed. Light may then be shed where previously darkness alone has prevailed.

"What is it then between us?" the poet asks? (5:54) The reader is once again thrust into shaky ambiguity. Does the narrator's "us" refer to the poet and his reader? or to the poet and the others? or to the poet and his own shadow world?

Fright intrudes. "I too felt curious abrupt questionings stir within me" (5:59). Uncertain of his sexual identity, the narrator confesses his fear of disclosing his sexual proclivities. These will mark him; they will stain his world. To *face* such a truth pains and haunts the poet, particularly when lying alone at night on his bed, with no escape from his thoughts.

> I too had been struck from the boat forever held in solution,
> I too had receiv'd identity by my body,
> That I was I knew was of my body, and what I should be I knew I
>   should be of my body. (5:62)

Anxiety intrudes as the poet's confession, aimed not only at the reader, but projected onto future generations, grows more personal, poignant, as well as erotic.

> It is not upon you alone the dark patches fall,
> The dark threw its patches down upon me also,
> The best I had done seem'd to me blank and suspicious,
> My great thoughts as I supposed them, were they not in reality meagre?
> Nor is it you alone who know what it is to be evil,
> I am he who knew what it was to be evil. (6:70)

Feelings of inadequacy corrode his being. More questions concerning his worth as a poet abound. Is he the great poet he believes himself to be? The harbinger of new forms and fresh ideations? Guilt intrudes as "dark patches fall," and the blackness of night, now identifies him with "evil." The narrator's knowledge that his homosexuality and masturbatory practices are unacceptable to the religious and social standards of the time encourages him to confess: "I am he who knew what it was to be evil" (6:70). While unburdening himself of his "guile, anger, lust, hot wishes," he further eroticizes the picture, his intention shifting from guilty confession to spurring the reader on to seek out the "curious" joys experienced in his secret "garden of delights." Then again, the narrator's disclosures take a more negative bent as he enumerates his "wayward, vain, greedy, shallow, sly, cowardly, malignant" ways (6:74). Cataloging his transgressions in confessional style, he saves the most excoriating — his escapades in Manhattan and his many sexual partners — for the last. But once again his tone changes. Titillating his readers by his use of tactile images, as would Jean Genet a century later, he ushers them into complicity with him — inviting them to join his world of the pariah.

> Was call'd by my nighest name by clear loud voices of young men as
>   they saw me approaching or passing,
> Felt their arms on my neck as I stood, or the negligent leaning of
>   their flesh against me as I sat,

Saw many I loved in the street or ferry-boat or public assembly, yet
   never told them a word,
Lived the same life with the rest, the same old laughing, gnawing,
   sleeping,
Play'd the part that still looks back on the actor or actress,
The same old role, the role that is what we make it, as great as we
   like.
Or as small as we like, or both great and small. (6:78)

Although role-playing creates problems between the narrator and
society, he does not have to resort to such devices with those of his
ilk, for they recognize his sexual identity instantly:

Gaze, loving and thirsting eyes, in the house or street or public
   assembly!
Sound out, voices of young men! loudly and musically call me by my
   nighest name! (9:108)

Like the actor and actress, the poet, his secrets known to only a
few, continues to play out the role he chooses for himself, adhering,
but only for relative peace of mind, to the "well-joined scheme."
Yet, when pondering his life, the narrator yearns to heal his frac-
tured and atomized psyche. Nevertheless, with eyes "downcast," he
continues his duplicitous ways, revealing his mask only: an image
of harmony, joy, and ebullience. Referring to his dual personality,
he sings: "About my body for me, and your body for you, be hung
our divinest aromas" (9:122). He will retain his secret bonding with
other men, despite the torments it causes, so as not to be forced to
live out a marginal existence.
   Whitman's intense internecine psychological conflict, as conveyed
in "Crossing Brooklyn Ferry," discloses a portentous awareness of
the evils inherent in both an overly puritanical ruling conscience
and an overly industrialized society. Each in its own way imposes
its rigid views and intransigent programs, treating any disruptive
or irrational happenings with feelingless rigor and machinelike
exactitude.
   A man for whom the democratic spirit took on virtually holy
significance, Whitman failed in his struggle to open himself up
to a society in which notions of propriety, health, and morality
marginalized homosexuals. Because of his inability to come forth
and disclose his sexual proclivities, "shame" ate away at his flesh
and soul — like a malignancy. To avoid further alienation and humiliation, he remained cautious, not only secreting his own sense of

inadequacy as a poet, but burying his "secret" from the "curious." Although he recasts his themes and perfected the formal elements of his poetry, Whitman, who had called to others to be forthright and open in their personal revelations, never had the courage to "Show a bold and brazen front!" Is it any wonder that Whitman's conflictual psychological situation gave rise, around the mid-1850s, to a period of deep melancholia?

"Song of the Broad-Axe" (1856, 1881)

Whitman energized global vistas in "Salut au Monde!," tramped along the paths of the world in "Song of the Open Road," and drew upon a machine to take him from one shore to another to convey life's joys and torments in "Crossing Brooklyn Ferry." Now in "Song of the Broad-Axe," he focuses on a tool to express humanity's positive and negative activities.

The broad-axe, one of the chief instruments of the American pioneer, was not only used to clear deeply forested areas, but to acquire lumber for the building of houses, towns, and cities. Wood was instrumental in the fabrication of objects necessary to the acculturation process of a land and the celebration of American democracy. From time immemorial, the ax had been employed for multiple purposes, both in the workaday world and as a symbol. The North American Indians, for example, used it both aggressively, as an instrument of war, and defensively, to protect themselves from their enemies. So, too, was this tool crucial to the construction of their habitations and totem poles. So powerful had it been considered by the Mayas — as replicator of thunder and lightning — that it was endowed with numinous powers. Certain ancient peoples, namely, the Mesopotamians and Aegeans, looked upon the ax as a sacrificial tool and as an emblem of the gods.

Mythical in dimension and historical in purpose, the double-edged symbol of the broad-axe was, for Whitman, an insignia of power. Usually identified with the male principle in that it was associated with strength, it was seen by Whitman as androgynous. The opening trochaic lines of "Song of the Broad-Axe" endow it with feminine as well as with masculine attributes. This self-reproductive weapon, therefore, takes on psychological ramifications.

Weapon shapely, naked, wan,
Head from the mother's bowels drawn,
Wooded flesh and metal bone, limb only one and lip only one,

Gray-blue leaf by red-heat grown, helve produced from a little seed sown,
Resting the grass amid and upon,
To be lean'd and to lean on. (1:1)

In keeping with nineteenth-century symbology, the adjectives used to describe the broad-axe — *shapely* and *wan* — associate this tool with woman. That its "head" emerges "naked" from the "mother's bowels" identifies it with the fertile and nutritive mother who feels "wan" after the effort expended in the birth process. Phallic images also abound, as attested to by the "head," used not only to represent the infant being born, but the "head" of the penis, which, when reaching a climax, or "red-heat," hardens like a "limb" or "metal bone," after which it ejaculates its "little seed," or semen, into the "lip," or vagina. Once the "seed" unites with the other "seed," or egg, they work together in the uterus, or by association, in the furnace of the metallurgist. After the completion of the gestation period, the growth process having come to term, the finished product is then expelled by the woman, thereby paralleling the male's ejaculation of his semen.

The analogies drawn with the birth act, be it that of the woman with the help of the man, or the poet's verbal creation, or the metallurgist's fashioning of the broad-axe in the smelting process, may also be identified with the felling of the tree and the role played by the tool in shaping its phallic handle.

The effort expended in the creative act, whatever its nature, is so enormous that it requires periods of rest in a fertile area, namely, in the grass, for the poet. "To be lean'd and to lean on" not only suggests the very act of lovemaking, but the existence of an emotional relationship between a mother who, after giving birth, nurtures her child both physically and creatively; and, by extension, with society as well.

The "wooded flesh" refers, in Whitman's complex of analogies, to both the tree and the handle of the tool. Both participated in the cutting down of forest lands by the pioneer, whose goal was not necessarily to divest a newly discovered land for lucre, although this might have been part of his plan, but, rather, to thin out an overabundant nature, thereby, paradoxically, encouraging it become even thicker and more lush.

Whitman views the ax not only animistically, that is, in the physical act of giving birth, or in the performing of "masculine trades," but as an abstraction, in the composition of a poem or in the musical arts, namely, that of the "organist."

> Strong shapes and attributes of strong shapes, masculine trades, sights and sounds,
> Long varied train of an emblem, dabs of music,
> Fingers of the organist skipping staccato over the keys of the great organ. (1:7)

Erotic images suggesting palpation are obvious in "Fingers of the organist skipping staccato over the keys of the great organ." Nevertheless, this same line takes on another cast: the poet's linkage of sensations of sight and sound with an "organ," usually identified with church services, lends a religious note to the image.

The felling of trees also has vast implications. To sever, cut, divide the whole into pieces, or the parts into smaller parts, transforms the ax into an agent of differentiation. The same reasoning may be applied to the structuring of a poem: the ability to cut various words or events depicted is to divide the mass into various parts. Such a severing process allows the individual to examine the entire work from a variety of vantage points. Thus is he given the opportunity to enlarge his or her perspective.

Tree symbolism is crucial to Whitman in "The Song of the Broad-Axe." That its branches reach toward the heavens identifies it with the spiritualization process; that its roots burrow deep within the earth suggests a source of strength and inspiration; and that its trunk links it to the earthly sphere serves to conflate seemingly dual forces: Heaven and Earth, spirit and matter, body and soul, conscious and unconscious.

Humanity in general is nurtured by the tree as a natural and as an aesthetic power. An American folklore hero, the Massachusetts-born Johnny Appleseed, traveled westward for fifty years preaching and handing out apple seeds to plant. Like this figure, Whitman seeks to implant his poetry in the minds and hearts of people. It has been claimed that the orchards of Pennsylvania, Ohio, Illinois, and Indiana were begun by Johnny Appleseed. Could not Whitman, as poet, be equally instrumental in the acculturation process, thereby taking on legendary stature and becoming part of the American democratic scene?

Reminiscent of Johnny Appleseed, Whitman sweeps his readers through American landscapes, plunging them into seemingly unending vistas. His use of complex internal and end-rhyme schemes, anaphoras, and repetitions emphasizes the enormous bursts of energy and excitement implicit in the creative process:

Welcome are all earth's lands, each for its kind,
Welcome are lands of pine and oak,
Welcome are lands of the lemon and fig,
Welcome are lands of gold,
Welcome are lands of wheat and maize, welcome those of the grape,
Welcome are lands of sugar and rice,
Welcome the cotton-lands, welcome those of the white potato and
     sweet potato. (2:10)

The poet's continuous use of caesuras to mark time are onomatopoeias calling to mind hatchet strokes cutting through matter.

Lands of mines, lands of the manly and rugged ores,
Lands of coal, copper, lead, tin, zinc,
Lands of iron — lands of the make of the axe. (2:22)

With biblical grandeur, the poet lists the virtues of the ax as a
builder of the nation.

The settlements of the Arkansas, Colorado, Ottawa, Willamette,
The slow progress, the scant fare, the axe, rifle, saddle-bags'
The beauty of all adventurous and daring persons. (3:34)

Whitman's pioneers, be they creators of concretions or abstractions, forge ahead as in biblical times — until they, too, reach their
Promised Land. Was it not said in Joel that "the mountains shall
drop down new wine, and the hills shall flow with milk, and all the
rivers of Judah shall flow with waters, and a fountain shall come
forth of the house of the Lord" (3:18)? Likewise, will America
build and enrich itself by welcoming refugees the world over to
work a land of "pine," "oak, "lemon," "fig," "gold," "wheat,"
"maize," "grape, "flats," "forests," "prairies," "mines," "ores,"
"coal," "copper," "lead," foods, metals — "lands of the make of
the axe" (2:24)?
     Again the narrator emphasizes the masculinity of the "adven-
turous" and "daring" ax-bearing men. He pauses to admire the
physical appeal of men at work.

The beauty of wood-boys and wood-men with their clear untrim'd
     faces,
The beauty of independence, departure, actions that rely on them-
     selves.... (3:36)

His enumeration of images of men cutting, bending, standing, "driving in pins, holding on by the posts," serves to link phallic with fruitful forces (3:49).

The orchestration of strident and unexpected staccato sounds intrudes while the men perform their various activities, supplementing the visual with aural artistry. Hatchet-wielding men severing branches, and cutting trunks by virtually eating into the bark with their implements, lend a visceral note to the entire flow of images describing the construction process.

> The floor-men forcing the planks close to be nail'd,
> Their postures bringing their weapons downward on the bearers,
> The echoes resounding through the vacant building;
> The huge storehouse carried up in the city well under way. (3:52)

In addition, a variety of syncopated sonorities underscores the industrious nature of workers involved in the building of factories, markets, girders, arches, railroads, and arsenals: the "continual click of the trowels striking the bricks" and "the brisk short crackle of the steel driven slantingly into the pine" (3:58).

Despite his celebrations of farming, mining, and building, Whitman deprecates societies that focus on material factors. "What do you think endures?" he asks rhetorically (4:99). Manufacturing, steamships, industry, "hotels of granite and iron" are all important. But such achievements "are not to be cherish'd for themselves," the narrator states (4:104). Objects, whatever they may be, play their part in time, pass before the public eye like so many performances. Reminiscent of *Macbeth* (V, 5), Whitman writes: "They fill their hour, the dancers dance, the musicians play for them, / The show passes, all does well enough of course, / All does very well" (4:104).

Whitman's use of parallel structure and alliteration throughout "Song of the Broad-Axe," emphasizes the savage nature of humanity's destructive side: "The hell of war, the cruelties of creeds.... The power of personality just or unjust" (3:91). Although he underplays the negative ramifications involved in the use of the broad-axe, the poet believes it has been instrumental in emasculating the American wilderness. Nevertheless, the implication is that the individual has not been to blame for the despoliation of vast forests; rather, the large companies, employing thousands of workers to cut down timber from New England to the Northwest, have been responsible.

As the ax-wielder's achievements continue to be reiterated with ever-increasing gusto, the stanzas take on cumulative power. They are most frequently characterized by a complex of joyous images and sonorities, but sinister undertones, frequently relegated to the background, emerge every now and then to work on the reader's soul and psyche.

The double-edged broad-axe, builder of cities, of incredible frameworks and skylines, of bridges and arches, has also given rise to murderers, suicides, shrouds, coffins, prisoners, courtrooms. Woodpiles, however, are assembled for home heating, and fields are cleared for the planting of crops and gardens of all types. The cataloging of trades and professions in which the broad-axe is instrumental is done swiftly in seemingly chaotic listings: butchering for food; making blazing fires for cooking and for forging iron and smelting steel used in building bridges, piers, ships, and trains. The broad-axe is also meaningful to Whitman as a lifesaver: to help firemen break windows and doors when extinguishing dangerous flames and rescuing people from burning buildings in New York City. In his enthusiasm for building cities, however, Whitman fails to allude to the dirt, grime, and dangerous conditions workers had to endure during their hours of labor in factories. Nor does he mention such industrial diseases as silicosis in mining, or tuberculosis in sweatshops.

The cumulative buildup of Whitman's enumerations at times parallels the stridulent rhythms, and grating tones of continuous hatchet strokes. The poet's onomatopoeias succeed in replicating the breathlessness of men at work who barely take time to inhale, so intent are they in achieving their goal. His telegraph or catalog style, used virtually continuously in "Song of the Broad-Axe," serves to sweep readers into his powerful rhythmic embrace, there to hold them as he pursues his historical résumé of the birth, passing, and future of great civilizations. To build a land, the poet reiterates, necessitates vision and courage, but also the ability to deal with imponderables. Polarities are again on the poet's agenda as he sings of both the "roughness of the earth and of man" and "the delicatesse of the earth and of man." Nor can the masculine exist without the feminine: cities are complete, for example, only when made up of "the greatest men and women" (4:107).

Whitman's enumerations are also built into the patternings of the poem for didactic reasons. Such a technique indulges his penchant for vast historical résumés to prove his belief in progress and utopianism. In so doing, the poet informs his readers of the various ways to which Egyptians, Assyrians, Romans, Goths, Celts,

and others, put the ax to use. A civilizing factor for some, it was
a death-wielding power for others.

> I see the clear sunset of the martyrs,
> I see from the scaffolds the descending ghosts,
> Ghosts of dead lords, uncrown'd ladies, impeach'd ministers, re-
>   jected kings,
> Rivals, traitors, poisoners, disgraced chieftains and the rest....
>
> I see the blood wash'd entirely away from the axe,
> Both blade and helve are clean,
> They spirt no more the blood of European nobles, they clasp no
>   more the necks of queens. (8:171)

Whitman considered the broad-axe, as used in America, to be
a purifying force, capable of ridding the New World of the dross
of old, worn, and effete traditions. The greatness of a city — and
the ax used to build it — depends in the last analysis on its inhabitants. Still, he is not blind as to the double-edged nature of this
tool: "The door that admits good news" does so for "bad news"
(10:236). Good and evil cohabit everywhere and in everything: it is
"a law of Nature" (10:248).

Like the ax, Whitman's pen is also viewed as a magic tool, enabling him to resurrect a past, to build his verbal cities, to depict
his multiracial and multiethnic populations, his traitors, his pari-
ahs, workers, rulers, statesmen, tradespeople, and intellectuals —
all inhabitants of his metropolis, together with their physical and
emotional yearnings, their acts of love.

Whitman's faith in the magic embedded in the broad-axe — like
the fetish for the shaman, the miracle-bearer for the believer — invited him to consider it instrumental not only in the shaping of
democracy, but also in the inspiration encouraging him to sing out
his love for America in hymnal fashion (12:250):

> (America! I do not vaunt my love for you,
> I have what I have.) (9:184)

"A Song for Occupations" (1855, 1881)

In this poem Whitman directs his attention to the "workmen and
workwomen!" who have made the new and growing industrial society possible. The uniqueness of American democracy rests, he
maintains, on the fact that all human labor, no matter the category,
is valued and appreciated. The use of direct address to confess his

love and admiration for his country, its workers, and their multiple trades and occupations is an ideal strategy to reach the reader. The dialectic between Whitman as narrator and the reader/stranger moves along in swift and successive cacophonous tropes, touching increasingly upon economic issues and social needs. Nor does the poet omit to mention of the potency of that hidden but crucial factor within the poem and the human being, instrumental in both the spiritual and sexual love-embrace: the "souls of men and women" (2:28). The inborn impulse toward a union of the disparate and conflictual will lead to the birth of a fully operative society — a polis in which the senses and mind awaken to the sound of the machine, discourse, music, and the aesthetics of a new language that will include traditional poetics along with colloquialisms, and slang, as well as gutter speech.

From approximately 1800 until 1880 it was believed that some of the ideas formulated by Jean-Jacques Rousseau in his *Discourse on the Origin and Bases of Inequality among Men* (1750) would be fruitful to American industrialists and humanists. While celebrating "natural man," Rousseau condemned the social factors in the political state that created the inequality and oppression of its citizens. In his *Social Contract* (1762), Rousseau stated that since no man has any "natural" authority over another, the individual becomes the basic political unit. By surrendering his rights to the state, on the other hand, he is assured of equal status with the other citizens. Idealistic, to be sure, he, along with Montesquieu, as attested to in the latter's *Spirit of Laws* (1748), believed that government should be determined by the finest practical, moral, and theoretical notions. Rousseau's ideological stand, his love of nature, his sensitivity to and ennoblement of emotions, and his rejection of the status quo endeared him to Whitman and to those other Americans who sought to conciliate utilitarian and Romantic points of view.

However, Rousseau was much more hostile to the consequences of industrialization than Whitman was. Along with such humanists as Thoreau, Audubon, Emerson, Melville, and Olmsted, Whitman believed that the development of science, mechanics, and industry was not only important in increasing personal incomes, but was crucial to the prosperity and welfare of the nation as a whole. Thoreau, who had built a cabin at Walden Pond on Emerson's land and had lived there for a little over two years, was no hermit. On the contrary, he entertained friends, while also recording his observations of nature in *Walden* (1854). Although he believed that people should simplify their existence so as to understand its meaning better, he did not suggest that they withdraw from life, and he in no way discounted the positive side of industry. In fact, he helped in his family's pencil-making business by utilizing a new process for purifying graphite about which he had read in a scientific review.

John James Audubon, the artist and naturalist whose detailed studies of birds in their settings became so popular, had received a fine humanistic education. While he explored the beauties of nature, responding to its sounds and colorations, he was averse neither to scientific discovery and mechanical inventions nor to the growth of commerce. Indeed, he was fascinated by these elements, considering them symbols of an expanding society. What he feared, along with Whitman, was the overrapid acceleration of the factory system and the dehumanization that arises with industry's unchecked growth — paradoxically, the very elements that brought America into being (Lewis Mumford, *The Myth of the Machine, 23*).

In "A Song for Occupations," Whitman expresses his respect and affection for workers, whatever their trades and vocations, be they farmers, sailors, housewives, or teachers, be they poor or rich. In so doing, he dignifies and lends meaning to each type of undertaking.

> A song of occupations!
> In the labor of engines and trades and the labor of fields I find the
>   developments,
> And find the eternal meanings. (1:1)

Compassion and understanding flow forth from the idealistic poet's pen. While valorizing a variety of trades, he also seeks to instill in both the laborer and the employer a sense of fulfillment in the work accomplished, as well as a notion of equality and of virtue. Nevertheless, Whitman is not blind to the fact that money is the motivating power behind labor. Yet he strives for balance between need and greed, hoping to even out the disproportions inherent in a society in which moral citizens should become politically and economically involved.

The poet also opens his arms to embrace each individual who is not part of the conventional laboring society: a "degraded" criminal, a prostitute, an alcoholic, or a person who is diseased — no matter the condition. All are loved by him; all are his equals.

> Is it you that thought the President greater than you?
> Or the rich better off than you? or the educated wiser than you? (1:22)

Nevertheless, Whitman's main object in this poem is to show his reader the greatness of a democratic land by singing his appreciation of workers and their work. To achieve the desired effect, he again has recourse to his cataloging strategy. The intensification and slackening of rhythms and parallelisms imbue the stanzas with a strangely — almost frighteningly — realistic, frenetic quality, implicit in an expanding and evolving industrial age.

> Blacksmithing, glass-blowing, nail-making, coopering, tin-roofing, shingle-dressing,
> Ship-joining, dock-building, fish-curing, flagging of sidewalks by flaggers,
> The pump, the pile-driver, the great derrick, the coal-kiln and brick-kiln. (5:103)

The speedy staccato proliferation of Whitman's enumerations, accentuated by his expert use of harsh consonants, and other viscerally oriented aural devices, brings him to the twentieth even the twenty-first centuries. The caesuras, for example, in "Iron-works," forge-fires.... Oil-works, silk-works, white-lead-works" add a telegraphic quality to the stanza and the workplaces focused upon. Onomatopoeias, with their sibilants and palatals, underscore brutal and aggressive tones, identified with the physical power needed to perform such tasks as "stone-cutting" or "calking-iron." Alliterations of labials and gutturals intensify the nerve-racking atmosphere of harsh factory noises, as in "brewery, brewing... brewers, wine-makers," "Goods of gutta-percha" and "glazier, glue-pot." Anaphoras — "Stave-machines, planing-machines, reaping-machines, ploughing-machines, threshing-machines" — emphasize the continuous hours spent in a mechanical environment.

In his use of neologisms ("blacksmithing"), and slang ("gutta-percha"), Whitman sought to introduce street talk, everyday speech, thereby playing up his vision of an egalitarian society. The addition of ancient and recently invented aids to working people — "tools of the rigger, grappler, sail-maker, block-maker . . . veneer and glue-pot . . . awl; and knee-strap . . . stave-machines" — serves to unify disparate time sequences (past and present) in accordance with the continuous, cumulative, and progressive nature of human endeavor. The resulting stridulating and throbbing sonorities lend a hypnotic note to the poet's lines, as in concrete music, which carries the reader along in ascending and descending wavelike sequences. Not ideology is of import here, but the manner in which language is used to intensify the poet's emotional involvement with his medium, and by extension, the reader's.

Whitman's cataloging of trades and human activities in general may be said to parallel musical stanzaic patternings, which succeed in arousing profound responses in the poet/performer's reader/audience. Indeed, the entire musical dimension of "A Song for Occupations," replete with harsh and metallic, but also mellifluous and velvety instrumentations, adds to its symphonic power. Its cacophonous and harmonious score establishes a dichotomy of moods: stabbing or smooth ejaculations from the brasses are interwoven with deafening or pianissimo pitches by the tympanists, thus previewing concrete, rock, and electronic music played at high decibel range.

> All music is what awakes from you when you are reminded by the
>   instruments,
> It is not the violins and the cornets, it is not the oboe nor the beat-
>   ing drums, nor the score of the baritone singer singing his sweet
>   romanza, nor that of the men's chorus, nor that of the women's
>   chorus,
> It is nearer and farther than they. (4:94)

Never forgotten in a Whitman score, whatever the music, was the life of each worker within the collective: each viewed as significant, each as beautiful, despite the fact that society in Whitman's day was becoming ever more complex, with industry taking large leaps forward and sweatshop labor increasingly in demand. It was to the individual that the poet addressed his words of comfort.

Nevertheless, a power struggle between the poet and the impersonal strangers to whom he was singing his poem invited him to wield his verbal weapons forcefully — his goal being to assault and menace but also to seduce and convert all those who still remained oblivious to the greatness of human activity.

When introducing himself to the individual or the collective reader, the poet takes on the allure of a divinity, becoming all things to all people. To define himself in this manner enhances his self-image, assuring his audience of his desire and ability to respond to their needs.

> I bring what you much need yet always have,
> Not money, amours, dress, eating, erudition, but as good,
> I send no agent or medium, offer no representative of value, but offer
>   the value itself. (2:41)

What he also offers his followers is a passionate appreciation of the infinite multiplicity of life in all of its sensual and aesthetic delights.

> The sun and stars that float in the open air,
> The apple-shaped earth and we upon it, surely the drift of them is
>   something grand,
> I do not know what it is except that it is grand, and that it is
>   happiness (3:53).

Sufficiently secure in his ideations, particularly from his vantage point as a poet, Whitman now began to adopt an increasingly critical look at the new industrialized society. No longer the starry-eyed idealist, he had a growing awareness that led him to deprecate the routine and regimentation of the expanding bureaucracy, and to expose war, as the sham of a materialistic approach to life.

Whitman was not oblivious to the psychological dangers involved in the growing schism between the workplace and the home. Similar dichotomies existed in the political arena, between self-governing groups and a representative body. Although Whitman did not go so far as to subscribe to Rousseau's doctrine as expressed in his *Discourse on the Origin and Bases of Inequality among Men,* he did believe in balance in "our Union grand, and our Constitution grand" (3:74). Rousseau's simplistic generalizations suggested that man was born good and that physical inequality alone was present in primitive societies. Social inequality and corruption of all types arose after the division of labor and the concomitant industrialization in capitalistic societies.

What Whitman did see was that atomization of the *whole,* be it in industrial, technological, governmental, or aesthetic spheres, together with an increase in the complexities accompanying an expanding economic and social order was lending further divisiveness to the individual's sense of identity. No longer did he take pride in his achievements — since he was only a cog in what would later be termed the assembly line. Everything accomplished in the workplace, then, was becoming an impersonal act, a monetary transaction. Not that Whitman took umbrage at money-making activities, since a catalyst was needed to set societies in motion, but to be obsessed and enslaved by a desire for more and more wealth was to misplace values and obscure the larger picture.

Will the whole come back then?
Can each see signs of the best by a look in the looking-glass? Is there
    nothing greater or more?
Does all sit there with you, with the mystic unseen soul? (5:98)

No, there would be no return to the past, to the fantasized primitive society depicted by Rousseau, and mocked by Voltaire and
other eighteenth-century philosophes. Nor would an idealized society based on the ethics, equity, and spiritual values for which
Whitman longed come into being. Disheartened by what he considered to be the failure of the Democratic party's Free-Soiler elements,
and disenchanted by the defeat of the multiple European revolutions of 1848, Whitman reverted to the tried-and-true principles he
had held early in life. He embraced the belief that countercurrents
within the collective would rectify inherent imbalances: if individuals could be inspired to find their own groundbed and thus discover
feelings of serenity and leisure, such self-enrichment could lead to
emotional and spiritual regeneration of people throughout the land.

What is crucial to Whitman, then, is theorizing or *speculation* on
a variety of subjects. The use of the word *looking-glass* or mirror
(in Latin, *speculum*), as quoted above, identifies the object being
examined with the act and art of speculation, contemplation, and
understanding. The looking glass's glimmerings, radiant luminosities, scintillae, and sparks are equated by Whitman with wisdom
and intuition, not necessarily with learning. To look into the mirror
(into oneself), then, encourages cogitation and evaluation, thereby
shedding light onto the paradox of life itself, and one's role in the
earthly experience as individual and as a member of the community
at large. "Strange and hard that paradox true I give, / Objects gross
and the unseen soul are one" (5:98).

If money rules an existence and is not simply understood as a
source of revenue, Whitman intimates, it becomes as dangerous as
any extreme or any disruptive act that puts democracy at risk. In
"A Song for Occupations," he seeks to reinject in the individual the
notion of pride and joy in the work undertaken. No revitalization
will be forthcoming from books or in discussions, only in what is
"nearest, commonest, readiest" (2:48).

What the narrator offers his followers is a passionate appreciation of the infinite multiplicity of life in all of its sensual and
aesthetic manifestations. His invocation of the sun and stars, and his
well-turned imagistic epithet, "apple-shaped earth," bring to mind
the Garden of Eden, bearing its heavenly fruits on earth (3:33).

The ignorance characterizing those enjoying the paradisaic condition does not enter into the poet's concern; he focuses on the choice given to humankind after the eating of the fruit from the Tree of Knowledge. The Fall into earthly existence, with all of its glee and sorrow, engendered *differentiation* and *speculation* about all of life's variegated trades, institutions, and landscapes. Although the stamp of the individual may no longer be visible in the uniformity of production, it may be present in the mind of the person participating in the collective act.

> Will you seek afar off? you surely come back at last,
> In things best known to you finding the best, or as good as the best,
> In folks nearest to you finding the sweetest, strongest, lovingest,
> Happiness, knowledge, not in another place but this place, nor for
>   another hour but this hour. (6:136)

Dissociation and alienation exist on many levels in modern social orders, as they did in ancient ones, Whitman notes. So, too, do antipathies cohabit within an individual's psyche and between a citizen and his government, a worker and a corporation. By balancing out the negative with the positive elements in each case, a dynamism is engendered, as it also is in the poet's depiction of competition — the active desire for gain that pits one individual against another. This dynamism serves to increase "speculative" activities, be they in the stock exchange or in the philosophical, aesthetic, and religious sphere. Such drive compels people to work courageously and efficaciously in the building of a niche for themselves — and by extension, the nation. Potential is there for everyone: "In them the development good — in them all themes, hints, possibilities" (4:132). Concluding on a note of optimism, Whitman writes: "I intend to reach them my hand, and make as much of them as I do of men and women like you" (6:151).

7

Sea-Drift

Whitman's collection of poems entitled *Sea-Drift* (1881), focusing mainly on childhood reminiscences, indicated a need on his part to return to his early days the better to assess his present torments. To take stock of his problematic existence — especially questions revolving around sexual matters, periods of creative aridity, unhappy memories of his relationship with his father, and his overly close rapport with and dependency upon his mother — might, he felt, help heal his still-bloody scars. The process of allegorizing and symbolizing his inner dramas, as well as the recollecting of past scenarios, afforded him the possibility of glimpsing new and varied perspectives.

That both the "sea" and the need to "drift" had always played a significant role in Whitman's life is brought into evidence in the following passage in *Specimen Days*.

Even as a boy, I had the fancy, the wish, to write a piece, perhaps a poem, about the sea-shore — that suggesting, dividing line, contact, junction, the solid marrying the liquid — that curious, lurking something, (as doubtless every objective form finally becomes to the subjective spirit,) which means far more than its mere first sight, grand as that is — blending the real and ideal, and each made portion of the other. Hours, days in my Long Island youth and early manhood, I haunted the shores of Rockaway or Coney Island, or away east to the Hamptons or Montauk. Once, at the latter place, (by the old light-house, nothing but sea-tossings in sight in every direction as far as the eye could reach), I remember well, I felt that I must one day write a book expressing this liquid, mystic theme. . . .

There is a dream, a picture, that for years at intervals, (sometimes quite long ones, but surely again, in time,) has come noiselessly up before me, and I really believe, fiction as it is, has enter'd largely into my practical life — certainly into my writings, and shaped and color'd them. It is nothing more or less than a stretch of interminable white-brown sand, hard and smooth and broad, with the ocean perpetually, grandly, rolling in upon it, with slow-measured sweep, with rustle and hiss and foam, and many a thump as of low bass drums. This scene, this picture, I say, has risen before me at times for years. Sometimes I wake at night and can hear and see it plainly. (*Specimen Days*, I, 138)

Psychologists have identified the water element (in Whitman's case, the "sea") with the amniotic fluid of the uterus and with the collective unconscious. In that this element is associated with the mother, everything is said to exist in potential in this preformal, preconscious, and undifferentiated liquid. As such, water is viewed as the source of life, and therefore of continuous regeneration. The Greek philosopher Thales considered water the principle of all things. In creation myths, as depicted in *The Kalevala* (the Finnish national epic), in "The Drunken Ship" by Arthur Rimbaud, and in certain dramas of W. B. Yeats, water lends an aura of the eternal. Because water has the power to dissolve hard matter, it has been looked upon as an agent capable of liquefying solid problematic conditions; of solving otherwise impossible quandaries by breaking them up into their component parts. For Whitman, who responded so viscerally to the sea's personality — its turbulence as well as its calming and lulling movement — water seemed the perfect image for his poetic anamnesis.

"Drift," equally suitable to Whitman's psyche, suggests a rootless and constantly altering condition. Tramping, journeying, and changing scenes were the poet's natural condition. The personality of the wanderer, conveyed psychologically, may be associated with a weakly structured ego that allows itself to be carried along by a current, breeze, or tendency — aimlessly, without direction. Cut off, unfixed, alienated from self and society, the poet as he emerges in *Sea-Drift* is one who has neither been in touch with his groundbed nor has come to terms with his conflicts. Included in *Sea-Drift*, however, are some of his best-known and finest poems, "Out of the Cradle Endlessly Rocking," "As I Ebb'd with the Ocean of Life," and "Tears."

"Out of the Cradle Endlessly Rocking" (1859, 1881)

Autobiographical in content and operatic in structure, "Out of the Cradle Endlessly Rocking," inspired by Whitman's walks on the Long Island beach, begins with an overture/introduction, followed by a long act divided into sequences of arias and recitatives.

The curtains part in the spring: in the fifth month, as the Quakers referred to the month of May. Nature is awakening. The stage is set.

Up from the mystic play of shadows twining and twisting as if they
    were alive....
From the memories of the bird that chanted to me,
From your memories sad brother, from the fitful risings and fallings
    I heard....
From those beginning notes of yearning and love there in the
    mist....
I, chanter of pains and joys, uniter of here and hereafter,
Taking all hints to use them, but swiftly leaping beyond them,
A reminiscence sing. (6)

As the narrator regresses and scenes drawn from his lonely childhood pass in review, he seems to take on two personalities: "A man,
yet by these tears a little boy again" (18). The mature bard, the
poem's author, progressively flooded by the emerging image of the
boy he once was, lives out two identities.

With utmost maternal solicitude (emphasized by clusters of dependent phrases and clauses identified with the referent "I" [20,
29, etc.]) the fatherly man seeks to console the sensitive and deeply
distressed little boy. In so doing, he may believe he can help him
cope with his misfortune. Distinctions between youth and old age
give rise to particularly poignant moments — sometimes as obscure
projections, in other instances as strong imagings.

The mature poet now resurrects a specific sequence in his past: he
sees himself as a "curious boy" who has just discovered some mock-
ingbirds nesting nearby. Although intent upon peering into their
secret world, he is very careful not to disturb the family's joyous
harmony:

And their nest, four light-green eggs spotted with brown,
And every day the he-bird to and fro near at hand,
And every day the she-bird crouch'd on her nest, silent, with bright eyes,
And every day I, a curious boy, never too close, never disturbing them,
Cautiously peering, absorbing, translating. (27)

The mockingbird is soon to become the focus of the drama enacted.

The clarity and lyrical quality of Whitman's verbal tones, as these
resound in the following lines, shed an atmosphere of foreboding
and distress. So intense is the bird's melodious interlude, ranging as
it does from highs to lows, so gripping are the images accompanying
its performance, that it may be viewed as a poetic transliteration of
an aria from *La Favorita,* which Whitman heard in New York City
performed by the contralto Marietta Alboni. The continuation of

the mockingbird's warblings and threnodies might also have been inspired by and paralleled to the passionate tones of the famous tenor Allesandro Bettini, singing the male lead in the same opera. About him Whitman wrote:

His voice has often affected me to tears. Its clear, firm, wonderfully exalting notes, filling and expanding away; dwelling like a poised lark up in heaven; have made my very soul tremble. — Critics talk of others who are more perfectly artistical. But the singing of this man has breathing blood within it; the living soul, of which the lower stage they call art, is but the shell and the sham. (Holloway, *Uncollected Poetry and Prose of Walt Whitman*, I, 257)

That Whitman's mockingbird took on human dimensions is not surprising, given the number of allegorical birds appearing in religious as well as in literary texts throughout the centuries: the Egyptian Book of the Dead (Horus), the Ramayana (Garuda), the Koran (Ababil), and Attar's *Conference of the Birds* (Simorgh), the Song of Solomon, not to mention the writings of such poets as Robert Browning ("Home-thoughts, from Abroad"), Emily Dickinson ("No ladder needs the bird. . . . "), Alfred Lord Tennyson ("The Eagle"), and Alfred de Musset ("May Night"). The latter's depictions of the allegorical pelican, a personification of the suffering and alienated poet, whose sorrows are transformed into food by the creative individual, may be regarded to a certain extent as a precursor of Whitman's stanzas.

As the focus of "Out of the Cradle Endlessly Rocking" changes, the father mockingbird and his family take center stage. His joyful aria now rings with masculine bravura, confident as he is in a life that has brought him thrilling and unending romance.

> *Shine! shine! shine!*
> *Pour down your warmth, great sun!*
> *While we bask, we two together.* (32)

Naively, the father bird rhapsodizes over his mate in glowing sonorities — over their eternal passion for one another and the beauty of their young love.

> *Two together!*
> *Winds blow south, or winds blow north,*
> *Day come white, or night come black,*
> *Home, or rivers and mountains from home,*

> *Singing all time, minding no time,*
> *While we two keep together.* (35)

Soon we learn in the recitative that fate has stricken its blow —
cruelly, incisively, and without warning. The she-bird has vanished.
The crash of breaking waves accompanies the revelation of the
event; their hissing sounds, reverberating in the distance, preludes
the blackness of night enclothing an atmosphere of doom. The rising moon's soft glow has a calming effect on the raging undulations
of the ocean, but only for a moment, after which they break out
more formidably than before: "the hoarse surging of the sea" (48).
The sibilants in the just-quoted line underscore the bird's sorrow
and its rage over life's unwarranted cruelty.

The boy, identifying with the bird's lamentations, is encapsulated
in the drama. His loss of identity mystifies him; his loss of self-
control wipes away the rest of the world from his focus. Wrapped in
silence, he listens to the bird's threnodies, which are now his own.
Gone are his former childlike excitement, his bounding energy, his
carefree ways. Deeply sensitive, he feels *into* the bird's mourning
cries: *"Blow! blow! blow!"* it warbles, apostrophizing the wind,
begging it to blow his mate back to him (52). Night descends, the
most painful of hours, finding the bird alone on the dunes, still
intoning his cry of despair.

Transfixed, the boy listens in silence to the rhythms of the pounding waves, which once had — but no longer — a cradling effect on
him, like a mother rocking and cradling her baby in her ocean-
uterus. Has the seemingly endless body of water now become an
ocean-coffin? The bird continues his vocalizations in true Romantic style, allowing his feelings, but only momentarily, to be lured
into the pleasures of past times, into the oblivion of the water's now
lulling effect.

> *Soothe! soothe! soothe!*
> Close on its wave soothes the wave behind,
> And again another behind embracing and lapping, every one close,
> But my love soothes not me, not me. (71)

The drama intensifies as harsh sounds again burst forth, paralleling the crashing noise made by the "slapping waves." Every shadow
the bird sees in the distance, every form, every decoy, and breaker
tossing its spray, raises his hope of finding his mate. *"Loud! loud!*
loud! / Loud I call to you, my love" (81).

Loneliness spreads its darkness over his soul. Hope has dimmed, strength ebbed. Even his song seems useless now, merely a replication of his protracted loss. Reverting to the past, in mourning tones he resurrects joys gone by, increasing the urgency and amplitude of his cry, which flows forth into impassable space.

> *O past! O happy life! O songs of joy!*
> *In the air, in the woods, over fields,*
> *Loved! loved! loved! loved!* (125)

Even though the poet has now made it clear to his readers that the bird's mate is never again to appear, and only tragedy can be the outcome, the still-glowing embers of hope compel the lonely bird to chant his anguish to empty heavens and heaving seas.

All the while the child, standing near the shoreline, watches and absorbs the harrowing drama — his own by projection — before him. With a sinking heart, he "listen'[s] long and long" to the mournful melodies. A strident, ugly, and foreign note intervenes as the mysterious murmurings of the sea spell increasing despair for the boy. Listening intently, he hears, "With angry moans the fierce old mother incessantly moaning" (133). The crashing waves, the bursting whitecaps, the bold rhythms accompanying the litany of grief, suggest a ferocity inherent in mother/sea. The reader learns more about this intrusive power: "The strange tears down the cheeks coursing.... The undertone, the savage old mother incessantly crying" (140).

Is the "savage old mother" who emerges from the sea a death-dealing entity? Although the answer is not yet forthcoming, to increase the stress of the emotional recitative, the poet alters time and phonemic schemes. The mood of despair is prolonged and intensified by opting for present participles (*moaning, rustling*), groupings of long vowel sounds (*u, o, a, i*), nasals (*moan, moan, moon*), rhyme patternings, and frequent use of onomatopoeias to describe the boy's heartrending pain.

Only now does the mature man, who has been observing the lad's sorrow via his identification with the bird, *know* what he *felt* as a child. Bereft of the positive, loving, warm, and nutritive feminine element, as symbolized by the mockingbird's mate, the mature man had been left with a "fierce old mother," a "savage old mother," demanding, domineering, always moaning and crying, accounting perhaps for his present sorrow.

The love in the heart long pent, now loose, now at last tumultuously
    bursting,
The aria's meaning, the ears, the soul, swiftly depositing,
The strange tears down the cheeks coursing,
The colloquy there, the trio, each uttering,
The undertone, the savage old mother incessantly crying,
To the boy's soul's questions sullenly timing, some drown'd secret
    hissing,
To the outsetting bard. (137)

Who was this bird that grieved so deeply? "Demon or bird! (said
the boy's soul)," attempting as best he could to understand the
powerful empathy racking his being (144). The anaphoric repetitions of "never more" that follow are, to be sure, reminiscent of
Poe's bird in "The Raven," referred to as "Demon" or "fiend."
Identified with a malignant spirit or genii of sorts, Whitman's
mockingbird, while prolonging his grieving sounds, ceremonializes
them as well. Thus are they transformed into a series of rites and
solemn acts, in accordance with the bird's own religious rules and
observances.

Identities have blurred. The mature poet speaking through the
boy, with whom he now identifies, begins to realize that the bird's
tragic tale, to which he was so drawn years back, is his own.

Is it indeed toward your mate you sing? or is it really to me?
For I, that was a child, my tongue's use sleeping, now I have heard
    you. (145)

His years of sorrow have taught the poet humility. Nor is he
naive, as he had been as a child. Having resurrected the inner boy,
the mature man begins to understand, through that pure and un-
developed part of himself, that solitude as well as suffering may
be nutritive for a poet, may revive the urge to create. Having accepted the sorrows of his childhood and youth as his own, he
understands that these are instrumental in shaping his feeling and
thinking realms, thereby his creative world. He will not seek to escape distress. Rather, he will mold and craft his pain, as he feeds it
to his verbal construct. But what theme, emotions, and phrases will
he vocalize? "O give me a clew!" he asks (157). The answer:

A word then, (for I will conquer it,)
The word final, superior to all,
Subtle, sent up-what is it? — I listen;
Are you whispering it, and have been all the time, you sea-waves? (160)

Because he is no longer blind to the dualities of life, both torment and joy are imbricated on his verbal palette. Not one without the other. His art, he assures himself, will enable him to meld pain and happiness into the poetic process. In a touching and loving apostrophe to the bird, he says:

> O you singer solitary, singing by yourself, projecting me,
> O solitary me listening, never more shall I cease perpetuating you....(150)

The raw experiences of life, the mature poet has learned, must now be transformed into the work of art: the personal crises and the original sensations that had stirred both the young boy and the mature man must now be impersonalized. To verbalize *feeling* involves discipline, vision, and the ability to formalize the informal.

Only now is the presence and message of the "savage old mother" clarified for the mature poet.

> Lisp'd to me the low and delicious word death,
> And again, death, death, death, death,
> Hissing melodious, neither like the bird nor like my arous'd child's heart,
> But edging near as privately for me rustling at my feet,
> Creeping thence steadily up to my ears and laving me softly all over,
> Death, death, death, death, death. (168)

As previously suggested, the archetypal mother/ocean figure is identified with the unconscious. So demanding a parent may she have become that her impact on her son may have taken on "savage" proportions. In Whitman's case, his great attachment to his mother had transformed a positive into a negative power. Indeed, he even sought to play the "mother" to her, helping her financially and emotionally to care for his siblings. So incapable was he of breaking away from her that he never succeeded in cutting the umbilicus. For the poet and man, such attachment spelled death!

The poem's macabre poundings of incessant waves fiercely crashing are metaphors for the heaving pulsations emanating from Whitman's subliminal spheres, endlessly spelling out the same message. Whitman has succeeded in imbricating his invasive conflictual emotions into the work of art.

> My own songs awaked from that hour,
> And with them the key, the word up from the waves,
> The word of the sweetest song and all songs,

That strong and delicious word which, creeping to my feet,
(Or like some old crone rocking the cradle, swathed in sweet
    garments, bending aside,)
The sea whisper'd me. (178)

No longer only a threatening power at the poem's conclusion, the immortal mother/ocean has become a wondrously comforting force, a nurturer of life. She, who had brought the bard into the world, had also been the one to have stirred his poetic voice. Now she invites the poet to awaken to a new world. Strengthened by his newfound inner harmony, he finds himself able to compose his message of faith in his creative powers.

A. N. Whitehead, deeply impressed by "Out of the Cradle Endlessly Rocking," commented on Whitman's imaginative dimension:

One of the finest love poems in the nineteenth century, Whitman's Out of the Cradle Endlessly Rocking, is expressed in such an image as Darwin or Audubon might have used, were the scientist as capable of expressing his inner feelings as noting "external" events: the poet haunting the seashore and observing the mating of the birds, day after day following their life, could scarcely have existed before the nineteenth century.... Almost all the important works of the nineteenth century were cast in this mode and expressed the new imaginative range: they respected the fact: they are replete with observation: they project an ideal realm in and through, not transcendentally over, the landscape of actuality. (Lewis Mumford, *Technics and Civilization,* 332)

"As I Ebb'd with the Ocean of Life" (1860, 1881)

When Whitman wrote "As I Ebb'd with the Ocean of Life," he had just been dismissed (but, characteristically, first withdrew) from his editorial position on the *Brooklyn Times.* Jobless, and without prospects, he naturally felt mounting uncertainty as to his future course. Other torments also left him listless and despondent: increasing self-doubt about his worth as a poet; guilt with regard to his sexual proclivities and the intense joys experienced in his love affairs.

The word *ebb'd,* so well chosen by Whitman, refers not only to the tide flowing back to the sea, but also to emotional factors. The once-optimistic and dynamic Whitman of "Song of the Open Road" had receded, weakened, declined in spirit as well as in activity. The extremes of his mood swings had become so evident that they could have been measured in Faustian terms: "From the heights of jubilation to the depths of despair."

The metaphor of the ocean ebbing, in the poem's title, suggests that currents of formerly pulsating energy are now lying apathetically within the poet's depths. In contrast to the individual drop of water, the ocean represents universal existence: "the ocean of life," as it occurs and recurs endlessly in the influx and reflux of tidal rhythms. What has ebbed within the poet, then, is a sense of connectedness with life as a whole.

"As I Ebb'd with the Ocean of Life" opens as had "Out of the Cradle Endlessly Rocking" with the poet walking on the Long Island beach. Rather than spring (when the latter poem begins), when youth lives in hope and in the belief that life burgeons eternally, it is late autumn. Defoliation and the bleak coldness of winter, identified with old age, are to follow. As the poet observes the continuously mobile waters before him, he is mesmerized by their lilting "ripples," thus setting the stage for a pacific frame of mind, harmony of spirit in the never-ending serenity of the undulating surface movements of the water.

But is everything calm and pleasurable? In addition to the soft and even sounds of gentle and barely visible waves, the narrator hears ominous sonations as well. To be sure, the harsh, grating, hissing tones in such lines as "Where they rustle up hoarse and sibilant" suddenly alters, yielding to a comforting and pleasurable mood, but this mood in turn changes, and the reader hears "the fierce old mother endlessly cries for her castaways," already metaphorized in "Out of the Cradle." The reader is left with ambiguous, even conflictual feelings: the imaging of a violent, cruel mother screeching out her eternal pain and loss at the death of those very beings she has abandoned or destroyed in shipwrecks or drownings. Unlike the "angry moans the fierce old mother incessantly moaning" in the previous poem, the cries of the mother in "As I Ebb'd with the Ocean of Life," are without anger, a passive acceptance of divestiture. Only her mechanical, irrational cries, the narrator says, are heard beyond the din of the waves.

As the narrator continues his meditations, gazing at the autumn scene, his thought takes another turn.

> I musing late in the autumn day, gazing off southward,
> Held by this electric self out of the pride of which I utter poems,
> Was seiz'd by the spirit that trails in the lines underfoot,

> The rim, the sediment that stands for all the water and all the land
>   of the globe. (6)

Something has galvanized within the poet, empowering him to
"utter" his poems, to sing out their "spirit" rather than attempt
to understand their meanings rationally. Electrified by the water's
circular rhythms, images, and tonalities, the poet's eye movement
follows their flow. Observing the infinite expanses before him, while
encapsulating heavens and waters in one visionary experience, his
eyes drop to the "lines underfoot," markings left on the sand by
receding tides.

What remains of the water's impact? he asks himself. Are the
"rim" and "sediment" before him symbols of civilizations and individual existences long since dead? Are they not also comparable
to the narrator's past — his memories? They, too, come into being
following the to-and-fro movement of life's compositioning experiences. Aren't his creations, molded from these inner sands of time —
his time — his legacy to the world?

> Fascinated, my eyes reverting from the south, dropt, to follow those
>   slender windrows,
> Chaff, straw, splinters of wood, weeds, and the sea-glutten,
> Scum, scales from shining rocks, leaves of salt-lettuce, left by the
>   tide.... (I. 10)

The poet questions the nature of his legacy: made up of "windrows," a row of dry leaves, dust that has been swept together by
the wind; "chaff," threshed or winnowed husks of wheat, straw,
anything that is worthless; "splinters," thin sharp pieces of wood;
"weeds," uncultivated and useless plants. The alliterations of *scum,
scales, shining,* and *salt,* like *undertow,* seem to keep reinforcing the
poet's negative view of himself and man and artist. Is his gift merely
detritus; merely residue?

Whitman's metaphoric artifacts, when examined more closely,
may in reality be understood as positive entities, particularly if identified with nature's cyclicality: death and renewal. Windrows, chaff,
weeds, and the rest of the experiential assortment of organic matter Whitman enumerates, are nourishing factors, used to enrich the
earth, as every event enriches the poet's life. Considering them as
negative forces at the outset of the poem, the narrator now comes to
view them as charges capable of energizing his literary listlessness.

That the narrator chooses the "fish-shaped island" of Paumanok
for his walk is indicative of physical and spiritual fecundity. Fish,

identified with nutritive powers of the mind, is also associated with Christ because of the miracle of the loaves and fish (Matt. 14:19). Representing, therefore, inner riches, fish are instruments of regeneration, always altering in consistency, renewing in form, ready to nourish those who seek them out. While water is the habitat of the physical fish; this same entity, when associated with the unconscious, may also stand for unchanneled subliminal thoughts and feelings that feed the poet when erupting into consciousness. However, killer fish also inhabit the deep. The Leviathan mentioned in Job, the antithesis of light, lurks about in darkened subliminal realms: "Canst thou draw out leviathan with an hook? or his tongue with a cord which thou lettest down?" (Job 41:1). Psychologically, the Leviathan may be identified with the narrator's shadow: those elements inhabiting his unconscious, or inner ocean, which his ego (center of consciousness) and society look upon as unredeemed and unregenerate.

Mesmerized, electrified, by the thoughts the image of "sediment" has evoked in him, the narrator pursues his walk, singing his dirges for the dead, which involve not only his personal past, but also humanity's. The mystery of the life-death cycle and the secrets hidden within the uncreated poem haunt him, like so many sea-drifts washed up on the sand. In sequences of exciting alliterations, the narrator speaks of his awe:

> O baffled, balk'd, bent to the very earth,
> Oppress'd with myself that I have dared to open my mouth,
> Aware now that amid all that blab whose echoes recoil upon me I
>   have not once had the least idea who or what I am,
> But that before all my arrogant poems the real Me stands yet
>   untouch'd, untold, altogether unreach'd.... (25)

"Baffled," but also "oppress'd" by his former arrogance, the bard is diminished by an overpowering sense of his smallness: "I perceive I have not really understood any thing, not a single object, and that no man ever can" (32). His self-interrogation, although veiled, takes on momentum as the narrator digs deeply into himself, despite his fear of society's "ironical laughter" that might follow any confession of his sinful sexual ways and pretensions as a poet.

"Because I have dared to open my mouth to sing at all" he suffers those Shakespearean "slings and arrows" of destiny (32). Deflated, he nevertheless understands that the wounds of life, painful as they are, have deepened his vision into himself. Aware of the existence of two *Me's* in himself — his *persona* (or social mask, the face worn for his readers and family) and his *underlying Me* (invisible to the world and unknown to himself until now) — he senses a way of cohabiting with them in the poetic process. By delivering up the sediment within the archaic part of himself, he will not only be lending depth to his poetry, while also increasing its turbulence, but will be exposing his wounds to a fresh lexicon of his own fashioning.

As the narrator apostrophizes the ocean, his pain takes on cosmic proportions: "We murmur alike reproachfully rolling sands and drift, knowing not why" (3:36). But rather than crushing him with its vastness and infinite energy, the ocean now paves the way for a mystical correspondence, lending his personal and ephemeral torment eternal and collective grandeur. He senses an affinity with the body of water before him: just as the ocean is driven to fulfill its destiny, so he, as poet, must write his song. Both the "trails in the lines underfoot" and the lines of the poem that these real trails also symbolize — "These little shreds indeed standing for you and me and all" — are meant to yield the meaning of their impress to the world (3:37).

In the harrowing conflict raging within the poet, fear of loneliness again arises, as does his yearning for love and understanding. His sense of deprivation encourages him to cry out for a father, although not necessarily for his own. Is it to God the Father, as remote and unfeeling as his own had been, to whom the poet addresses his pitiable words?

> I throw myself upon your breast my father,
> I cling to you so that you cannot unloose me,
> I hold you so firm till you answer me something.
>
> Kiss me my father,
> Touch me with your lips as I touch those I love,
> Breathe to me while I hold you close the secret of the murmuring I
>   envy. (45)

The love beseeched is not forthcoming. God or nature, personal or impersonal, is impassive. Nevertheless, the life experiences contained within the poet, like "little corpses," have, paradoxically awakened. He can speak his feelings — "my dead lips the ooze exuding at last" — in "prismatic colors glistening and rolling"; forever "buoy'd" from within by conflictual moods, forever invited to partake of "a dab of liquid or soil," from which he can fashion his work. Whether he sobs the "dirge of Nature" or the "blare of the cloud-trumpets," whatever "capricious" feelings take hold of him will be infolded in the written poem.

The interaction between past and present tenses in the various sections of "As I Ebb'd with the Ocean of Life" reinforces the continuity of the water image by yielding cyclicality to the poetic voice. Indeed, as manifested in the continuous nature of the act of writing and rewriting, of dredging up the sediment of each emotional reaction to a past event and segmenting it to a present experience, the poet's subliminal world, like the ocean floor, is home to infinite amounts of matter lying in its depths, although invisible to the naked eye. Glistening as it emerges, primal matter becomes the essence of the work of art.

"Tears" (1867, 1871)

Although the waters of "As I Ebb'd with the Ocean of Life" have diminished in extent, in "Tears" they have condensed in amplitude. The extraordinary interplay of light and blackness, of transparencies and opacities, in addition to the complex rhythmic effects, is masterfully accomplished in "Tears."

The drops that emerge from the narrator's eyes flow forth as tangible manifestations of emotional pain and then evaporate, but like the inner layers of the palimpsest, although they are invisible they retain their vigor. Parallelisms between these tears and the "dripping" waters "suck'd in" by the sandy "white shore" emerge in all of their saltiness. Unlike brilliant stars, constellations symbolizing the source of light and intuition as set against a blackened night, they emerge from the remote "dark and desolate" vault of a "muffled" mind/psyche. Multiple memories and buried events, like many "ghosts" lingering in the mind's eye, erupt into present time schemes, like a "shapeless lump" the poet might have seen "crouch'd there on the sand."

As the drama becomes increasingly poignant, rhythms accelerate via Whitman's expert use of multiple caesuras placed between each cry, increasing in diapason and stridulence. Like a breaking storm, the tonalities, whimperings at first, burst forth into solo sobs, only to aggravate the emotional power of the sequence, now personified as "embodied, rising, careering with swift steps along the beach!"

Only at night, however, does the "wild and dismal night storm" give vent to its desperation. In contrast, the daytime persona is "sedate and decorous . . . with calm countenance and regulated pace." Severed from and antagonistic to one another are the narrator's personalities — depicted not as slumbering entities within the same soul (as in "As I Ebb'd with the Ocean of Life"), but as highly volatile powers inhabiting the same soul, and unloosening their gargantuan explosive anguish in the form of minuscule drops of liquid.

Thematically, Whitman's need to walk on a beach, there to recapture and perpetuate episodes in his past, was far from innovative. Romantic poets, such as Lamartine, Hugo, Wordsworth, Keats, Shelley, and so many more had all identified their emotions with a landscape. Nevertheless, Whitman's replay in free verse, divested of many traditional artifices, allowed his cadenced and measured lines to stress and thereby reactivate what had lain dormant in his subliminal spheres. Moreover, the mood of abandon in "Tears," resulting from his use of poetic modes to excite visceral contact with sand and sea, awakened him to a sensate world, allowing him to *feel* happenings rather than *think* them.

That Whitman chose the title *Sea-Drift* for his collection of eleven poems dealing with reminiscences suggests the crucial correspondence he felt between word as object, and word as replicator of inner feelings. His imagistic seas and oceans allowed him, at least temporarily, to free himself from increasingly mortifying terrors. To commune with nature, be it in terms of "sediment" left from a time past or other aspects of the seashore, allowed him to step out of his individual and mortal time scheme and leap into pleromatic spheres. Forever altering in form and consistency, in vision and perception, in thought and in feeling, the poet is that one who observes while absorbing; who dilates while diminishing — a paradox of multiplicity in oneness.

8

Autumn Rivulets

Although some of the poems included in *Autumn Rivulets* had appeared as early as 1855, the final edition published in 1881, comprised thirty-eight works. Gravely ill when composing *Autumn Rivulets,* Whitman was motivated to see it through in order to reiterate his undying faith in the future of America. Supportive of its "Modern Spirit" and of its "Kosmic Spirit," ready and able to "launch humanity into new orbits," he had a vision of the years to come that imbued him with strength and his poetry with purpose.

Whitman was aware of the symbolistic effect of the cluster's title. "Rivulets," streams or brooks that flow slowly in the "autumn" of life, he says in his preface, both suggest meanings and are at the origin of other meanings. One of the poems in this intriguing collection, "There Was a Child Went Forth," recalls the excitement as well as the trauma experienced by a child awakening into adolescence and maturity. Poems with a decidedly musical flavor — "Vocalism," "Italian Music in Dakota," "Proud Music of the Storm" — sweep readers into the tremulously beautiful world of America's vastness. "Passage to India" defines humanity's achievements in terms of larger cosmic purposes. A more esoteric work, "The Sleepers," deals with the fascinatingly mysterious world of the unconscious.

"There Was a Child Went Forth" (1855, 1871)

Whitman's autobiographical poem depicting his birth into consciousness, or the passage from childhood to maturity, takes on the stature of an archetypal awakening. On a universal scale, it suggests a replication of nature's own cyclicality: birth, growth, and decay. What adds to the poem's authenticity is its syntax and structure. The repetition of single words and catch phrases, and the cumulative power this and other rhetorical devices engenders, gives the impression that the technique *itself* was instrumental in liberating the poem's form and its thematics. The disclosures of childhood experiences written in free verse, for example, take on such fluidity that content and structure seem to meld together from the outset, each growing and gathering strength from the preceding line — as a plant takes life from its own roots. Instrumental in creating the above effect is the poem's stanzaic patterning: four, six, eight, three, eighteen — each cluster reflecting the child's halting, straining, growing, depleting, yet relentless need to cope with the difficulties involved in the maturation process.

While the narrator in the opening lines of the poem observes a lonely shore and countryside, a second image imposes itself: a child gazing at the beauty of the pristine landscape.

> There was a child went forth every day,
> And the first object he look'd upon, that object he became,
> And that object became part of him for the day or a certain part of
>   the day,
> Or for many years or stretching cycles of years. (1)

In keeping with the introductory lines, which set atmosphere and tone, Whitman builds on the idea of solitude, isolation, and love — for a world lying outside of the child's understanding. The unknown beckons to him, entices him to wander about, to begin to pick and choose rather than to accept everything in toto. Drawn to beings and things viewed around him, he reaches out to them with excitement. Rejoicing in the new sensations triggered by objects sequentially framed within his vision, he begins to identify with these novel entities.

> The early lilacs became part of this child,
> And grass and white and red morning-glories, and white and red
>   clover, and the song of the phoebe-bird....(5)

A double movement follows: the enumeration of flowers during the course of the child's discoveries and the poet's communication of the enrichment such joy afforded him. The child's growth during the bursting into bloom of nature suggests that animate and inanimate worlds are nourished by a subsoil common to both. No longer dominated by feelings of loneliness, the child now senses that he belongs to, and is an intrinsic part of, the earth's heritage.

Growing into awareness, the child slowly becomes conscious of his identity as an individual. In Whitman's Darwinian terms, he begins to ascend the ladder of evolution — "Or for many years or stretching cycles of years" — he progresses from an understanding of the inanimate world to an understanding of the human one (4). He is taken aback when he learns that although he is part of nature's world, he is no longer the center of the unlimited expanse before him. Centroversion has yielded somewhat to objectivity.

Fish suddenly come into view: "And the fish suspending themselves so curiously below there, and the beautiful curious liquid" (8), Representing fecundity, inner riches, instruments of regeneration, fish live, psychologically, like unformed thoughts, within the waters of the unconscious. Always altering in consistency, fish/thoughts may be understood as capable of nourishing those who seek them out. They rise from the sea as do ideas, sensations and inspiration, while also dredging up what some consider negative factors: unchanneled and unredeemed forces within the human being.

Enchantment grows as time passes, "the Fourth-month and Fifth-month." The child becomes aware of, and enumerates, other aspects of a bewitching environment:

> Winter-grain sprouts and those of the light-yellow corn, and the esculent roots of the garden,
> And the apple-trees cover'd with blossoms and the fruit afterward, and wood-berries, and the commonest weeds by the road....
> And all the changes of city and country wherever he went. (12)

But as he increasingly abandons narcissistic self-contemplation for a new process of mentation, he reaches out to a world of duality. As differentiation sets in, so, too, do comparisons. Linear and no longer solely cyclical time frames are manifest. In the face of these developments, the child, perhaps intimidated at first, experiences a sense of reserve and humility; deflation clouds the formerly ebullient atmosphere.

Sequences of parallel images and activities are enumerated concurrently with the growth of the child's ego (center of consciousness). Detaching himself little by little from the ever-expanding world before him, he continues along the path of his evolutionary process into manhood. Human and nonhuman factors are interwoven into the stanzas: the birth of the child from semen and ovum replicates the plant's development from the seed. The notion of life and death, metaphorized in the burgeoning, budding, and depleting process, takes on contour as inner and outer worlds unfold before the reader, expanding and contracting in dimension and in keeping with the rhythmic pattern of the individual scene and the intricate symphonic movement of the poem as a whole.

No longer the center of the world, and having distanced himself from the *oneness* he had known, the child observes that just as there are numerous varieties in nature (fruits, vegetables, flowers), there are many different types in the human domain (drunkard, schoolmistress, friendly or quarrelsome boy).

> And the old drunkard staggering home from the outhouse of the
>   tavern whence he had lately risen,
> And the schoolmistress that pass'd on her way to the school,
> And the friendly boys that pass'd, and the quarrelsome boys.... (14)

The child's own home is brushed into view, revealing a charming but painful portrait of family life.

> The mother at home quietly placing the dishes on the supper table,
> The mother with mild words, clean her cap and gown, a wholesome
>   odor falling off her person and clothes as she walks by,
> The father, strong, self-sufficient, manly, mean, anger'd, unjust,
> The blow, the quick loud word, the tight bargain, the crafty
>   lure.... (22)

Polarities take on substance as the personalities of mother and father subvert each other: the former all good, the latter, "mean, anger'd, unjust" (22, 24). No longer in the idyllic atmosphere of babyhood, the child faces an antagonistic home environment, which he as yet cannot fathom. Although awareness has expanded in objective areas, his relationship with his parents still remains subjective. Increased discernment takes time and trauma: evidenced when the child is able to probe the cutting edge of actions and reactions.

With "swelling heart," the reader understands the child's yearning for affection. Rather than being offered love, the emotionally troubled lad is plagued by "The doubts of day-time and the doubts of night-time" (27). Questions remain unanswered: "Whether that which appears so is so or is it all flashes and specks?" (28) Anxiety grows as uncertainties mount. What is he to make of the outside world: the countless people lining the streets, "the facades of houses, and goods in the windows" (31)?

Each step forward into the empirical world requires endurance, strength, and motivation. As the child assesses his observations, a panoply of animate and inanimate entities catapult into view: vehicles, ferries, schooners, waves cresting, clouds, the flying sea crows. No longer one-dimensional, each object takes on a variety of contours. Fear intrudes as the child, now a young man, becomes cognizant of the fact that social masks, worn by almost everyone, hide a whole shadowy and invisible dimension, perhaps even that fearful, insalubrious world of sexuality.

The joys and sorrows experienced by the lad in his initiatory process into manhood are accompanied by moods of inflation and deflation, frustration and exhilaration, each significant in his attempt to understand the ever-elusive world that he inhabits. Antithetical images, such as purity and mud, depict the difficulties with which the young man must contend. No longer living in a state of identification or dependency, nor rejecting the world for the pain he must endure, he understands that dichotomies are implicit in the life experience. "These became part of that child who went forth every day, and who now goes, and will always go forth every day" (39).

"Vocalism" (1860, 1881)

In Whitman's 1876 preface to *Leaves of Grass and Two Rivulets,* he says that thought, poetry, and melody possess "a certain fluid, aerial character, akin to space itself." Boundless, limitless, music extends in all directions — within or outside the human being. The *great* artist, then, has to descend into the deepest levels of his subliminal spheres and/or ascend to exterior climes, to the heights of the earth's atmosphere, to draw inspiration. Such duality — within and without — serves to catalyze a variety of moods and melodies, as well as to arouse unsuspected verbal combinations.

The title "Vocalism" suggests the poem's signifier: the voice used in speech or lyrics, in the art of singing exercises; in creating the poem. The voice, appealing to the most untutored, was a passion with Whitman even prior to his love affair with opera. Beginning his poem rather didactically, he instructs his readers on the importance of discipline and drive in the development of their vocal potential.

An advocate of vocal study by all Americans, not only singers, Whitman felt that the exercise of vocal cords, even if this comported only basic elements, had physical as well as psychological implications. It served to limber up the voice's melodious qualities and capacities while also inviting its timbre and speech patterns to evolve. The development of voice in general, he contended, effects an individual's personality and temperament.

What vocalism most needs in these States, not only in the few choicer words and phrases, but in our whole talk, is ease, sonorous strength, breadth, and openness. Boys and girls should practice daily in free loud reading — in the open air, if possible.... Open your mouth — sound copiously and often such rich sounds as *oi* and *wu* — let your organ sound loudly without screaming — don't specify each syllable or word, but let them flow — feel the sentiment of what you read or say, and follow where it leads. (Faner, 57)

The voice, as is true of any muscle, is not merely servant of the will, but, as mentioned above, acts and reacts in consort with the body and psyche. A potent emotional force, it works differently on different people: relieving some of personal anguish, helping others to accept certain unpalatable facts of life; such as the horrors Whitman had witnessed during the Civil War. That vocalizing may open an individual up to the influx of divinity is evident in such biblical texts as Exodus, Job, Psalms, Matthew, Acts, and Galatians — and in Whitman's case is a truism.

A bridge to the world, vocal music transcends the rational domain. Striking a powerfully responsive chord in the sensitive individual that Whitman was, it accounted in part for the excessively musical quality of his work. "O what is it in me that makes me tremble so at voices?" (2:12).

Wasn't it the voice of William D. O'Connor, one of Whitman's earliest literary friends, that first endeared him to the bard? "He was a gallant, handsome, gay-hearted, fine-voiced, glowing-eyed man," Whitman wrote (*PW*, I, 690). Indeed, Whitman frequently judged an individual's personality by his voice's tonal qualities.

To be born with a beautiful voice is not sufficient, Whitman emphasized. "Where is the practis'd and perfect organ? where is the develop'd soul?" (2:17). Voice must be studied in the same way as poetry: range, modulations, nuances, and impact must be perfected. Singers — like poets in the process of creating — must not only listen to their heartbeats, but to the potent or latent resonances within the caverns of their subliminal realms.

"Italian Music in Dakota" (1881)

Although Whitman never traveled to the Dakotas, he did commemorate his affective reactions to a musical event in "Italian Music in Dakota." Whether the poem's genesis was in a concert he heard by the "Seventeenth Regimental Band" or in some similar musical entertainment, his involuntary recall system was aroused. Chantings of long-since-vanished peoples and cultures also emerged into the poet's mind and psyche, along with his own memories of such lyrical scores as Bellini's *La Sonnambula* and *Norma*.

"Through the soft evening air enwinding all, / Rocks, woods, fort, cannon, pacing sentries, endless wilds" (1), speaks to him directly and in moving terms. A world of concretion awakens to the poet, as it had for Orpheus centuries earlier.

As the music's melodious progressions flow into Whitman's lines, infiltrating body and psyche, they affect his every fiber with their "sounds, echoes, wandering strains," endowing him with a sense of belonging both to himself and to the cosmos.

"Proud Music of the Storm" (1869, 1881)

Reminiscent of Beethoven's thunderous storm sequence in his *Pastoral Symphony,* Whitman's "Proud Music of the Storm" also recapitulates an archetypal vision of nature in the process of unleashing its furious winds and rain. During the unfolding drama, objects are both abstracted and concretized, enabling the viewer to experience viscerally a panoply of vicissitudes.

As if preluding such tone poems as Richard Strauss's *Death and Transfiguration,* Whitman orchestrates the fluctuating and rhythmical nuances during nature's "music of the storm." Readers grow increasingly receptive to the tempest's blusterings, both near and distant, as well as to the under- and overtones imbricated into his poetic structure. Onomatopoeias transform sound into sight, filling the emotional landscape with strident, hissing, thunderous claps as well as mellifluous sonorities: "whistling across the prairies," the "hum of forest tree-tops," the "sounds of distant guns with galloping cavalry," "bugle-calls," "roar of pouring cataracts," "galloping cavalry." While dim and hidden shapes fuel the scene, appearing as individual "phantoms" and undulating in chaotic rhythmic formations, they are, like a giant conflation, perfectly orchestrated in the text: "Blending with Nature's rhythms all the tongues of nations" (1:6).

Passing from objective to subjective mode, Whitman speaks of "entering my slumber-chamber," not alone, but accompanied by a variety of music: marriage marches, love duets, dirges, festive sequences, played by flutes, harps, drums, organs, violins, or other instruments. Multiple centuries, each introducing their most popular types of performers, make their way into the lyrical interludes, inviting minnesingers, minstrels, troubadours, and operatic voices to vocalize their feelings:

> The players playing, all the world's musicians,
> The solemn hymns and masses rousing adoration,
> All passionate heart-chants, sorrowful appeals,
> The measureless sweet vocalists of ages....
> A new composite orchestra, binder of years and climes, ten-fold
> renewer....(41)

Music bursts forth from all quarters of the verbal scape, and "every instrument in multitudes" fills the atmosphere, regaling readers with heteroclite sonorities, linking them to earth and Heaven, binding them to liquids and solids, to evanescent fire and air.

The impress of vastness gives way to an individualized vision. The poet recalls the serene music he had heard as a child: "My mother's voice in lullaby or hymn" (3:61). Comforting, soothing, and nurturing, her tones, antithetical to that of the storm, are the ones for which he longs. "(The voice, O tender voices, memory's loving voices, / Last miracle of all, O dearest mother's, sister's, voices)" (63). Virtually divinized, this distilled motherly voice emanating from within and without the poet, and now diffused into the cosmos by organic and inorganic nature, has become embedded into the stanzas themselves.

Music, for Whitman, was a means of reentering *primal oneness:* of taking him out of the anguished world of the adult. The power of melody may be interpreted psychologically, as the poet's way of gaining reentry into the birth canal, thereby divesting himself of the world of conflict. Tone, sonority, rhythm, vocalization, allowed him to be welcomed, warmed, and embraced by not only his personal mother, but his collective mother as well: singer of nature's musical language.

Returning to his objective narrative, Whitman enumerates operas — *Norma, Lucia di Lammermoor, Ernani, I Puritani, La Favorita, La Sonnambula, Lucrezia Borgia, Faust, William Tell, Huguenots, Don Juan* — emotionally stirring in their tragic intensity. Orchestrated religious compositions — Rossini's *Stabat Mater,* Haydn's *Creation* — also inspire him to compose.

"Passage to India" (1871, 1881)

That Whitman again broached the thematics of death in "Passage to India," when believing himself close to his end, may serve to explain his inclusion of the word *passage* in the poem's title. *Passage,* suggesting an initiation ritual — a journey from one sphere of being to another — sets the tone for his own experience: the death of his profane and temporal self and the rebirth of his eternal aspects in his poetry.

Initiation ("to go within") amounts to a descent into Self (total psyche; psychologically speaking, an equivalent of God): the passing from one level of consciousness to another. Such a *katabasis* empowered Whitman to reconnect not only with his own past, but, concomitantly, with humanity's primordial existence.

In place of the ebullience and sensuality of Whitman's early poems, "Passage to India" creates a more intellectual and studied Apollonian climate, the fervor of youth having diminished. Although this later poem is replete with images and symbols that were used more effectively in previous poems, its philosophical exegesis is of interest because of Whitman's belief in a "cosmic purpose" and in humanity's higher destiny. In a very modest way, "Passage to India" could be compared to some of Victor Hugo's epic visions in *The Legend of the Centuries* (1859), a body of poems narrating worldly events from biblical to democratic times, within the framework of great civilizations.

Unlike Hugo's vast apocalyptic work, however, Whitman's single poem begins not with the past, but with the "great achievements of the present." Proudly, the American poet iterates the possibilities of increased trade through better communication, namely, the establishment of the transoceanic cable (1866), the transcontinental railroad (1869), and the Suez Canal (1869). These achievements have served to link Africa, Europe, America, and Asia, thereby spanning both time and space, thus indicating "God's purpose from the first" (2:31).

Like many of Hugo's poems in *The Legend of the Centuries,* Whitman's "Passage to India," is a deeply spiritual document, an enunciation of his faith in a providential cosmic force present in the mystery called life. Utopianism, as previously indicated, also marked Whitman's and Hugo's points of view. Scientific, technical, and industrial advances were considered harbingers of future progress, both with regard to democracy and the peace and freedom that would ensue with this form of government.

Bleak and dark times are not considered by Whitman to be wholly negative. Rather, they are nurturers of the modern world of *light*.

The Past — the dark unfathom'd retrospect!
The teeming gulf — the sleepers and the shadows!
The past — the infinite greatness of the past!

> For what is the present after all but a growth out of the past?
> (As a projectile form'd, impell'd, passing a certain line, still keeps on,
> So the present, utterly form'd, impell'd by the past). (I:10).

The word *projectile* includes both the notion of "project," an undertaking or action planned for some future time, and the image of something thrust or hurled forward. The latter interpretation may also be envisioned as an icon: a metaphor for an instrument used to penetrate or open onto a lighted area, such as thought and or creativity. A "projectile," then, may be understood as something that helps clarify what lies in darkness. In that it also serves to penetrate a space/time continuum, "projectile" allows the poet to experience the simultaneity of past, present, and future.

Whitman's broad-swept allusions to myths, legends, religions, and historical facts from Asia, Africa, Europe, and America come as no surprise. "The deep diving bibles and legends, / The daring plots of the poets, the elder religions" (2:22). Also enumerated in the poet's visions are sequences of juxtapositions in time: historical facts presented alongside modern achievements.

> I see in one the Suez canal initiated, open'd,
> I see the procession of steamships, the Empress Eugenie's leading the
>   van....
> I pass swiftly the picturesque groups, the workmen gather'd.
> The gigantic dredging machines (3:43).

A double image comes into focus as Whitman plays out his roles of narrator and observer of the speeding Pacific railroad. While eye contact with the train is maintained as it spans an entire continent, the observer/narrator is outside the train, and he sees it and the landscape through which it passes as forever altering in form and contour. Moments later, however, one finds him within the mobile train as it rushes along the expanses of land. The accelerated movement through time and space, as experienced from both within and outside the train, enables the observer/narrator to penetrate the transpersonal fourth dimension, thus giving the impression of transcendence. Not only are "the three or four thousand miles of land travel" bridged, but iconographically, the poet has also linked "The road between Europe and Asia" (3:64).

Entering the realm of history once again, Whitman calls upon the "Genoese," Christopher Columbus, who, though searching for a passage to India, came upon America. Fame, but also "dejection, poverty, death," followed. Nevertheless, his dreams had been realized in a wholly unexpected and spectacular manner: he had helped humanity circumnavigate the globe. Vasco da Gama and other heroic sailors and captains are also called upon by Whitman — "down the slopes, / As a rivulet running" (4:72) — to substantiate his thesis of progress. Wanderers all, "yearning, curious, with restless explorations" they were the ones who made it possible to "Alternate light and day and the teeming spiritual darkness" (5:84).

Great discoverers, be they explorers, scientists, chemists, geologists, ethnologists, inventors, or creative spirits in the arts, were and are forever sounding out theories, beliefs, and faiths, *querying* always:

> With questionings, baffled, formless, feverish, with never-happy hearts,
> With that sad incessant refrain, *Wherefore unsatisfied soul? and Whither O mocking life?* (5:91)

For Whitman, "the true son of God" is no longer Christ, but "the poet [who] shall come singing his songs" (5:105). Binder of time and space, as well as of purpose; the poet is the recorder of the evolutionary process; the singer of the great epics and spiritual lessons of the past.

Guiding his readers across vast landscapes and time schemes, the observer/narrator points to the Caucasus, "soothing cradle of man," to the Euphrates, to the Indus and the sacred waters of India's Ganges, where "primal thought" originated. Cultures are also revisited: those of China, Persia, Arabia, Bengal; heroes are likewise enumerated: Alexander the Great, Tamerlane, Marco Polo, Batouta "the Moor"; as are deities, philosophers, and religious figures and texts: Brahma, Buddha, the Vedas. Heroes, those restless and "repressless" souls, are all subject to "slander, poverty, death" (6:161). Yet each, "full of the vastness of Space," surges forth on his own "Passage to India" — through the trinity of sequential spheres of "Time and Space and Death" (8:207).

Imbricated within the poem, and adding to its frenetic and all-encompassing climate, are the elements — fire, air, earth, and water — working as catalysts, enabling the observer/narrator to bathe, breathe, walk, and burn in God's mystery. As a "moral spiritual fountain," Deity has given the observer/narrator the love and affection forever wanting in his life, thereby leading him to his spiritual center: "mightier centre of the true, the good, the loving" (8:197).

Although the observer/narrator's "passage," or initiation, has been completed, still "blood burns in my veins!" In a desperate apostrophe he speaks out, in terms reminiscent of Charles Baudelaire's poem "The Voyage," when, at the end of life's trajectory, the Captain, a personification of Death, says "It's time! hoist the anchor!" So Whitman urges the restless, dissatisfied soul-force within his psyche to carry him into his own inner seas:

> Away O soul! hoist instantly the anchor!...
> Sail forth — steer for the deep waters only....
> O farther, farther, sail! (9:243)

The epic quality of the early stanzas of "Passage to India" projects a vision of a united world flying the banner of democracy and equality. By way of contrast, the last sections, particularly the bard's invocation to his soul, affirm his personal yearnings. The finale, a Hegelian dialectical synthesis, binds history, geography, and time/space in one conclusive vision. A need to forge ahead and pierce life's mysteries emerges; for the struggle to clarify its enigmas and to chant its conflictual "passages" is what yields the poet the most intense joy. It is at such crossroads that the crucial dialogue between him and his beloved soul — his inspiration — takes root ("O soul thou pleasest me, I thee") and the actual poem is able to be written (8:184).

"The Sleepers" (1855 1881)

One of Whitman's most fascinating poems, "The Sleepers," recounts his journey into subliminal spheres. Richard M. Bucke, one of his earliest biographers, and himself a psychologist, indicated that "The Sleepers" was a meticulous

representation of the mind during sleep — of connected, half-connected, and disconnected thoughts and feelings as they occur in dreams, some commonplace, some weird, some voluptuous, and all given with the true and strange emotional accompaniments that belong to them. Sometimes (and these are the most astonishing parts of the poem) the vague emotions, without thought, that occasionally arise in sleep, are given as they actually occur, apart from any idea — the words having in the intellectual sense no meaning, but arousing, as music does, the state of feeling intended. (*Norton Anthology,* 424)

Considered somewhat "surrealistic" because of the catapulting and seemingly irrational nature of the images, "The Sleepers" depicts, with ostensible freedom and abandon, the peregrinations of a dreamer's dream. Autobiographical in essence, the poem discloses the joys and sufferings of a sensitive young man whose sexual proclivities, unbeknownst to him at the outset of the poem, become increasingly clear during the course of his visionary expeditions. While subjected to the desolation of the pariah, he also celebrates, both viscerally and aesthetically, the intense pleasures gleaned when gazing upon and palpating a body beautiful.

Other factors intrude. The dreamer bonds with the mother figure, who, creating a symbiotic relationship with the lad, imprisons him in her world, and thus he experiences her as a destructive force. Themes of parting and of death, rejection and love, interwoven in the fabric of the poem, are poignantly dramatic.

As the poet recapitulates the happenings during periods of reverie and stress, gazing at the throngs of images flashing forth, he suddenly loses hold, and confusion mounts.

> Stepping with light feet, swiftly and noiselessly stepping and stopping,
> Bending with open eyes over the shut eyes of sleepers,
> Wandering and confused, lost to myself, ill-assorted, contradictory,
> Pausing, gazing, bending, and stopping. (1:2)

The dreamer's unordered rovings, rather than offering serenity, security, and enrichment, create chaos, disorientation, and loss. The atmosphere of solemnity permeating the sleeper's world instills feelings of anxiety and fear. In an ontogenetic descent through the space/time continuum, the poet follows his own return to childhood, pausing every now and then to observe outward earthly realms: for example, children with whom he identifies.

> How solemn they look there, stretch'd and still,
> How quiet they breathe, the little children in their cradles. (1:6)

As the poet continues descending into his earliest life, he experiences the original stage of primal oneness prior to the birth of consciousness, but the expected harmonious interaction with nature does not come to pass. The troubling impress of the dreamer's natural inclinations indicates a difficult course ahead. Plagued with frustration, heteroclite images parade before him: lives wasted in boredom, drink, insanity, perversion; the "sick-gray faces of onanists"; corpses spread over battlefields. Happier visions are also visible: married couples in their beds, "he with his palm on the hip of the wife, and she with her palm on the hip of the husband"; sisters sleeping together "lovingly"; mothers with their babies; and men "lovingly side by side" (1:11).

Pausing, gazing at these figures, the poet longs to make their idyllic existences his own. Instead, he stands alone. "I stand in the dark with drooping eyes by the worst-suffering and the most restless" (1:23). That he stands "in the dark" and "with drooping eyes" suggests the sorrow of the onanist. Masturbation, considered an overwhelming and debilitating problem in Whitman's day, could only be mentioned in secret, never in public; nor ever clarified or explained. Unable to open his eyes onto the subject, he finds himself incapable of becoming enlightened about the problem. As long as the act of masturbation is "imprisoned" within him, closeted in his shadowy world of thoughts, he can neither be vilified for indulging in it, nor considered a social outcast.

Whitman's use of the hand image — "I pass my hands soothingly to and fro" — is significant (1:24). Like a child's pacifier, repeated rhythmical massagings yield pleasure and soothe disquietude — but only momentarily, since the terrifying fear of divine retribution is forever present. Nevertheless, the sleeper's admission of guilt for the erotic pleasures visited upon him after ejaculation has served to liberate him for the time — thereby amplifying the observer/dreamer's vision. Facades have been shorn. As God uttered "It was good," following nearly each of his creative acts in Genesis, so Whitman enumerates the changes that have come over him during his subliminal and paradoxically light-bringing trajectory.

> Now I pierce the darkness, new beings appear,
> The earth recedes from me into the night,
> I saw that it was beautiful, and I see that what is not the earth is
> beautiful. (1:26)

No longer living in a *participation mystique,* the observer/dreamer, having passed beyond the womblike security of the infant, understands the difficulties involved when forced to cope with multiple as well as conflictual situations. He knows the meaning of agonizing over choices to be made and consequences to be expected. No longer the passive observer who lives in fear of isolation, the poet, having experienced sexual fulfillment, having accepted his sexual proclivities, seeks to begin playing an active and positive role in the workaday world — as healer.

Like the sages or the medicine men in shamanistic and tribal communities, or doctors in modern societies, the observer *knows* that experience, in addition to his natural empathetic personality, has enabled him to gain insight into the world of others and, concomitantly, into his own. So close does he feel to suffering, particularly that of the war victims to whom he devoted so many years, that he has come to absorb their visions — making them his own. No longer harboring feelings of rejection, nor obsessed with destructive notions of guilt, he claims, like the clairvoyants and telepathists, to be able to penetrate into the thoughts of others, while also propelling his own into their soul/psyches.

Transference has come to pass, and with it, a loss of identity on the healer's part. The qualities he observes in others, responsive to an inner need, now exist in himself: subject and object have blended into one. That an ever-increasing diminution of the sleeper's identity follows is not surprising, energy having flowed from subject to object: projection to recollection. Divested of feelings of anxiety and self-deprecation, the former pariah is ready to live life with abandon: "I am a dance — play up there!" (1: 32). Having shed his Apollonian stance, he now enclothes himself in Dionysian revels: "I am the ever-laughing — it is new moon and twilight" (1:32).

Not only the healer of others, he becomes the healer of his own wounded psyche. Liberated from the sexual ban — and concomitant banishment — he is free at last, like Faust, to enjoy the pagan, unchristian pleasures of the Walpurgisnacht. "Onward we move, a gay gang of blackguards! with mirth-shouting music and wild-flapping pennants of joy!" (1:40). Reminiscent of the lusty Greeks and Romans, the observer/dreamer, be he of the working class or any other, will initiate the adolescent into a world where nothing is relegated to darkness or secreted in shame (1:36). Every crease of the body beautiful, be it that which lies in darkness or in light, will be exposed for every eye to see. No longer eliciting torment, it will invite merriment, joy, ecstasy.

Liberated from constraints, so long as he lives out his transference and remains the healer of multitudes, contentment flows into the dreamer/observer's being. That "I reckon I am their boss and they make me a pet besides" (1:38) introduces yet another note into the observer/dreamer's scenario. Now that he feels that all beings exist within him, he experiences an even greater dissolution of the ego. "I am the actor, the actress, the voter, the politician, / The emigrant and the exile, the criminal that stood in the box" (1:42). Shifting from the *one* to the *atomized* personality has allowed him to depart from the world of sorrow into one of festivity. Important in the alteration of focus is his newly acquired ability to shed sexual identity. Now that *he* has become *she*, the dreamer has succeeded in divesting himself of the last vestiges of constraint. Delirium follows. "I am she who adorn'd herself and folded her hair expectantly, / My truant lover has come, and it is dark" (1:46).

Yearning for so long to play the passive role in a love relationship, with the complicity of "darkness," now a protagonist, the dreamer's wish has been fulfilled: he *is* loved and *is* fondled. Even more affable and bountiful in his womanly ways than as the masculine lover he once had been, he apostrophizes night, his perfect mate: "Darkness, you are gentler than my lover, his flesh was sweaty and panting, / I feel the hot moisture yet that he left me. / My hands are spread forth, I pass them in all directions" (53).

Darkness is seduction and comfort. It is also a return to pre-consciousness: the world prior to sex differentiation — before the instigation of social taboos. All is acceptable in this homoerotic and heteroerotic sphere. Soothing pleasures, his only values now, encourage the observer/dreamer to penetrate ever more deeply into this wondrous subliminal world. Instinctively, darkness directs his hand, paving the way for the orgasm and ecstasy in ejaculation. The "heart-beat" follows the body's rhythms, intensifying that moment sublime, which then fades into oblivion (1:59).

Hands, conveyors of the observer/dreamer's thoughts, are also enactors and promulgators of desire. It is they, therefore, that dominate a situation; they that perform the work; they that intervene or refrain from so doing; they that transform the uncreated desire or need into the manifested act. The hand, as used by men of the cloth, blesses as well as condemns; heals as well as sickens; protects as well as destroys. Whitman, who refers to it frequently in this and other poems, approaches it, under the cloak of darkness, as performer of the sexual ritual. Hidden from the light of reason, sexuality's arch-executioner, the hand functions efficaciously in tenebrous regions, inviting the observer/dreamer to touch, feel, enter into physical contact with others.

No sooner does the observer/dreamer awaken from his trance and return to the reality of his act than he suffers anew from guilt and fear: "I descend my western course" (2:60). Darkness's antagonist, daylight, accompanied by linear time, has entered into the picture. The truth of the present appears. No longer young and vibrant, he now sees himself as old, his "sinews flaccid," his male or female "face yellow and wrinkled" (2:62). What remains? A morbid fear of death.

> A shroud I see and I am the shroud I wrap a body and lie in the coffin,
> It is dark here under ground, it is not evil or pain here, it is blank here, for reasons. (2:67)

Death, now equated with darkness, may lead to the poet's salvation. Not unlike Emily Dickinson in thought, although antipodal to her dense, taut style, Whitman's observer/dreamer also experiences himself lying in his coffin and looking out at the living. No longer participating in earthly events, he now has fantasies that revolve around death. He first sees himself as a youthful Promethean — a "beautiful gigantic swimmer swimming naked through the eddies of the sea" — whose undaunted sexual energy seems unlimited. But death, having claimed this youth in a shipwreck — "his beautiful body is borne in the circling eddies, it is continually bruis'd on rocks" — has transformed him into a corpse. "Swiftly and out of sight is borne the brave corpse" (3:80). Death also dominates the sequences to follow, including mention of the slaughter of countless young men during Washington's defeat in the battle of Brooklyn Heights; of the killings "of the southern braves" during the Civil War.

Separations of all types are painful, as attested to by the story the poet's mother had told him about a beautiful Indian squaw who visited her home when she herself was just a child.

> My mother look'd in delight and amazement at the stranger....
> The more she look'd upon her she loved her,
> Never before had she seen such wonderful beauty and purity. (6:106)

Saddened by the squaw's departure, the observer/dreamer's mother yearned in vain for the return of this national icon. Although the vignette related was personal, it had vast implications: her disappearance signaled the loss of America's indigenous heritage. Empathizing with his mother's sense of bereavement after the Indian woman's departure, the poet feels a vacuum in his own life, resulting perhaps from a familiar feeling of deprivation caused by his mother's inability to give him love, and his father's hostility.

The poet's sense of helplessness and frustration, as disclosed in "The Sleepers," may be transformed into revelry and fulfillment in the dream, as well as in the work of art that is the poem. Inner chaos and frustration, guilt, and the tremulous fear of angering and disappointing those around him have led to a reconciliation — in the verbal domain — with what society labels the dark side of a personality: those turbulent instinctual powers. The poet, now able to live in reality, discards the wishful-thinking worlds delineated in religious texts. No longer does he expect to experience an ordered universe with God seeing to it that everything is in its place, as Descartes and Newton had proclaimed: a message that is so often given to assuage the fears of the gullible. What is to be humanity's fate? "The twisted skull waits, the watery or rotten blood waits" (7:157). Relief from protracted anguish may occur when gazing upon the exquisiteness of the body. "The sleepers are very beautiful as they lie unclothed, / They flow hand in hand over the whole earth from east to west as they lie unclothed" (8:162).

Earthly nights, equated with vast and dimensionless dream-worlds, alone help alleviate life's sorrows: "I stay a while away O night, but I return to you again and love you" (8:178). Embedded in the poet's underground repository are the not yet burgeoning seeds of creativity — where the unknown is transformed into the known by the wizardry of the artist's genius.

When at the poem's conclusion the sleeper finally returns to the daylight realm with all of its inconsistencies and sorrows, and utters, "I will duly pass the day O my mother, and duly return to you," he reveals a still-unhealed wound — an inability to deal openly with torment (8:185). As an infant sucks on the pacifier, he finds solace only in a restoration of the infantile mother/son bonding.

Deservedly admired for Whitman's innovative journey into a dream state replete with free associations, "The Sleepers" anticipates, on some levels, James Joyce's stream-of-consciousness style: the poet leading the reader into the heart of his own oedipal narcissistic drama.

PROSE

Begin my visits among the camp hospitals in the army of the Potomac.... Out of doors, at the foot of a tree, within ten yards of the front of the house, I notice a heap of amputated feet, legs, arms, hands, &c., a full load for a one-horse cart. Several dead bodies lie near, each cover'd with its brown woolen blanket. In the door-yard, towards the river, are fresh graves, mostly of officers, their names on pieces of barrel-staves or broken boards stuck in the dirt.... No cots [in the hospital], seldom even a matress. It is pretty cold. The ground is frozen hard, and there is occasional snow. I go around from one case to another. I do not see that I do much good to these wounded and dying; but I cannot leave them.

— *Specimen Days*

9

"Few of Life's Days Are Ever Noted"

Although Whitman is best known as a poet, some of his prose works, *Democratic Vistas* and *Specimen Days and Collect* in particular, are outstanding for their esthetic, historical, and cultural worth. Specific passages in the latter-mentioned volume are so lyrical in quality and rhythmic in beat, so palpable in their colorations and so dramatic in the interplay of dark and light shadings, that they could be identified as prose poems.

Memorable for his times, and perhaps even more so for modern readers, are Whitman's eyewitness accounts in *Specimen Days* of his daily visits to hospitals in Washington, D.C., and its environs during the Civil War. His deeply moving depictions of, and dialogues with, the wounded and dying soldiers are documents of the soul.

Whitman's articles as journalist, editor, and critic, as well as his works of fiction, may also give one pause for the light they shed on his subjective reactions to the climate of his day.

FICTION

Most of Whitman's twenty-four tales, written from 1841 to 1848, were either autobiographical in nature and/or identified with a cause. Their essentially didactic and polemical style, their sentimental protagonists, their actions and reactions slanted to suit *truth* as he saw it, divests them of both depth and individuality. Conventional, as well, was his all too superficial treatment of psychological motivations and of environmental conditions. Because he sought to please his readers, Whitman's tales, revolving around workaday events and people, were forever garnished with melodramatic events aimed at heightening suspense. Although the ring of authenticity sounds in the spoken language of Whitman's characters, modeled on and in keeping with their natures and their specific environments, his plots are contrived and self-indulgent. Nor, save in rare instances, did his realistic style circumvent the pedestrian. If, as it has been contended, Whitman was inspired by and therefore imitated Poe and Hawthorne, he did so poorly indeed.

Since he considered himself the spokesman for causes and addressed himself to the masses, his tales militated against poor working conditions for adults; fought to eradicate child labor, child abuse, starvation, and corporal punishment in the schools; deplored the breakup of families; and denounced the accumulation of capital and power by business and religious institutions. Rather than effecting a frontal attack on the collective in order to remedy such problems, Whitman believed that he could be most influential in pointing up the ethical and moral evils in a loveless society through fiction.

Of importance to Whitman were the sociological and psychological components of his tales. He wanted to prove that a good family relationship was not only significant in resolving personal problems, but was also instrumental in creating conditions of harmony nationwide. Because of his conviction that popular literature could play an important role in elevating the mores of the people by raising their standards and values, he felt that specific protagonists in works of fiction should be endowed with redeeming characteristics, and that plots should point up a moral. Whereas parables and fables had been used in biblical and other religious texts to teach piety and inculcate readers or hearers with high moral standards, Whitman contended that fiction was also important in conveying to people the beauty of their system. To some extent, then, his tales may be looked upon as teaching devices: each having a theme and goal; each being a civilizing agent capable of elevating and improving the American people and nation.

"The Child and the Profligate" (1841)

Whitman's tale may be seen as a protest against inhumane labor laws and human degradation. The plight of a poor widow and mother is fleshed out by highlighting the pain she feels as she watches her thirteen-year-old son, employed by an abusive master, work himself virtually to death. Heartrending is Whitman's depiction of the mother's agony at "the thought of a beloved son condemned to labor — that would break down a man — struggling from day to day under the hard rule of a soulless gold-worshipper; the knowledge that years must pass thus; the sickening idea of her own poverty, and of living mainly on the grudged charity of neighbors." For Whitman, expostulator against the pain, humiliation, and feelings of powerlessness endured by both mother and child, the situation had to change. The author, therefore, called another character, the Profligate, into being. Essentially good-natured, this man, who had always yearned to be loved and to love, had succumbed to drink and an overwhelming need for gain. Redeemed eventually by the child, symbol of futurity and purity, he is reborn through temperance and love. Adopting a social course based on love and kindness toward others, it is he who frees the child from his enslaving master and provides for the mother, while also founding a family of his own.

"Bervance; or, Father and Son" (1841)

Autobiographical in nature, "Bervance," one of Whitman's most intriguing tales, is a dramatization of a father's love for an older son and hatred for Luke, his younger progeny. The greater the father's aversion toward Luke (who by a strange happenstance looks just like him), the more this "eccentric, and high tempered" lad rebels against the tyrannical man. Father and son, as is to be expected, eventually come to blows. The doctor called in on the case is unaware of the prevailing climate of rage and hatred. He judges Luke's behavior from a strictly medical point of view and diagnoses him as insane. At the father's insistence, Luke is committed to a mental institution. After some weeks, the doctor feels the lad sufficiently recovered to be released. The father disagrees, insisting that he is still dangerous. So dominated does the older man become by feelings of guilt from what he now admits to be the iniquity of his acts, that one evening, alone in the house, he finds himself hallucinating. He happens to look into a mirror before him and the figure he sees is that of an "unwashed, tangly-haired, rag-covered" man, whose eyes, "vacant and glaring," wear the "wild look of a maniac." Ambiguity reigns. Is the father looking at Luke or at himself? Not such a farfetched question, since father and son do look alike. The reader is benumbed when the father suddenly turns around and recognizes this ghastly face to be that of his son. Unbeknownst to everyone, Luke had escaped from the mental institution. Moments later, the son vanishes, never to be seen or heard of again.

"Bervance" was a "strange" story, Whitman noted, depicting "unsoundness of mind," resulting from a son's "morbid and unnatural paternal antipathy." So horrific were the events in this macabre and somewhat Poe-like tale that Whitman felt they might "serve as a not useless lesson" to some parents.

"Death in the School-room (A Fact)" (1841)

Whitman's thesis in this story focuses on a repudiation of corporal punishment meted out to students by teachers. The incidents related are based on what took place in a Long Island school where Whitman had taught when he was seventeen. The author dramatizes a teacher's uncontrollable rage against a student for a minor infraction of the rules. He not only beats him to death, but continues to brutalize him even after the lad has stopped breathing.

A reformer in every way, Whitman sought to appeal to the hearts of his readers by underscoring the need for self-control and for the inculcation of high moral and spiritual values in both teacher and student — not by the imposition of inflexible and biased laws or actions, but through compassion and understanding.

"Wild Frank's Return" (1841)

"Wild Frank's Return," also based on fact, allows Whitman to narrate the plight of an ill-fated family, and by extension, a nation, when love is in short supply. An unfeeling father, reminiscent of the father in "Bervance," favors an older son, Richard, over the younger son, Frank. When the father insists that a mare called Black Nell belongs to Richard, although she is really his brother's, Frank, enraged by the injustice of the situation, leaves to join the navy, and Frank has second thoughts. He feels bad about the concern he must have caused his parents and writes to them, announcing his return. On his way home, he meets his brother by chance in a village tavern. Regretting the altercation, Richard lends Black Nell to his brother to ride home. On the way, Frank grows tired, takes some cord that he ties to Black Nell's saddle and to his own wrist, and falls asleep under an oak tree. A storm breaks and the frightened animal bolts. In a powerful description worthy of a Robinson Jeffers, Whitman writes:

The blast blew sweepingly, the lightning flash'd, and the rain fell in torrents. Crash after crash of thunder seem'd to shake the solid earth. And Black Nell, she stood now, an image of beautiful terror, with her fore feet thrust out, her neck arch'd, and her eyes glaring balls of fear. At length, after a dazzling and lurid glare, there came a peal — a deafening crash — as if the great axle was rent. God of Spirits! the startled mare sprang off like a ship in an ocean-storm! Her eyes were blinded with light; she dashed madly down the hill, and plunge after plunge — far, far away — swift as an arrow-dragging the hapless body of the youth behind her!

When the animal stops in front of Frank's parents' home, the parents behold "on the ground near her [the horse] a mangled... mass — the rough semblance of a human form — all batter'd and bloody."

In mysterious Poe-like manner, Frank, working in consort with destiny, has punished his parents for his pain-wracked childhood. The domineering and unfeeling father had made the mistake of not teaching "his children love of one another," and the feeble mother had been destructive in her very passivity. At her by projection, but in reality toward himself, Frank aimed his venomous wrath and the hideous form of his revenge.

Franklin Evans; or, The Inebriate, a Tale of the Times (1842)

Franklin Evans is a thesis novel dedicated to the Temperance Society. Enjoying enormous popularity in 1842, this group organized feasts, speeches, and testimonials throughout the states trying to dissuade rum sellers from dispensing their poisons. Frequently they succeeded in their endeavor, encouraging or forcing shops selling their evil spirits to close their doors. Thanks to its subject and to the laudatory and partisan reviews, one of which Whitman himself wrote, *Franklin Evans,* composed for remuneration, sold twenty thousand copies. Despite the fanfare, however, the plot was trite and unimaginative, revolving around a young man from Long Island who arrives in the big city. Naive, without friends or money, he rents an attic room in a boardinghouse and comes under the influence of "evil" young men who teach him the joys of gin and the pleasures of the brothel. After having undergone many unpleasant events, he is saved when pledging himself to "temperance," and finally, to "total abstinence."

"The Last of the Sacred Army" (1842)

This story is intended to remind Whitman's countrymen never to forget those who fought in the American Revolution, for they were the "WARRIORS of our FREEDOM!" The memory of these noble souls must be guarded, the author writes, with "a holy care," for they are the "Soldiers of Liberty."

George Washington and General Lafayette, both of whom Whitman idolized, had fought hard against "kingcraft and priestcraft" and were, he stresses, "benefactors of a people." To recall their values and their courage in "The Last of the Sacred Army" will, Whitman believes, make it impossible for Americans to ever again be enslaved.

"Richard Parker's Widow" (1846)

Despite the marked influence of this story on Melville's *Billy Budd* (written 1886, published 1924), an extraordinary novella of love and justice, Whitman's tale is contrived. Its single point of interest to modern readers is the widow's necrophilism. After suffering a business failure and going through a period of despondency, the hero/antihero, Richard Parker, scion of a good Scottish family, leaves his wife to become a common sailor. Well-bred, "and the bravest of the brave," he is chosen by the crews of several warships to lead a mutiny against the British government for nonpayment of wages and for obliging sailors to live under oppressive conditions. In time, Parker and the other mutineers are overpowered, brought to trial, and sentenced to death. When a petition sent to the king to spare Parker's life is denied, Mrs. Parker travels to London. After her husband's execution and burial, she waits around the churchyard until dusk, after which she climbs over the wall, finds her husband's grave, digs up the body with her own hands. "She clasped the cold neck, and kissed the clammy lips of the object of her search!" This "extraordinary woman" brought her husband's body back to her London room. Only when the authorities promised that her husband's remains would be interred "decently at Exeter, or in Scotland," did she agree to part with the corpse. The "hapless sailor was inhumed in White-chapel churchyard."

Whitman's emphasis on Mrs. Parker's strength and determination suggests his admiration for this kind of powerful wife/mother figure, who is able, when necessary, to rectify a wrong. The details Whitman provides of Parker's corpse indicate a morbid bent in the writer that will become increasingly obvious when he vividly records the infections, gangrenous legs, and skin diseases of the wounded soldiers he visited in the Washington hospitals.

Certainly Whitman's tales did not measure up philosophically, psychologically, or aesthetically to those of Poe, Hawthorne, or Melville. Nevertheless, their reserved, controlled, and confessional narrative style does hold the reader's attention, if only momentarily. More importantly for the author than for his reading public, was the fact that Whitman's fiction enabled him to verbalize his antipathy toward the father figure. His focus on sibling rivalry in "Bervance" and "Wild Frank's Return" also had a cathartic effect upon him. Relatively complex in nature, the latter tale not only dramatizes outerworldly events, in a manner reminiscent of such Gothic novels as Ann Radcliffe's *The Mysteries of Udolpho* and Horace Walpole's *Castle of Otranto,* but it also fleshes out ambiguous love/hate feelings toward a mother.

NONFICTION

Democratic Vistas (1870)

Whitman was in a position to follow postwar events at close range during his tenure as clerk in the office of the attorney general. He attended the highly charged congressional debates on Reconstruction and followed the arguments with rapt attention. His progressive disenchantment with government officials and bureaucrats may have been caused in part by his proximity to them. He saw many officials yielding to political pressures, to special interest groups, and most particularly to their own egotistical wants. Is it any wonder that he described them and American society in general as "canker'd, crude, superstitious, and rotten" (*PW,* 2, 369)?

The evolution in Whitman's political thinking becomes evident in his rebuttal to Thomas Carlyle's essay "Shooting Niagara: And After" (1867). Known for his attacks on hypocrisy and on excessive materialism, as well as for his distrust of democracy and the mob, Carlyle took the opportunity to vent his spleen on America, its Civil War, and the "Settlement of the Nigger Question" by assaulting Benjamin Disraeli's Reform Bill, which granted the vote to British working people. Whitman's immediate reaction to Carlyle's vituperative attack on democracy was one of anger. A year later, however, in his essay "Democracy," incorporated in *Democratic Vistas,* along with two others, "Personalism" and "Orbic Literature," he altered his stand. Nothing is either black or white, he reasoned; nuances exist in all fields, political, social, or otherwise. When questioning his own reactions to Carlyle's statements, he decided that the Britisher had not been *completely* misguided in his judgments. So significant were the changes in Whitman's thinking that when he prepared the final version of "Democracy," he deleted many of the abusive remarks he had made about Carlyle in his earlier drafts.

The problems preoccupying Whitman for the most part during

the Reconstruction era were the necessity for Americans to work toward healing racial hatreds; "the depravity of the business classes," the politicians "saturated in corruption," and the "tainted" judiciary; and the safeguarding of individualism (later alluded to as personalism) while unity in the collective sphere was maintained.

Whitman could no longer adhere to Madison's optimistic views as conveyed in his *Federalist Paper X,* in which he stated, in contradiction to the opinions of eighteenth-century political theorists, that if a people were committed to a central government of its own choosing and were intent upon working toward the common good of its citizenry, differences between factions would be ironed out and national unity would prevail. When a period of chaos followed the Civil War, Whitman, among others, feared that America's immense size, in addition to its pluralistic society, giving rise to a diversity of opinions on so many subjects, would make political cohesion impossible. America, he felt, lacked that "common skeleton."

Whitman's remedy for unifying America's powerful schisms lay in the creation of a national poetry of epic quality. It alone would have the power to save the United States from progressive atomization. Art, he maintained, had the power to fuse races, obliterate distances and differences. Poetry could do more to unify a land "than all its Constitutions, legislative and judicial ties" (*PW,* II, 368). What he found wanting were

native authors, literatures, far different, far higher in grade, than any yet known, sacerdotal, modern, fit to cope with our occasions, lands, permeating the whole mass of American mentality, taste, belief, breathing into it a new breath of life, giving it decision, affecting politics far more than the popular superficial suffrage, with results inside and underneath the elections of Presidents or Congresses — radiating, begetting appropriate teachers, schools, manners, and, as its grandest result, accomplishing (what neither the schools nor the churches and their clergy have hitherto accomplished, and without which this nation will no more stand, permanently, soundly, than a house will stand without a substratum), a religious and moral character beneath the political and productive and intellectual bases of the States. (*PW,* II, 365)

Rather than trusting organized churches and clergy, which the poet felt did more harm than good, Whitman sang out his own religious credo. By *religious,* he did not mean adhering to a certain sect or group, but rather, in keeping with eighteenth-century Deist tradition, a profound feeling of *oneness* among human beings, nature, and a God who had neither become manifest supernaturally in history nor immanently in nature. "A new Literature, perhaps a new Metaphysics, certainly a new Poetry," must come into being, Whitman stated, for these are "the only sure and worthy supports and expressions of the American Democracy" (*PW,* II, 416).

Whitman considered himself the epic bard who would single-handedly have the power, talent, and wisdom to unite the disparate and equalize the hierarchical differences in society. As "the poet of the modern," he would conserve what was so precious to Americans — their individuality — while also implementing the moral and aesthetic values of the collective. For Whitman this meant a perpetual re-creation of the American spirit as it had been conceived by the founding fathers.

The highly intuitive Whitman was forever attempting to re-order his ideas and affective reactions to altering situations and movements. At times, as noted, he called upon Hegelian dialectics to substantiate his views. What appealed to Whitman in Hegel's doctrine was its ascending process of history. No matter the difficulties involved, and even because of life's baffling contradictions and paradoxes, at least the notion of continuous progress remains constant.

Perhaps because of Whitman's Hegelianism, the optimistic poet accepted the perils inherent in his democratic land as part of an ascending historical process. He admitted again and again that hypocrisy, dishonesty, and greed are implicit in the process. Nevertheless, Whitman's increasing concern for America's future became evident: "We sail a dangerous sea of seething currents, cross and under-currents, vortices — all so dark, untried — and whither shall we turn?" (*PW,* II, 422). Still, Whitman's other, wide-eyed side — the impractical, imaginative, and sensitive poet that he was — spoke out forcefully and positively until the end. Like his hero Lincoln, he would not give up the ship, but would continue his verbal fight unabashed. Never would he shy away from deprecating what did not suit his plan: the "system of inflated paper-money currency," for example, which he believed not only invited dishonesty, but served to increase the disparity between rich and poor, while also destroying the heretofore heroic values of America's founding fathers.

Always mobile, always saturated with a variety of impressions and ideological views, Whitman questioned the problematics — seemingly eternal ones — of immigration and automation. Perceptively, he anticipated extreme mechanization and industrialization, "the long series of tendencies, shapings which few are strong enough to resist, and which now seem, with steam-engine speed, to be everywhere turning out the generations of humanity like uniform iron castings" (*PW*, II, 424). Whitman also foresaw the difficulties involved in governing America's vast land: "Unwieldy and immense, who shall hold in [this] behemoth?" (*PW*, II, 422). As poet of the future, he dreamed of creating a new language, an American myth capable of fusing distant localities, diverse races, and ethnic groups.

A believer in the common man and in gender equality, Whitman resisted the dominance of an elite class. Hence he was convinced that the reconstruction of America, on both an individual and collective basis, rested upon the inner riches and motivating factors of each human being. Nor would intellectual, knowledge, without its application in the marketplace, solve the problems facing America. Whitman's solutions to America's problems lay to a great extent in the reestablishment of a past ideal, the visions rooted in Jeffersonian democracy.

As an early advocate of women's rights who argued in favor of their presence in the workplace, Whitman believed that women should not live fossilized existences, but should develop themselves both physically and intellectually. Along with men, they should be politically informed, and participate in the running of the government as well as in their own affairs. He opposed Catherine Beecher's view of women — as depicted in her *A Treatise on Domestic Economy* (1842) — as all-giving Christian feminine beings. On the other hand, he favored Margaret Fuller's approach to the emancipation of women, as described in her *Women in the Nineteenth Century* (1845). Whitman was convinced that one day women would be

raised to become the robust equals, workers, and, it may be, even practical and political deciders with the men — greater than man, we may admit, through their divine maternity, always their towering, emblematical attribute — but great, at any rate, as man, in all departments; or, rather capable of being so, soon as they realize it, and can bring themselves to give up toys and fictions, and launch forth, as men do, amid real, independent, stormy life. (*PW*, II, 389)

Thus would the United States be insured of "a strong and sweet Female Race," and, Whitman added, much to the dismay of many a twentieth-century feminist, "a race of perfect Mothers." That he should have included the latter statement may be understandable, given his deep love for his mother.

Lewis Mumford's commentary on *Democratic Vistas* was most lucid.

No critic ferreted out the weaknesses and pettinesses of America with a surer nose than Whitman tracked them down in his Democratic Vistas: what could be said against his dream, Whitman said, with the staunch candor of a friend. But his thought and his vision were unshaken; the promise of America had not disappeared. If it was absent from the immediate scene, it had nevertheless taken form in his poems; and his poems were still waiting to shape a new America. (Norton, *Anthology,* 853).

Specimen Days and Collect

Although published in 1882, much of *Specimen Days and Collect* was written earlier. The first section includes sketches and brief commentaries on his youth and his later years; the second comprises accounts of his more than six hundred hospital visits, with descriptions of some gruesome cases, and notations about the advice and comfort he gave to nearly a hundred thousand sick and wounded Civil War soldiers.

In an altogether-different vein are the exquisitely written random meditations on nature also gathered in *Specimen Days and Collect.* Clouds and constellations, as well as animal and insect worlds, drawn from his Timber Creek notes and his trip to the West and Canada, add an artistic dimension to the work. Exciting verbal scenes conjure forth for the reader an entire sphere of sensual delight: visual, audible, tactile, olfactory, even gustatory. The feeling of *being there,* of accompanying the artist/writer in all of his discoveries and joys is imbricated into what has already been alluded to as prose poems.

An idyllic period was resurrected by Whitman whenever he glanced back to his youth and to family life on Long Island. Forgotten were his problematic relationship with his father, the questions revolving around family health and finances. Now that he was old and infirm, the difficulties that had caused him such anxiety in the past seemed inconsequential. Wistfully he recalled those moments of seemingly perfect repose when he breathed in "the cool of the sweet and slightly aromatic evening air." So strong were the sensations evoked by the images of the past that they intruded into his present reality: his lungs expanded with each breath he took, filling his whole being with fervor and delight. The absorption of sunsets into himself awakened him to a newfound spirituality and physicality. He recalled the times in his youth spent clam digging, inhaling "the perfume of the sedge-meadows" and viewing with wonder and joy the isolated "bare unfrequented shore." It was there that, "after bathing," he loved "to race up and down the hard sand, and declaim Homer or Shakespeare to the surf and sea-gulls by the hour." Life was just beginning then. The future was open, bright, excitingly positive (*PW*, I, 1–12).

Although Whitman reveled in country landscapes, city life also fascinated him. At an early age, he had developed a "passion for ferries" taking him across the Hudson. Whitman's powerful response to water, as already manifested in his verse, is also implicit in the nature descriptions of *Specimen Days*. "What oceanic currents, eddies, underneath — the great tides of humanity also, with ever-shifting movements" (*PW*, I, 16). Not only did this eternally mobile element nurture his poetic soul, but its continuous and volatile activity paralleled his own inner turmoil.

Nor does Whitman omit the jaunts he took on the omnibus or the stagecoaches up and down Broadway, Fifth, and Madison Avenues. These precious moments, which brought him close to the young and handsome drivers to whom he was so powerfully drawn, afforded him some of his greatest pleasures, as have been described earlier in this book. The "comradeship, and sometimes affection" of these drivers, as well as the escapades Whitman enjoyed with them, "undoubtedly enter'd into the gestation of *Leaves of Grass*" (*PW*, I, 18, 19).

What makes *Specimen Days and Collect* unique, remaining indelibly engraved in readers' minds, is the writer's account of the "volcanic upheaval of the nation" (*PW*, I, 24–25). Whitman's personal account of the conflagration takes his readers through the early days of the Civil War, the unexpected loss of Union troops at the conclusion of the battle of Bull Run (July 21, 1861), and his bitter realization that the North had reached a crossroad.

Most shocking of all to Whitman, not surprisingly, were the horrors of the makeshift hospitals that supposedly served the wounded. The hundreds of deaths daily could not, he learned, be blamed on the war alone, but on the impossibly poor sanitary conditions in these places, not to mention an almost total lack of amenities: few cots, rarely any mattresses, and virtually no protection from icy temperatures in winter. Illness and death from all types of diseases was so prevalent that Whitman was frequently overcome with feelings of utter powerlessness. Yet he felt driven to continue his daily visits to the wounded and the sick, to try to comfort them in his own small way. "I do not see that I do much good to these wounded and dying," he wrote, "but I cannot leave them" (*PW*, I, 33). That he could not leave them tells one a great deal about his empathy and compassion for others. Heretofore he had experienced his own brand of emotional pain, narcissistic in part, self-indulgent to a certain extent. Now, however, he was facing the real world: observing physical suffering, real agony that no word, no medicine, save for the most potent narcotics, could assuage. What he discovered in the process, and probably unconsciously, was his ability to *feel* deeply into the lives and wounds of others; to identify with their pain, which was, on another level, his own. When the limbs of young men were being amputated, when bodies were being slowly corroded by gangrene, and when infectious diseases such as osteomyelitis, erysipelas, pyemia, diarrhea, typhoid, and pneumonia were ravaging the hospital wards, the poet was there. He held the hands of the wounded and diseased, patted their faces, and kissed their cheeks, decanting words of warmth, comfort, and love to those in need. No sight was too gruesome, no odor too repugnant, no cry too bruising to keep this compassionate visitor away. (In fact, if no doctor or nurse were available, and he were called upon, he washed and dressed the soldiers' wounds himself. So expertly and with such gentleness did he accomplish his task that some patients wanted only him to tend to them.)

Whatever small gifts he could provide — candy, fruit, writing paper, tobacco, money — were brought to the soldiers whenever he could afford it. Or he would simply read to them whatever they wanted to hear (poetry, passages from the Bible that he would then discuss with them) or would tell them stories. The tenderness of his voice seemed to work wonders in assuaging their torment.

When a soldier in the throes of agony, paralyzed, or weakened by disease looked at him from his bed, searching for human contact and tenderness, Whitman would take him into his arms, cradle him, and nurture him with gentle words, his entire being suddenly flooded by that exquisite pleasure known to those who *feel needed*; to those who *feel they can help*. In so doing, Whitman not only strengthened the soldiers' will to live, but discovered some incredible factor within himself: *he was a healer.* There might be more to the story. Was he also playing, perhaps unconsciously, the role of lover to those whose lives were ebbing? Whatever the motivations for his acts, he experienced a sense of camaraderie for which he had been searching all his life. Whitman the loner, the wanderer, now belonged to someone: to many. Someone counted on him; was dependent upon him for his well-being. Some unknown force had been stirred and awakened in Whitman's depths. Never had he lived such thrilling moments.

In addition to his role as healer and possibly lover, was he not, perhaps, playing father to multitudes of lonely and suffering young men? Unlike his own father, Whitman was a helpful force. But, was he not also playing the part of a nurturing mother figure? A "mother-man" was the epithet used by so many of his friends to describe him as he went about his hospital work. He had been endowed with a very special talent: the ability to talk to young men on a most intimate level, that of *feeling*. Never had this emotionally deprived individual enjoyed such a relationship with his parents.

In an essay in *Specimen Days* called "A New Army Organization Fit for America," Whitman was harshly critical of the "current military theory, practice, rules and organization" of the army. Blaming much of the slaughter on the crucial errors committed by those in charge, he pointed to their outmoded tactics, modeled on European-style battle, which were unsuitable to American democratic ideals and American terrain. Moreover, the kind of trench warfare used during the Civil War, which pitted large armies against each other, relied a good deal upon volunteers for soldiers, which meant that frequently, the same families were fighting on opposite sides. Nor were the military leaders considerate of their own men: in fact, many Northerners had been killed as the result of the indifference or ineptitude of their own officers. Although democratic in principle, many a Union officer brought up with the old-time aristocratic beliefs, namely, that foot soldiers are relatively unimportant, paid little attention as to whether or not they were being butchered.

The fighting at Fredericksburg and at Chancellorsville (which Whitman had not witnessed), was particularly violent and the wounded were many. Consumed with horror by the scenes about which he had heard, and by others he had witnessed, Whitman, the narrator/journalist, spared not a macabre detail in his observations. When unable to bear the horror, he looked toward nature in its cosmic dimension for succor: considering the sight of carnage not as an individual event, but as part of an eternal round of cause and effect, death and rebirth.

One man is shot by the shell, both in the arm and leg — both are amputated — there lie the rejected members. Some have their legs blown off — some bullets through the breast — some indescribably horrid wounds in the face or head, all mutilated, sickening, torn, gouged out — some in the abdomen. . . . Such is the camp of the wounded . . . while over all the clear, large moon comes out at times softly, quietly shining. Amid the woods, that scene of flitting souls — amid the crack and crash and yelling sounds — the impalpable perfume of the woods — and yet the pungent, stifling smoke — the radiance of the moon, looking from heaven at intervals so placid — the sky so heavenly — the clear-obscure up there, those buoyant upper oceans-a few large placid stars beyond, coming silently and languidly out, and then disappearing — the melancholy, draperied night above, around. (*PW*, I, 47)

To make his points, Whitman described individual cases explicitly. John Mahay, for example, who had been shot through the lower abdomen, had been agonizing in a hospital for two years.

The bladder had been perforated by a bullet going entirely through him. ...The water ran out of his eyes from the intense pain, and the muscles of his face were distorted, but he utter'd nothing except a low groan now and then. Hot moist cloths were applied, and reliev'd him somewhat. He never knew the love of parents, was placed in infancy in one of the New York charitable institutions, and subsequently bound out to a tyrannical master in Sullivan county, (the scars of whose cowhide and club remain'd yet on his back.)...He found friends in his hospital life, and, indeed, was a universal favorite. (*CW*, I, 84)

A nineteen-year-old Confederate soldier, whose leg had been amputated, had to be given morphine to make his pain endurable —

very affectionate — held on to my hand, and put it by his face, not willing to let me leave....Visiting him daily for about two weeks after that, while he lived, (death had mark'd him, and he was quite alone,). I loved him much, always kiss'd him, and he did me. (*PW*, I, 107)

He lingered, suffered, and finally died.

The years Whitman spent tending the ill in the army hospital, although physically taxing on him, taught him the profoundest of lessons: "It arous'd and brought out and decided undream'd-of depths of emotion" (*PW*, I, 113) — such as anguish, at the sight of

dead and living burial-pits, the blackest and loathesomest of all, the prison-pens of Andersonville....The dead, the dead, the dead — *our* dead — or South or North, ours all, (all, all, all, finally dear to me)...they crawl'd to die, alone, in bushes, low gullies, or on the sides of hills....Their skeletons, bleach'd bones, tufts of hair, buttons, fragments of clothing, are occasionally found yet. (*PW*, I, 114)

Whitman's attachment to some soldiers awakened in him the profoundest love — emotions he had not heretofore allowed to flow forth. His letters to them, in many instances, supplemented the feelings only alluded to in his statements concerning the specific young men in question.

O what a sweet unwonted love (those good American boys, of good stock, decent, clean, well raised boys, so near to me) — what an attachment grows up between us, started from hospital cots, where pale young faces lie & wounded or sick bodies. My brave young American soldiers — now for so many months I have gone around among them, where they lie. I have long discarded all stiff conventions (they & I are too near to each other, there is no time to lose, & death & anguish dissipate ceremony here between my lads & me) — I pet them, some of them it does so much good, they are so faint & lonesome — at parting at night I kiss them right and left — The doctors tell me I supply the patients with a medicine which all their drugs & bottles & powders are helpless to yield. (*CORR*, I, 122)

Love always prevailed for Whitman, even when the stench coming from a gangrened wound, or the urine trickling from a bladder that had been pierced by a bullet, or the delirium of a highly fevered patient was devastating. About one of his loves, Lewy Brown, a patient at the Armory Square Hospital, Whitman wrote: "When I came away, he reached up his face, I put my arm around him, and we gave each other a long kiss, half a minute long" (Miller, *Selected Letters of Walt Whitman*, 55). Lew's answers were welcomed with intense joy by the poet "as any thing from you will always be, & the sight of your face welcomer than all, my darling" (Miller, *Selected*, 55, 72).

Deeply disturbed, even torn, by the sight of human suffering, Whitman had nevertheless been fascinated by his hospital work. "It was a religion with me," he told Traubel years later. "Every man has a religion ... something which absorbs him, possesses itself of him, makes him over in its image" (Traubel, *With Whitman in Camden*, III, 581). Rather than emphasizing the political and ideological side of the Civil War, he focused mainly in *Specimen Days* on the individual soldier and his one-to-one relationship with him, thereby adding a poignant note, but also a democratic one in which he proved to his readers that for Southerners or Northerners (and both were responsible for the carnage), no matter the class nor the family status, agony made no distinctions.

The ten years of intense emotional upheaval that had been Whitman's during his stay in Washington took their physical toll. On

January 23, 1873, he suffered a nearly fatal stroke. His mother's death, on May 23, left him utterly dejected. Paralyzed and unable to work, Whitman moved into his brother George's home in Camden, New Jersey. His meeting and friendship with the young Harry Stafford, an illiterate farm boy, proved to be a beneficial experience for the poet. He accepted the lad's invitation to live at his parents' farm at Timber Creek, about thirteen miles from where it entered the Delaware River. At the Stafford farmhouse Whitman grew stronger and increasingly mobile, and it was there that he wrote some of the extraordinary depictions of nature included in *Specimen Days and Collect.*

The warm and friendly atmosphere of the Stafford home, and its isolation — surrounded by woods, a pond, and calamus — renewed Whitman physically and emotionally. A factor not to be omitted in Whitman's return to health was the healing program he instituted for himself: healthy foods, long walks, mud baths, and nude sunbathing, all of which endowed him with a new sense of livingness. Even more important, was Harry's presence.

Of all the Stafford sons, it was Harry whom Whitman loved. It was he with whom he wrestled, and from whom he drew strength enough to hold him down. *"If I had not known you* — if it hadn't been for you & our friendship & my going down there summers to the creek with you, I believe *I should not be a living man to-day* — I think & remember these things & they comfort me — & you, my darling boy, are the central figure of them all" (*CORR,* III, 215).

Although Whitman did not use overt metrical structures or obvious rhyme schemes in his verbal transpositions of nature in the Timber Creek pieces, he did imbue them with balance, a variety of subtle and brash rhythms, a medley of tones, and multiple figures of speech. The highly dramatic effects he achieved, in addition to his panoply of succulent images, was an artistic expression of inner movements of energy and primal human forces worked into a precise literary form.

Because Whitman dug deeply into the animistic world about him, nature took on an existence of its own, its redolence becoming a fact of life for the poet. His concrete yet analogically abstract language tingled with excitement at the birth of a new day; rhythms were set into place when delineating trees, bushes, brushes, and grasses swaying and bending with awe as oncoming winds preluded a fierce storm revealing for him and the reader a whole unspoken language. Nature's mysterious tonal responses, as in birdcalls or the rustling of an animal foraging for food, were at times dissonant and at other moments harmonious. Altering colorations, depending upon the sun's radiance and the moon's glow, marked life's ebb and flow. All the while, the poet was taking nature's powers unto himself, both artistically and viscerally, drawing sustenance from the living forms about him that his poetic imagination then transposed into the *word*.

Whitman's return to "the naked source — life of us all — to the breast of the great silent savage all-acceptive Mother," allowed him, as it had Jean-Jacques Rousseau when writing his *Reveries,* to revert to the very fundamentals of existence (*WP,* I, 122). While apostrophizing nature in his "jottings" and "babblings," which were "carelessly pencilled in the open air" as the spirit moved him, he purposefully omitted consecutive dates, thereby introducing into his prose poems a sense of timelessness. His personifications of inanimate forces served to humanize nature's energies, which the poet then befriended, taking them into his heart and mind (*WP,* I, 122). When looking about, he wondered how many people there were who had wandered too far away from natural life to make their return to it a possibility.

Nature in all of its variegated manifestations mesmerized the poet. When his thoughts suddenly alighted on "Birds Migrating at Midnight," they tingled; or, responding to melody and its undertones, as in "Bumble-Bees," they stopped, listened attentively to the droning "noisy, vocal, natural concert" reverberating throughout the forest; or were catalyzed, inviting imagination to roam wild; or when inhaling the rich aromatic perfumes and "the fresh earth smells" of the forest, were overwhelmed by feelings of well-being; or were enlivened when gazing relentlessly at "the delicate drabs and thin blues of the perspective" and the nuanced palette of green grasses drenched in morning dew.

Whitman's sequences on "Cedar-Apples" and "Sundown Perfume-Quail Notes — the Hermit Thrush" introduce a different realm, perhaps not as joyful as the previous sequences, because of his emphasis on solitude and nature's interlocking shadows and recesses, but, nevertheless, sparkling with life and electrifying in their fresh and buoyant rhythms and images. Corresponding to the poet's inner topography, he writes of "dappling glimpses of the water," the "warty, venerable, oak," and "the dual notes of the quail, the soughing of the wind through some near-by pines."

Particularly arresting are his jottings on trees. Not only does Whitman personify these natural forces, endowing them with eloquence, but like the shamans of old, he provides them with a soul of their own to which he relates.

What suggestions of imperturbability and *being,* as against the human trait of mere *seeming.* Then the qualities, almost emotional, palpably artistic, heroic, of a tree; so innocent and harmless, yet so savage. It *is* yet says nothing. How it rebukes by its tough and equable serenity in all weathers, this gusty-temper'd little whiffet, man that runs indoors at a mite of rain or snow. (*PW,* I, 130)

As they had for the Gauls and the Celts, trees for Whitman also possessed sensuality and spirituality. Phallic and divine symbology pervades all of the poet's writings on trees: as energizing powers, they trigger inspiration; as divine forces, they lift him out of his ego-centered world into collective mystical arenas. Because Whitman humanized trees, each took on a personality of its own, inviting him to enjoy their presences in the three or four favorite spots he singled out to rest.

I have selected, besides the hickory..., strong and limber boughs of beech or holly, in easy-reaching distance, for my natural gymnasia, for arms, chest, trunk-muscles. I can soon feel the sap and sinew rising through me, like mercury to heat. I hold on boughs or slender trees caressingly there in the sun and shade, wrestle with their innocent stalwartness — and *know* the virtue thereof passes from them into me. (Or maybe we interchange — maybe the trees are more aware of it all than I ever thought.) (*PW,* I, 153)

Although scientists would scoff at Whitman's ramblings about trees, rocks, and the earth in general, including the whole animal and insect kingdom, great moral lessons may be learned from each of these animate or inanimate entities, for they conceal, Whitman wrote, "humanity's invisible foundations" (*PW,* I, 131). Each time he dipped into nature, a sympathetic relationship was established between him and life in general — inner vibrations of the heart melding with outer vibrations of the cosmos.

Lights and shades and rare effects on tree-foliage and grass — transparent greens, grays, &c., all in sunset pomp and dazzle. The clear beams are now thrown in many new places on the quilted, seam'd, bronze-drab, lower tree-trunks, shadow'd... at this hour — now flooding their young and old columnar ruggedness with strong light, unfolding to my sense new amazing features of silent, shaggy charm, the solid bark, the expression of harmless impassiveness, with many a bulge and gnarl unreck'd before. In the re-vealings of such light, such exceptional hour, such mood, one does not wonder at the old story fables...of people falling into love-sickness with trees, seiz'd extatic with the mystic realism of the resistless silent strength in them — *strength,* which after all is perhaps the last, completest, highest beauty. (*PW,* I, 131)

Animated, as well, were nature's light-yellow butterflies. Outerworldly for Whitman, he saw them as "spiritual insects: straw-color'd Psyches !" When he observed their fluttering yellow wings blanketing the landscape, dipping here and there, oscillating about, they endowed the scene with "a curious animation." Singled out for his meditation were their "color, fragility," and "peculiar motion, and that strange, frequent way of one leaving the crowd and mounting up, up in the free ether, and apparently never returning" (*PW,* I, 178). Suddenly, however, Whitman injected an element of fear into the atmosphere, by introducing "the distant guttural screech of a flock of guinea-hens," their shrill tones introducing a condition of malaise, of discomfort, into the surroundings, and through projection, himself.

Nowhere has Whitman conveyed his dialogues with nature more intensely than in the Timber Creek pieces. Everything about his world at this time in his life dazzled him: be it the soft hum of the birds or the harsh squall of winter winds biting into his cheeks; the flamboyant colors shooting through the branches of the trees or the leaden tones of haze and clouds. The parched or moisture-filled fields, each in its own manner, reflected a mood, a thought, a sensation, enriched by glazed colorations — awakening him to new marvels of life.

Alchemical qualities are also implicit in Whitman's Timber Creek pieces. The ancient alchemists' recipes for transformation and cosmic evolution, as embedded in their scientific experiments and coded writings, revolved around their belief in a mysterious identity of essences, in a theory of correspondences, and in mystical notions of reincarnation. It was the alchemists who viewed primordial unity in the unmanifest sphere as diversity in the workaday world. So, too, were Whitman's symbolistic depictions allied to those of the alchemists. On the seashore, for example, there existed, he wrote, a "dividing line, contact, junction, the solid marrying the liquid — that curious, lurking something (as doubtless every objective form finally becomes to the subjective spirit,)...blending the real and ideal, and each made portion of the other" (*WP,* I, 138).

First viewed as distinct substances, opposites in nature are melded into a union by Whitman, the verbal alchemist, in an integration

of antagonistic forces, of inner movements, which in due course
he transmutes into the word. Such movement is understandable,
since he is projecting his inner drama onto outside forces. Once
opposing polarities are welded together in his mind's eye, everything within the cosmos — and within himself — seems to form
a cohesive whole, thereby preparing the terrain for a *renovatio* to
take place. "Come, ye disconsolate, in whom any latent eligibility is
left — come get the sure virtues of creek-shore, and wood and field"
(*PW,* I, 150).

Particularly sensual are Whitman's bathing sequences and the
elation he feels in his newborn sense of cleanliness and nakedness.

Partially bathing in the clear waters of the running brook...stepping
about barefooted every few minutes now and then in some neighboring
black ooze, for unctuous mud-bath to my feet — a brief second and third
rinsing in the crystal running waters — rubbing with the fragrant towel.
(*PW,* I, 151)

Nor does Whitman ever shy away from arguing this antipuritanical
approach to nakedness. No! the body is not indecent, as repressed
sin-ridden people would one believe, he intimates. Nor is there
a double standard for men and for women. On the contrary, although many may consider nudity vulgar and unchaste, the Greeks,
Whitman declares — models for Western culture, having reached
"the highest heights and deepest depth known to civilization in
those departments" — did not. Because God created the body, it
is, whether clothed or unclothed, a manifestation of Divinity.

For Whitman, God is all-encompassing. Unlike the typical West-
erner, who approaches Divinity with arms outstretched toward the
heavens, forever requesting redemption or beatitude, Whitman experiences Divinity in a more Buddhistically oriented manner in that
he absorbs the numinous unto himself, inhales this sacred presence
and essence into his very depths.

As if for the first time, indeed, creation noiselessly sank into and through
me its placid and untellable lessons, beyond — O, so infinitely beyond! —
anything from art, books, sermons, or from science, old or new. The
spirit's hour — religion's hour — the visible suggestion of God in space
and time — now once definitely indicated, if never again. (*PW,* I, 174)

Nature's palette also invites Whitman to free-associate. A pond,
set out as "flat spread, without a ripple," is compared most ap-
propriately to "a vast Claude Lorraine [sic] glass." Did Whitman

know that Claude Lorrain had actually developed his own ideal radiant landscape? The poet was drawn to this French painter's depictions of broad skies impregnated with delicate golden tints of dawn and/or sunset, visible at times as they flickered through a thin sheet of haze. Rather than pointing to a moral or praising a hero, Claude had created mood pieces bathed in an atmosphere of stillness and calm. Whether he was painting a seaport or a wooded area, misty plains or forested land, palaces, columns, and trees were used by this artist to frame a landscape, so as to enable him to focus better on a central light. He knew, as did Whitman, how to draw the viewer's eye into nature's visual, hence its spiritual depths. What perhaps attracted Whitman most particularly to Claude was his nostalgic moods, the vibrancy of his lighting effects, and the ambiance of subdued silence embedded in his softly modulated scenes, as in his "Morning Landscape" and "The Marriage of Isaac and Rebekah."

The canvases of Jean-François Millet also captured Whitman's fancy, and triggered bouts of free association. He identified with the Frenchman's "The Gleaners" and "The Angelus," featuring farm laborers and humble folk, who knew the joy of work and of quiet evening peace. Although the men and women he painted seemed to have been dwarfed by events, they were, nevertheless, depicted as strong and impressive figures set against a flat land and sky. They would be the ones to gain stature and dignity in the coming centuries. Although aware of Millet's socialist credo and his romanticized approach to the poor, the poet empathized with the grandeur and solemnity of his figures — for they had been inspired with a sense of purpose.

Whitman's democratic ideals were stirred by Millet's ethical visual echoings — "the long precedent crushing of the masses of a heroic people into the earth, in abject poverty, hunger" (*PW*, I, 268). Millet knew just how to endow his country scenes, Whitman wrote, with a "sublime murkiness and original pent fury," transforming them into a kind of pictorial narration of elements that brought on the French Revolution. Although momentarily oppressed, Whitman knew humanity to be strong, "titanic" in nature, waiting patiently for the moment of vengeance. Millet's canvases, as well as Claude's — and nature itself — were for Whitman part of a Divine scheme. Of import to him was to keep everything in perspective, so as to understand how each individual or inanimate entity, could best fulfill his, her, or its earthly mission.

With Whitman's fiction, *Democratic Vistas,* and *Specimen Days and Collect,* one virtually spans a lifetime. Having always had to confront reality (except for moments of reverie when the creative pen took over), having witnessed the monumental suffering caused by the Civil War; and having observed the growing disparity between rich and poor, and the growing conflicts between capital and labor (in the railroad strike of 1877, federal troops were called upon to stop the violence), the once-idealistic Whitman was considerably less so than he had been. An admirer of the French Enlightenment, which furnished the fodder for the French Revolution of 1793, Whitman noted thoughtfully:

The American Revolution of 1776 was simply a great strike, successful for its immediate object — but whether a real success judged by the scale of the centuries, and the long-striking balance of Time, yet remains to be settled. The French Revolution was absolutely a strike, and a very terrible and relentless one, against ages of bad pay, unjust division of wealth-products, and the hoggish monopoly of a few, rolling in superfluity, against the vast bulk of the work-people living in squalor. (*PW,* II, 528)

Frighteningly prophetic were Whitman's fears about the kind of democracy that might prevail in America in the years to come: economic conflict between the minority of wealthy and the masses of poor people might occur; educational systems and training centers designed to teach trades might be increasingly inadequate; materialism might take increasing hold. Cautionary was his tone when noting the importance of a national art or characteristic music as being crucial to the mental, spiritual, and economic health of a land. Is there anything more alarming, Whitman questions, than the complete lack of "fusion and mutuality of love"?

Conclusion

Whitman was unique in his time, and he still stands as a unique figure in ours. A poet of the rhapsody, of joy and energy, he reached deep into nature, embracing its human and nonhuman facets. Each day was for him an awakening into life; each minute of every hour, an enrichment. A poet who made body and soul one, he was a uniter of the disparate: of mentation and feeling, good and evil. He was a man whose wonderment at life remained a constant. Whether losing himself in ecstatic contemplation of vast inland landscapes, bodies of water, or vacant beaches, gazing heavenward into infinite space, or stopping to marvel at a tiny petal on a flower, or a bumblebee sucking out honey during its daily routine, he took it all in.

Whitman's approach to life was physical; primarily visible, and not abstract. Yet he was spiritually oriented, expressing his ethereality in brilliantly toned and concretely shaped images. A cosmic poet, he belonged to Earth and to Heaven. The energetic charges leaping out from within his words conveyed emotions of dread and even terror, as well as of veneration for that infinite and ineffable Deity, that intensely exciting mystery surrounding the creator of everything.

A mystic in the true sense of the word, Whitman wrote poetry that induced feelings of awe and universal love. His catalogings, imagings, symbols; his harsh or mellifluous tones, sweeping rhymes and rhythms, and outwardly simple vocabulary, which included slang and regional dialects, revealed only an outer core. Hidden behind the mask lived an ebullient and dazzling but also deeply secretive and distressed individual, a throbbing soul. "Camerado, this is no book, / Who touches this touches a man," he wrote in "So Long!"

A pantheist and pagan, Whitman sang the phallus: that fertile, procreative, and sexualized aspect of nature. "I shall look for loving crops from the birth, life, death, immortality, I plant so lovingly now," he wrote in "A Woman Waits for Me." And in "From

Pent-up Aching Rivers," he sang of "the muscular urge and the blending."

Yet Whitman did not withdraw from the workaday world into nature. On the contrary, he was engaged in life's every course. His poetic voice intoned both personal and impersonal worlds, real and imaginative powers, that which is heard and that which remains silent. His hypnotic sonations held his readers spellbound, dilated their framed spheres. Whether ushering them into subliminal spaces, as in "The Sleepers," in which he anticipated James Joyce's interior monologue–stream-of-consciousness style; or inviting them on a journey of discovery, as in "Salut au Monde!"; or dealing with the thematics of death, as in "Passage to India"; or facing agony ("I know every one of you, I know the sea of torment, doubt, despair, and unbelief"), as in "Song of Myself," Whitman kept his devotees enthralled — while others found him repellent.

A man of the pen, he was also a man deeply committed to humanity. A healer, most particularly during the ten years he spent in Washington, D.C., caring for the wounded of the Civil War, he gave unstintingly of himself. At the bedside of the ill and dying whenever he was needed, he exuded warmth, compassion, and tenderness. He knew how to communicate with those in agony, to assuage their suffering, for he *felt* deeply and authentically — directly from the heart.

Whitman's words were at times prophetic. In *Democratic Vistas,* he foresaw some of the difficulties ahead for the United States.

The problem of the future of America is in certain respects as dark as it is vast. Pride, competition, segregation, vicious wilfulness, and license beyond example, brood already upon us. Unwieldly and immense, who shall hold in behemoth? who bridle leviathan? Flaunt it as we choose, athwart and over the roads of our progress loom huge uncertainty, and dreadful, threatening gloom. It is useless to deny it: Democracy grows rankly up the thickest, noxious, deadliest plants and fruits of all — brings worse and worse invaders — needs newer, larger, stronger, keener compensations and compellers.

Thirsting for balance and harmony in a world that lived and breathed continuous contradiction, Whitman lusted for the open road, where the discovery of ever-widening vistas electrified his soul. His belief in progressive self-realization for the individual as well as for society, in artistic freedom, in equality of the sexes, and in human dignity helped him deal with the vagaries of everyday existence.

Unlike some of the scholastic, intellectual, and puritanical American poets following him — for example Pound, Eliot, and Robert Lowell — whose worlds revolved around sin, sacrifice, and sorrow, Whitman, despite periodic bouts of self-doubt and anguish, sang his full-throated passion in magical incantations for all to hear.

Who, then, were his progeny? Those who also fed on rapturously lush and wild greenery, autumn colorations, or denuded country-sides with their skeletal trees silhouetted against a charcoal gray sky, or sun-drenched scenes heightened by the crystallized hues of new-fallen snow. Poets and prose writers who lived the living mystery of life — D. H. Lawrence, Stephen Crane, Dylan Thomas, Vachel Lindsay, Henry Miller, Hart Crane, Carl Sandburg, Thomas Wolfe, E. M. Forster, William Carlos Williams, Allen Ginsberg, Karl Shapiro — all these and others are literary and spiritual inheritors.

The poet of America and of democracy, of country and city, of time and space, Whitman orchestrated his words, sang his scenarios, composed his complex metrics of sound and thought, when intoning the songs of scientists, philosophers, prophets, musicians; of workers in industries and on farms. A visionary who celebrated a New Age, he chanted a New Consciousness in personal but also in universal distillations, and fresh verbal alloys.

> Smile O voluptuous cool-breath'd earth!
> Earth of the slumbering and liquid trees!
> Earth of departed sunset — earth of the mountains misty-topt!
> Earth of the vitreous pour of the full moon just tinged with blue!
> Earth of shine and dark mottling the tide of the river!
> Earth of the limpid gray of clouds brighter and clearer for my sake!
> Far-swooping elbow'd earth — rich apple-blossom'd earth!
> Smile, for your lover comes.

Bibliography

Abbreviations

CORR	*The Correspondence.* Edited by Edwin H. Miller, 1961–69.
CPW	*Complete Prose Works.* Edited by R. Bucke, T. B. Harned, Horace L. Traubel, 1902.
DBN	*Daybooks and Notebooks.* Edited by William White, 1978.
EPF	*The Early Poems and the Fiction.* Edited by T. L. Brasher, 1963
FCI	*Faint Clews and Indirections.* Edited by C. Ghodes and R. G. Silver, 1949.
GF	*The Gathering of the Forces.* Edited by Cleveland Rodgets and John Black, 1902.
NYD	*New York Dissected.* Edited by E. Holloway and R. Adimari, 1936.
PW	*The Collected writings of Walt Whitman.* Edited by F. Stovall, 1963, 1964.
UPP	*The Uncollected Poetry and Prose of Walt Whitman.* Edited by Emory Holloway, 1921.
WWC	*With Walt Whitman in Camden.* Edited by Horace Traubel, 1906–1982.

Primary Works

The Complete Writings of Walt Whitman. Edited by Richard M. Bucke, Thomas B. Harned, Horace L. Traubel. New York: G. P. Putnam's sons, 1902. 10 vols.

With Walt Whitman in Camden. Horace Traubel. vol. 1. Boston: Small Maynard, 1906; vol. 2. New York: Appleton, 1908; vol. 3. New York: M. Kennerley, 1914; vol. 4. Philadelphia: University of Pennsylvania Press, 1953; vol. 5. Carbondale: Southern Illinois University Press, 1964; vol. 6 Carbondale: Southern Illinois University Press, 1982.

The Gathering of the Forces: Editorials, Newspaper Contributions, etc. of Walt Whitman. Edited by Cleveland Rogers and John Black. New York: G. P. Putnam's Sons, 1920.

The Uncollected Poetry and Prose. Edited by Emory Holloway. Garden City: Doubleday Page and Co., 1921.

New York Dissected. Edited by Emory Holloway and Ralph Adimari. New York: Rufus Rockwell Wilson, 1936.

Faint Clews and Indirections: The Manuscripts of Walt Whitman and His Family. Edited by Clarence Gohdes and Rollo G. Silver. Durham: Duke University Press, 1949.

The Wound-Dresser. Edited by Richard Maurice Bucke. New York: Bodley Press, 1949.

The Collected Writings of Walt Whitman. General editors, Gay Wilson Allen and Sculley Bradley. New York: New York University Press, 1963–.

The Correspondence. 6 vols. Edited by Edwin H. Miller, 1961–77.

Daybooks and Notebooks. 3 vols. Edited by William White, 1978.

The Early Poems and the Fiction. Edited by Thomas Brasher, 1963.

"Leaves of Grass" Comprehensive Reader's Edition. Edited by Harold Blodgett and Sculley Bradley, 1965.

"Leaves of Grass": A Textual Variorum of the Printed Poems. 3 vols. Edited by Sculley Bradley et al., 1980.

Notebooks and Unpublished Prose Manuscripts. 6 vols. Edited by Edward F. Grier, 1984.

Prose Works. 2 vols. Edited by Floyd Stovall, 1963–64.

Leaves of Grass. Edited by Sculley Bradley and Harold W. Blodgett. New York: A Norton Critical Edition, 1973.

The Portable Walt Whitman. Edited by Mark Van Doren. New York: Penguin Books, 1977.

Selected Letters of Walt Whitman. Edited by Edwin H. Miller. Iowa City: University of Iowa Press, 1990.

Secondary Sources

Allen, Gay Wilson. *The Solitary Singer: A Critical Biography of Walt Whitman.* New York: Macmillan, 1955.

Aspiz, Harold. *Walt Whitman and the Body Beautiful.* Urbana: University of Illinois Press, 1980.

Asselineau, Roger, *The Evolution of Walt Whitman.* Cambridge: Harvard University Press, 1960.

Black, Stephen A. *Whitman's Journeys into Chaos: A Psychoanalytical Study of the Poetic Process.* Princeton: Princeton University Press, 1975.

Blodgett Harold. *Walt Whitman in England.* London: Oxford University Press, 1934.

Bloom, Harold. "The Central Man: Emerson, Whitman, Wallace Stevens." In *The Ringers in the Tower.* Chicago: University of Chicago Press, 1971.

———. *Modern Critical Views Walt Whitman.* New York: Chelsea House Publishers, 1985.

Briggs, Arthur E. *Walt Whitman: Thinker and Artist.* New York: Philosophical Library, 1952.

Bucke, R. M., *Walt Whitman.* Philadelphia: David McKay, 1883.

Cady, Edwin H. and Louis J. Budd. *On Whitman. The Best from "American Literature."* Durham: Duke University Press, 1987.

Cavitch, David, *My Soul and I: The Inner Life of Walt Whitman.* Boston: Beacon Press, 1985.

Chari, V. K., *Walt Whitman in the Light of Vedantic Mysticism.* Lincoln: University of Nebraska Press, 1964.

Chase, Richard. *Walt Whitman Reconsidered.* New York: William Sloane Associates, 1955.

Crawley, Thomas. *The Structure of "Leaves of Grass."* Austin: University of Texas Press, 1970.

Davidson, Marshall B. *The Artists' America.* New York: American Heritage Publishing Co., 1973.

Emerson, Ralph Waldo. *Essays.* New York: U.S. Book Company., n.d.

Erkkila, Betsy. *Walt Whitman among the French.* Princeton: Princeton University Press, 1980.

———. *Whitman the Political Poet.* Oxford: Oxford University Press, 1989.

Faner, Robert D. *Walt Whitman and Opera.* Philadelphia: University of Pennsylvania Press, 1951.

Gould, Stephen J. "The Birth of the Two-Sex World," *New York Review of Books,* June 13, 1991.

Hollis, C. Carroll. *Language and Style in "Leaves of Grass."* Baton Rouge: Louisiana State University Press, 1983.

Hutchinson, George B. *The Ecstatic Whitman: Literary Shamanism and the Crisis of the Union.* Columbus: Ohio State University Press, 1986.

Kaplan, Justin. *Walt Whitman: A Life.* New York: Simon and Schuster, 1980.

Killingsworth, J. M. *Whitman's Poetry of the Body: Sexuality, Politics, and the Text.* Chapel Hill: University of North Carolina Press, 1989.

Kuebrich, David. *Minor Prophecy.* Bloomington: Indiana University Press, 1989.

Laqueur, Thomas, *Making Sex: Body and Gender from the Greeks to Freud.* Cambridge: Harvard University Press, 1991.

Miller, Edwin H. *Walt Whitman's Poetry: A Psychological Journey.* New York: New York University Press, 1968.

———, ed. *A Century of Whitman Criticism.* Bloomington: University of Indiana Press, 1969.

Miller, James E., Jr. *Walt Whitman.* Boston: Twayne Publishers, 1990.

Mumford, Lewis. *Technics and Civilization.* New York: Harcourt, Brace and Company, 1934.

Pearce, Roy Harvey, ed. *Whitman: A Collection of Critical Essays.* Englewood Cliffs, New Jersey: Prentice-Hall, 1962.

Rubin, Joseph Jay. *The Historic Whitman.* University Park: Pennsylvania State University, 1973.

Stern, Madeleine B. *Heads and Headlines. The Phrenological Fowlers.* Norman: University of Oklahoma Press, 1971.

Stovall, Floyd. *The Foreground of "Leaves of Grass."* Charlottesville: University of Virginia Press, 1974.

Taupin, René. *L'Influence du symbolisme français sur la poesie américaine (de 1910 à 1920).* Paris: Champion, 1929.

———. *The Influence of French Symbolism on Modern American Poetry.* Translated by William Pratt and Anne Pratt. New York: AMS Press, 1985.

Thomas, M. Wynn. *The Lunar Light of Whitman's Poetry.* Cambridge: Harvard University Press, 1987.

Waskow, Hoard. *Whitman: Explorations in Form.* Chicago: University of Chicago Press, 1966.

White, William, *1980: "Leaves of Grass" at 125: Eight Essays.* Detroit: Wayne State University Press, 1980.

Woodress, James, ed. *Critical Essays on Walt Whitman.* Boston: G. K. Hall, 1983.

Zweig, Paul, *Walt Whitman: The Making of the Poet.* New York: Basic Books, 1984.

Index